Comprehension

During Guided, Shared, and Independent Reading

by
Patricia M. Cunningham, Dorothy P. Hall,
and James W. Cunningham

Carson-Dellosa Publishing LLC
Greensboro, North Carolina

Caution: Before beginning any food activity, ask families' permission and inquire about students' food allergies and religious or other food restrictions.

Credits

Copy Editor: Bernadette Batliner

Editors: Jennifer Weaver-Spencer and Barrie Hoople

Layout and Cover Design: Van Harris

Inside Illustrations: Lori Jackson

Carson-Dellosa Publishing LLC
PO Box 35665
Greensboro, NC 27425 USA
www.carsondellosa.com

ISBN 978-1-936024-22-3
335101151

Table of Content

Collaborative Formats

Part One

Teaching Comprehension During Guided Reading

A Peek into Classrooms Where Comprehension Lessons Are Taught During Guided Reading

In the first chapter, we visit classrooms at an exemplary elementary school. This chapter shows you how you can tailor your Guided Reading instruction to the needs of your class, grade, and teaching style while focusing on comprehension.

Using Thinking Strategies and Text Structures to Help Students Comprehend

The second chapter provides an overview of the thinking strategies and text structures that you must acknowledge while teaching comprehension during Guided Reading. Students must use these strategies to think their way through the materials you will use in your classroom.

Materials for Teaching Guided Reading

The third chapter describes the variety of materials you might include in your Guided Reading program. Different types of literature require different comprehension strategies. When students read stories, they must follow the story structures and think about the characters, settings, events, and conclusions. Informational text contains special features such as headings, bold print, maps, charts, and glossaries that students need to understand to navigate the text easily. These special features help comprehension only if students know how to read and interpret them. Poetry, plays, and directions have their own structures. With poetry, plays, and directions, students must use different thinking strategies than the strategies they use with stories and informational text.

Chapter 1

A Peek into Classrooms Where Comprehension Lessons Are Taught During Guided Reading

Guided Reading in elementary classrooms is difficult to describe because it looks different from grade to grade, class to class, school to school, and day to day. Teaching comprehension also varies. The older the student is, the more text you read for the lesson and the more comprehension strategies you teach during the year. The purpose of this book is to share this variety of instruction and to help you understand why teachers decide which materials to use, in which formats to have students read, and which comprehension strategies to stress with particular reading selections and groups of students. This instruction is rich with possibilities, as proven by hundreds of creative teachers who make Guided Reading a successful and enjoyable experience.

We begin this book with an imaginary visit to Exemplary Elementary School. Claire Leider is a reading resource teacher from another school and has been helping the teachers at her school improve their comprehension instruction during Guided Reading. Claire's sister, Melodie Leider, is a music teacher at Exemplary Elementary. When Melodie discovered what Claire and the other teachers were working on, she arranged for Claire and two other teachers to spend a Wednesday during their school's spring break visiting Exemplary Elementary classrooms during Guided Reading. "I don't know the details, but all of our teachers seem happy with however they are doing Guided Reading. They talk about how good comprehension does not mean just *small groups* and *leveled readers*. And, they love to show off their success," Melodie explained. Melodie, Claire, and the visiting teachers arrive at Exemplary Elementary at 7:45 A.M. on a chilly spring morning.

The principal, Mrs. Best, greets her guests and talks about what the teachers will be doing and what they can expect to see in the classrooms. As she hands Claire a school map and a schedule, she says, "Have a terrific day. I'll catch up with you at lunch." Claire and her fellow teachers smile as they head down the hall to find the first-grade classroom that is first on the schedule. She was surprised to see that different classrooms do Guided Reading at different times—including in the afternoon. The principal and Melodie assured Claire and the visiting teachers that this is the normal schedule and that the teachers have good reasons for scheduling the way they do. At Claire's school, scheduling is a big problem because all of the teachers think that language arts instruction should happen at the beginning of the school day. Claire hopes she can find some convincing reasons for changing the schedules at her school.

Here is the schedule that Claire is given:

Time	Teacher	Grade Level	Room No.
8:20 A.M.–9:00 A.M.	Dennis Write	Grade 1	Room 33
9:00 A.M.–9:30 A.M.	Bea Ginning	Kindergarten	Room 22
9:30 A.M.–10:00 A.M.	Gay Smiley	Grade 1	Room 32
10:00 A.M.–10:30 A.M.	Deb Webb	Grade 2	Room 36
10:30 A.M.–11:00 A.M.	Laura Reading	Grade 2	Room 38
11:00 A.M.–11:45 A.M.	Frank Goode	Grade 4	Room 3
11:45 A.M.–12:15 P.M.		Lunch	Cafeteria
12:15 P.M.–12:45 P.M.	Diane Duright	Grade 3	Room 17
12:45 P.M.–1:30 P.M.	DeLinda DeLightful	Grade 3	Room 15
1:30 P.M.–2:15 P.M.	Will Teachum	Grade 5	Room 11

8:20 A.M.–9:00 A.M.   Dennis Write   Grade 1   Room 33

Claire arrives early for her first observation. The class has not begun their Guided Reading lesson. Students are busy in the centers around the room. Mr. Write is an excellent reading teacher who is known for teaching writing in first grade. He is sitting at a small table with five students reading an easy version of *The Gingerbread Man*. After talking about the pictures on each page, Mr. Write says, "Now, read the page to find out what is happening to the gingerbread man. Read it to yourself first. Then, I will choose someone to read it aloud."

The students read the page, pointing to each word and whispering it to themselves as first graders often do. Three students read more slowly than the others, getting stumped on and skipping a few words. Two students read fluently. When the students finish reading to themselves, Mr. Write calls on Ryan to read the page aloud. He reminds everyone that one purpose of the group is for each student to learn how to be a word coach, and he says that he hopes Ryan will have at least one word with which he needs coaching. Ryan reads the page and comes to a word with which he needs help. Mr. Write coaches Ryan to figure out the word, and the whole group cheers when Ryan reads the word! Mr. Write then leads the group in a quick retelling of what they have read and has students read the page chorally before moving to the next page.

At 8:15 A.M., the timer on Mr. Write's table rings. Mr. Write pushes the "play" button on a CD player and a bouncy song blares. Students immediately begin cleaning up their centers while singing along with the song. The students in Mr. Write's group place bookmarks in their books to show where they will start reading the next day. The students notice that they have only three more pages of *The Gingerbread Man* to read. One student observes that they will probably finish reading it tomorrow and read the whole book again on Friday. Another student asks Mr. Write what book they will start on Monday and if she can be in his Reading for Fun Club again. Mr. Write smiles and tells the student that the next book is a surprise and that he will consider her request to be included in the club again. He reminds her that everyone wants to be in the Reading for Fun Club and that she cannot be in the club for every book. "Will *The Gingerbread Man* books be in the reading crates on Monday?" a third student asks. Mr. Write assures her that he will place one copy of the book in each crate. "Good," says the student, "because I am going to read it all by myself!"

At 8:20 A.M., the music ends and students sit on the rug facing Mr. Write and the board. Mr. Write compliments students on how well they came in that morning and how nicely they worked in and cleaned up the centers. One student comments that cleaning is more fun with music to sing and dance to and that it is fun to see if they can finish cleaning up their centers before the music stops. Mr. Write says, "Yes, using music for center cleanup is another great idea from my 'virtual' friends on my favorite first-grade teachers' Web site." One student asks, "Do you have any more good ideas from your Web friends?" "Not yet," says Mr. Write, "but I'm sure I will get another one soon, and we will try it!"

"Now," says Mr. Write, "we should start Guided Reading for today because we have a fun activity to help finish our reading of *Are You My Mother?* by P. D. Eastman. On Monday, after we looked at the pictures and made predictions about what would happen in the story, you read with partners to see which predictions happened. Then, yesterday, you read the story again in groups and we did the Beach Ball. Today, we will act it out!" Students cheer and clap as Mr. Write pulls out the laminated character card necklaces that he uses to designate characters when students act out stories—a very popular activity with all of his students.

Mr. Write directs the students to chorally read the story with him. As they finish reading each page, he asks if the page has any new characters. As students tell him the name of each character, he writes the name with a marker on a character card. When the class finishes rereading the story, 11 character cards are lined up along the board ledge.

"There are 11 characters and 21 of you," says Mr. Write. "We will act out the story twice so that everyone can play a character." As he says this, he shuffles some index cards labeled with the students' names. He pulls the card with Kevin's name on it and asks him to choose a character card from the board. Kevin, looking amazed to be the first student picked, puts the snort card around his neck. In less than a minute, Mr. Write has called 11 names and 11 students are standing in front of the board with character cards around their necks.

"Now," says Mr. Write, "our characters will act out the story while the rest of us read the pages aloud." The students who are not characters read the pages chorally with Mr. Write, while the characters come to the front of the room and act out their parts.

Hurriedly, Mr. Write collects the character cards and pulls the rest of the students' names from his index card set to determine the second cast of characters. Once again, the audience chorally reads with Mr. Write while the characters act out the story.

Claire, who has been entranced throughout her visit in Mr. Write's class, hurries to the door when she notices that it is a few minutes past nine. As she leaves, she hears Mr. Write remind students that he is putting the character cards in the dramatic play center the next day so that they can "do the book" again if they choose that center.

9:00 A.M.–9:30 A.M.   Bea Ginning   Kindergarten   Room 22

At 9:04 A.M., Claire enters Miss Ginning's kindergarten classroom. Melodie had told Claire that Miss Ginning is a new teacher, having taken over this kindergarten class at the beginning of January. Miss Ginning had been the student teacher in the classroom last autumn. She graduated from college after the first semester this year and became the teacher when the previous teacher decided to stay home after her maternity leave ended.

As Claire enters, students are sitting on the carpet in front of the young teacher and looking at the big book *Is Your Mama a Llama*? by Deborah Guarino. Students are looking at the cover of the book and talking about llamas. Miss Ginning points to the title of the book, the author's name, and the illustrator's name. "The illustrator of this book is Steven Kellogg," she says as she points to his name on the cover. "What does Steven Kellogg do?" she asks. One little girl answers quickly, "He makes cereal!" Claire thinks about how wonderful young students are, how smart they feel when they make a connection, and how they want everyone to know they know! Miss Ginning chuckles and says, "There is a cereal brand by that name, but it says on the cover that Steven Kellogg is the illustrator. What does an illustrator do?" Several students chime in that an illustrator draws or paints the pictures.

Next, Miss Ginning opens the big book and asks students to take a Picture Walk through the book. They talk about the pictures on each page and discuss the animals (bat, swan, cow, seal, kangaroo, etc.) as Miss Ginning turns the pages of the big book. "Can you tell what this story will be about?" Miss Ginning asks. Students answer, "A llama and lots of other animals."

Miss Ginning points to one of the pages and asks, "What do you notice on this page?" Seth answers, "There is only one word on the page, and it is written in big letters. I can read it! It's *bat* and there is a picture of a bat." Miss Ginning and the class continue the Picture Walk, and each time they come to a page with one word and a picture of an animal, some students look at the beginning letter and the picture clue and read the word aloud.

After the Picture Walk, Miss Ginning reads the story to the class and asks students to count how many animals the llama asks, "Is your Mama a llama?" After reading the story to the class, having them answer the focus question ("How many animals . . ."), and talking about what happens in the story, Miss Ginning asks students to share the reading of the book by reading it aloud with her. Some students read in loud voices—proud they can do it! Other students chime in when they can—those big, bold words, one on a page, being the easiest to read! Everyone can see Miss Ginning point from left to right, do a return sweep to the left, and read from the top of the page to the bottom.

After the shared reading of the big book, Miss Ginning says, "I heard some rhyming words in this book. Did you? Let's read the book again and listen for rhyming words." She rereads the book, and students identify the rhyming words, which Miss Ginning writes on a piece of chart paper for students to see. When they finish Rounding Up the Rhymes, Miss Ginning and the class read the rhyming words together.

9:30 A.M.–10:00 A.M.   Gay Smiley   Grade 1   Room 32

Guided Reading is already in progress when Claire enters Room 32. Miss Smiley is sitting in front of the board with six students, five pairs of partners are working together, and five students are reading by themselves. They are all reading *Cats* by Helen Frost from the All About Pets series. Claire knows from this class arrangement that they are doing a Three-Ring Circus.

Claire observes the teacher's group first. As Miss Smiley turns each page, she asks students to remember what they just talked about when the whole class did a Picture Walk. The students tell her what they see in each picture, and she repeats their responses and prompts them for other things in the picture. Miss Smiley also asks students to say and stretch out one word, decide which letters they expect to see in the word, and find that word on the page before reading it. The students echo read each page. Miss Smiley reads each sentence and cups her hand behind her ear as she listens to students read it back. As they finish reading each page, they talk about what they learned on that page and where that information belongs on the cat web they are making. Claire watches them read several pages, each time using the same procedure of continuing the Picture Walk, identifying one difficult word, Echo Reading the page, and deciding what can be added to the web. She notices two students who attempt to echo read the pages and listen but do not contribute to the discussion, and she wonders if these students are just learning to speak English.

Next, Claire walks around and watches the partners read. Claire notices that these students have been taught how to partner read. They take turns with each page, one student reading and the other pointing to the words. At the end of the page, the reader asks the pointer what can be added to the web and where. Their eyes turn to the web, which has been started on the board, and they make suggestions. As the partners take turns, it is clear that struggling readers are paired with partners who can help them. Claire is amazed to notice, however, that the partners do not tell each other the words but coach each other to figure them out. In one partnership, the student who is the better reader cannot figure out a word, and her partner says, "Keep your finger on the word and finish the sentence. Then, we will go back and pretend it's Guess the Covered Word. We have the beginning letters." The helping partner does not know the word either, but he does know some strategies that will help them figure it out!

At 9:55 A.M., just a few minutes before Miss Smiley signals for students to gather at the web, several sets of partners and almost all of the individuals have finished reading. They all have index cards and have been writing what they think should be added to the web. Miss Smiley and her group go to the web, and as Claire once again hurries to her next observation, she notices that all students—including those with whom the teacher echo read—are eager to contribute to the web.

10:00 A.M.–10:30 A.M.   Deb Webb   Grade 2   Room 36

Claire is on schedule as she enters Deb Webb's second-grade classroom. Students are sitting on the carpet in front of Mrs. Webb's rocking chair. Yesterday, the class finished reading a story about the book/TV character Arthur. Today, Mrs. Webb is giving her class four Arthur books from which to choose for Book Club Groups. Using the story map they filled in for the Arthur story they read as a class, Mrs. Webb explains, "Arthur is the main character in all of his books. But, just like in *Arthur's Pet Business* by Marc Brown, there are other characters in his stories. For the setting, the places are sometimes different, but the time is always the present. What changes from story to story is what the problem is and how it is solved. So, as you choose a book and form Book Club Groups, think about what you believe Arthur's problem will be." Mrs. Webb explains to students that their task is to preview the four books and decide which will be their first, second, and third choices to read. She suggests that they look at the pictures and read a few sentences—not all of the words on every page—to find out if they can read the book and will enjoy it.

Next, Mrs. Webb sends five or six students to each stack of Arthur books placed in a corner of the room. After students have spent four to five minutes with a book, the timer rings, and each group heads to the next stack of books. There is a soft buzz in each group, but when Claire visits the groups, she is surprised that students are on task, reading or talking about Arthur and which book they like best.

After students have previewed all four books, Mrs. Webb gathers students on the carpet, asks them to think about the books as she passes around index cards, and tells them to write the titles of their first, second, and third choices on the cards. Mrs. Webb overhears some students say that they cannot decide—they liked all of the Arthur books. Mrs. Webb tells them not to worry about their choices, because all four books will be in the book baskets for Self-Selected Reading next week. This allays the students' anxiety, and they quickly make their choices.

10:30 A.M.–11:00 A.M.   Laura Reading   Grade 2   Room 38

Laura Reading is using *Weekly Reader* for her Guided Reading lesson as Claire enters her classroom at 10:30 A.M. Although the weekly newspaper is written especially for second-grade students, some students find it difficult to read—especially because this week's issue is about frogs, and they don't know much about frogs! (Even if they don't know much about them, children are interested in frogs and other topics covered in this weekly newspaper.) *Weekly Reader* enables Mrs. Reading to help students learn how to read informational text, and she uses this student newspaper for Guided Reading one day each week. She is especially grateful that she has these newspapers, because the reading series she uses contains good stories but little informational text. Mrs. Reading tells students, "Some grown-ups read newspapers to learn about the world, and so do we!"

Next, Mrs. Reading tells students with whom they will work today. As the names of two students are called, they sit together on the floor and immediately begin previewing the pictures and reading the captions. Claire notes that this format must have been used before because everyone knows what to do without much direction from Mrs. Reading. When all partners are sitting together, Mrs. Reading reminds them of their purpose: "Work together to read each page, talk about what you learn, and think about what you can add to our frog facts list."

Mrs. Reading circulates from pair to pair as students read and talk. Claire notes a happy buzz in this second-grade classroom as students find new and interesting facts about frogs. Soon a timer rings, and students return to the carpet in front of Mrs. Reading. They are eager to share their new information about frogs. Mrs. Reading calls on one student in each pair to share something he has learned. As students share, Mrs. Reading types the frog facts list on the classroom interactive whiteboard. Students watch the interactive whiteboard screen and read the sentences as Mrs. Reading types them. Each pair of partners seems very pleased as their information is added to the list. One student asks if the class will receive copies of the information she is typing, and Mrs. Reading explains that she will include it in next week's parent newsletter.

11:00 A.M.–11:45 A.M.   Frank Goode   Grade 4   Room 3

As Claire settles into a rocking chair at the back of Room 3, she wonders if Melodie mixed up the schedule or if Mr. Goode changed the schedule. Students are reading science books and raising hands. Some students have two hands raised. "They must be eager beavers," Claire thinks. "I am glad to see many of you with both hands raised," says Mr. Goode, "because the purpose I gave you for reading this page was indeed a two-hander. I asked you to find the two ways your body fights germs. Sophia, tell us one way." Sophia explains that a fever helps the body fight germs.

"Very good," responds Mr. Goode. "Who can read aloud the sentences in the text that told Sophia that fevers help you fight germs?" A boy sitting near Sophia quickly locates the text and raises his hand. "Grant, please read those sentences for us," Mr. Goode says. When Grant finishes reading, Mr. Goode calls on another student who says that white blood cells help fight germs too. Then, Mr. Goode chooses a fourth student to read the parts in the text that describe how white blood cells fight germs.

As the lesson continues, Claire realizes that she did come in at the right time and that Mr. Goode is doing a Guided Reading lesson with a portion of the science text. He is using the ERT format (Everyone Read To . . .), and most of his questions require students to connect text information with what they already know and to make inferences. The class reads several pages using this format, and Mr. Goode asks students to get out their science notebooks.

"That was a lot of new information about germs," he says. "Let's write a summary together that you will all have in your notebooks so that you can review the most important facts before our unit test."

As Claire is leaving, Mr. Goode and his students construct a summary. Mr. Goode writes on the interactive whiteboard as students write in their notebooks. Claire is amazed that integrating Guided Reading and focused writing with other subjects can be so easy and natural. She wonders why she and the other teachers at her school have talked about it but have never done it!

11:45 A.M.–12:15 P.M.   Lunch with Melodie

During lunch, Melodie tells Claire that Diane Duright is a champion for Guided Reading. Diane always has the answer for teachers when they ask about this block. Although the local school system has adopted a reading series, teachers are allowed and encouraged to use other materials—and Diane does. After their lunch in the cafeteria, Claire waves good-bye to her sister and hurries to see Mrs. Duright.

12:15 P.M.–12:45 P.M.   Diane Duright   Grade 3   Room 17

At 12:15 P.M., Claire enters Mrs. Duright's room. It is neat and orderly in spite of the fact that there are books everywhere—on bookshelves, in plastic bins, and near every bulletin board and display! From the mural on a large bulletin board in one corner of the room, Claire can see that these third graders are studying the water cycle in science. Students' drawings illustrate the water cycle, and the parts of the cycle are neatly numbered and labeled in the students' best handwriting.

Mrs. Duright tells the class that today they will go on an imaginary field trip with a famous teacher named Ms. Frizzle. Mrs. Duright explains that this field trip is imaginary because they are going with their eyes and minds as they read a book. She tells students that knowing about the water cycle will help them read the book.

Mrs. Duright asks students what they know about water from their science lessons. "Water is a liquid," says one boy. Someone else adds, "It is a solid when it freezes and becomes ice." Another student adds, "If you heat it, water can become a gas." Mrs. Duright begins a column on a large sheet of chart paper and lists what students know about water. Next, she tells them that they will learn more facts about water from this book.

Mrs. Duright gathers students around her, and together they read a big book version of *The Magic School Bus at the Waterworks* by Joanna Cole. They talk about the different kinds of information on each page—illustrations, text bubbles that show what people are saying and thinking, boxed text that gives facts about water, quicktext (labels, captions, etc.) under pictures and in diagrams, and the regular text. They decide on an order to look at and read these different kinds of information— visuals (pictures or illustrations) and quicktext captions first, then regular text, bubbled text after that, and the boxed informational text last. Mrs. Duright leads the class through the reading of the book. She invites students to join in the reading with her, and she lets volunteers read the dialogue in the thinking and speech bubbles.

Students discuss what they are learning and connect new knowledge to what they already knew about the water cycle. After they finish, Mrs. Duright asks students to take out their reading response logs and write something they learned about the water cycle from this book. She ends her lesson by having several students read their sentences aloud.

"I learned that clouds are made of water."

"I learned that people store water in reservoirs."

"You have to purify water before you can drink it."

"Most of the water on Earth is salt water in the oceans."

"Clear water is not always clean water. We can't see germs."

"Water pressure forces water through the pipes in our homes and at school."

12:45 P.M.–1:30 P.M.   DeLinda DeLightful   Grade 3   Room 15

When Claire enters Room 15, students are sitting at their desks with their reading textbooks open to a biography of Eleanor Roosevelt. Mrs. DeLightful is reading aloud to them, and she stops every few sentences, points to her brain, and stares into the distance. She says, "That reminds me of when

I was little. I had to go into the basement to get things from our freezer, and if it was late at night, I was always afraid that someone would be down there." She continues to "think aloud" and says,

"I can't imagine how she felt when she was only eight years old and her mother died. She must have been very lonely. I feel like crying myself when I think about it."

"It says she was a sad and lonely child. I wonder how she became such a wonderful first lady. I can't wait to see how she changed as she grew up."

Students are amazingly quiet and thoughtful as Mrs. DeLightful reads aloud, looks away, points to her brain, and tells the class what her "brain is saying to her." When Mrs. DeLightful finishes reading and "thinking aloud" the first three pages, she closes the book, opens and closes her eyes, and looks amazed to see her students. They laugh and have clearly been anticipating her doing this, although it is quite a surprise to Claire! Mrs. DeLightful congratulates students on remaining so "invisible" that she forgot they were there. Then, she asks students to recall what she was thinking as she read the first few pages of the biography. Students tell her that she connected things to her own life when she remembered going into the basement to get things out of the freezer, that she felt so sorry for Eleanor when her mother died that she almost cried, and that she wanted to read more and find out how Eleanor became a great first lady.

Mrs. DeLightful tells the class that they were so quiet while she was reading and thinking aloud that they almost became invisible, but that it was clear that they were still there, listening to every word. She tells them that they will read the next six pages of Eleanor Roosevelt's biography in Play-School Groups (heterogeneous groups). As they read, they should think about what their brains are telling them. She reminds students that the first few times they did Think-Alouds, they were only trying to make connections. Then, they added predictions and finally, images. "Who can explain what connections, predictions, and images are?" she asks. Students tell her about how they connect what they are reading to themselves, to things they know about the world, or to other books they have read. They also tell her how they predict when they think they know what will happen or when they don't know but they wonder about how something happened. Finally, students explain that when they "image," it is like they are really there. They can see how something looks, hear the sounds, and maybe even smell, taste, and feel things.

Claire is amazed that these third graders understand so much about how their brains think when they read. She imagines that Mrs. DeLightful has done many Think-Alouds and gradually introduced the three different thinking strategies. As Claire tries to make sense of this, Mrs. DeLightful separates students into Play-School Groups. Each group has a "Teacher" who is given three laminated index cards: a blue card that says *Connect*, a yellow card that says *Predict*, and a green card that says *Image*. Mrs. DeLightful tells students to echo read the sentences and stop after each paragraph to see if anyone's brain is "talking" to him—telling him any connections, predictions, or images.

Students quickly get into their appointed groups of four or five. The Echo Reading begins with the Teacher reading each sentence and having the rest of the group echo the sentence. The Teacher stops at the end of each paragraph and asks what students are thinking. The students in the group, including the Teacher, point to their brains, gaze into the distance, and tell their thoughts.

When the groups finish reading the six pages, they begin talking about their most interesting thoughts and negotiate the Think-Aloud they will share with the class.

The Guided Reading time ends with each group sharing their most interesting Think-Aloud. Everyone in the group reads aloud the sentences that precede the Think-Aloud, and one student stares into the distance, points to her brain, and tells what her brain is saying. Students enjoy this, and each group tries to outact the others. Claire walks out, shaking her head in amazement at the level of thinking and involvement she observed in this classroom.

1:30 P.M.–2:15 P.M.   Will Teachum   Grade 5   Room 11

Claire is exhausted when she arrives for her last observation of the day. She doesn't know how she can be so tired from sitting and watching all day. She thinks, *My brain is on overload. I will need a vacation to get over my vacation.*

Claire finds Mr. Teachum's students in animated discussion in small groups. They all have copies of *Because of Winn-Dixie* by Kate DiCamillo and are engaged in talking about it. As Claire approaches the groups, she notices that students have bookmarks on which they have written questions. These questions are guiding their discussions, and Claire notices that all of the questions begin with *how* or *why*.

At 1:45 P.M., the timer buzzes and Mr. Teachum tells the groups that they have exactly one minute to pick the best *how* or *why* question to ask the rest of the class. The groups argue amongst themselves and quickly vote when they cannot decide which question to include. Claire is amazed, as she has been all day, that students know just what to do. She realizes that small-group discussions are often unfocused and a waste of time and that a lot of time and modeling has gone into teaching these students the procedures and what is expected.

When one minute has passed, Mr. Teachum asks the first group for their best question. One member of the group reads the question and calls on three students from three different groups for responses. This procedure is followed as each of the five groups asks a question and calls on three students from other groups.

Next, Mr. Teachum tells students that they will have the rest of the Guided Reading time to read the next chapter in the book. Just as they have done before, their task is to come up with two good *how* or *why* questions for their small-group discussions tomorrow. Mr. Teachum also tells students that today's reading will be a You'se Choose format—they can read by themselves, with partners, or with him and his group. "Remember," he warns, "with choices come responsibility. If you choose to read by yourself or with a friend, you must be able to make up two good questions for tomorrow. If you make a bad choice today, you will lose the privilege of making a choice tomorrow."

Students scramble around, and in less than two minutes, they are all settled and reading. Six students choose to read by themselves. Five pairs of partners read together. Ten students join Mr. Teachum. Claire circulates and notices that all students are involved with their reading. Several students reading with partners stumble over some words, but their partners coach them to figure out the words.

All students have bookmarks and stop periodically to write a *how* or *why* question. Claire notices that Mr. Teachum stops students every few pages and asks, "Does anyone have a good question?" He writes their suggested questions on the board and asks them to wait until they are finished reading before choosing the best ones. Once they finish reading, they pick the two that they like best and write them on their bookmarks. The group that reads with Mr. Teachum includes some struggling readers as well as some able readers. Claire concludes that some students are there because they know they need the help, and other students would just rather read with the teacher than by themselves or with a partner.

As 2:15 P.M. approaches, some students have finished reading and have returned to their seats. Most students begin working on their math homework, but a few are reminded that "begin your math homework if you finish reading before the time is up" is the rule—and has been all year. Mr. Teachum's group runs about five minutes over, but by 2:20 P.M., all students are in their seats and preparing for the 2:25 P.M. dismissal bell. Claire notices that students have bookmarks in their Harry Potter books with *how* and *why* questions on them. Some questions intrigue her, and she is tempted to return the next day. But, she quickly changes her mind when she remembers that Melodie is taking a personal day, and they are spending the day together! Claire decides that she's devoted enough of her vacation to work.

After tagging along on Claire Leider's visit to Exemplary Elementary, hopefully you are intrigued by what you learned and have a lot of *how* and *why* questions to which you'd like answers. If your brain, like Claire's, is on overload, take a little break before continuing to the next chapter to begin exploring answers to those questions.

Chapter 2

Using Thinking Strategies and Text Structures to Help Students Comprehend

When you read, you do two things simultaneously: you say the words, and you think about what you are reading. Saying the words aloud or to yourself is the word identification part of reading. Understanding the meaning that the words convey is the comprehension part. Word identification is necessary for comprehension, but word identification does not guarantee comprehension. How do you comprehend the meanings of sentences in which you identify the words? Comprehension is accomplished in your brain as it processes the word meanings and language structures of the text. In simplest terms, your brain thinks about what you are reading and have read. But, what is thinking and how does it occur? What do you mean when you say, "Think about this"?

For more than a century, psychologists have tried to determine the exact nature of thinking, and there are many possible components of thinking. Because thinking is a complex process, it is difficult to describe. Nevertheless, because thinking is how your brain allows you to comprehend what you are reading, it is important to have an understanding of some of the possible components of thinking.

Thinking Strategies

This chapter describes seven strategies that play a large part in how your brain thinks as you read. Using a magazine article about Mia Hamm, a retired professional female soccer player, this chapter helps demonstrate how your brain comprehends by connecting, predicting/questioning, summarizing, inferring, monitoring, visualizing/imagining, and evaluating/applying.

Connecting

As soon as you see the title of the Mia Hamm magazine article, before you start reading, you begin to connect some things that you already know about soccer, the Olympics, and female athletes. You may think the following:

I never played soccer, but my kids did.

Mia is my sister-in-law's name.

You begin to read and learn that Mia was born in Florence, Italy.

> *Soccer is popular in Italy.*

You read that Mia went to the University of North Carolina at Chapel Hill (UNC), where they already had a championship soccer team, and you may think,

> *I knew that the university's men's basketball team was a powerhouse, but I didn't know that it also had a championship women's soccer team.*

You read about the U.S. soccer victory in the 1996 Olympic Summer Games in Atlanta, Georgia.

> *I remember the bombing and how tragic it was. I was recovering from surgery at the time and watched a lot of the events. I don't remember watching any soccer though.*

Connecting is probably the most pervasive thinking strategy you use while reading. You connect what you are reading to your life, to what you know about the world, and to other things you have read. Connecting is so integral to reading comprehension that you may forget that fledgling readers need some prompting to make the personal, world, and intertextual connections that are critical to comprehending.

Predicting/Questioning

Another thinking strategy you use while you read is predicting/questioning. This strategy also begins when you see the title and accompanying pictures.

> *I think that she is a soccer player.*

> *She was probably on the U.S. Olympic team.*

> *I wonder how well she did.*

As you read, your mind thinks ahead about where the text is going and what it might tell you. Sometimes, you have a specific prediction about what will happen. You read about the University of North Carolina's outstanding women's soccer team.

> *I think that's where she will go to college.*

You read about the injuries to the World Cup team in 1995 and think,

> *They probably won't win.*

Sometimes, you don't have a specific prediction about what will happen, but you have a question about the direction the text will take. Often, your questioning includes a voice in your brain starting sentences with *I wonder*, *How*, and *Why*.

Why does she look so excited?

How will she make the play?

I wonder what she will do next.

I wonder what she is doing today.

Connecting as well as predicting/questioning are strategies that your brain uses to make sense of, enjoy, and learn from whatever you are reading. In addition, predicting/questioning has a motivating effect. Once it occurs to you that something might happen, you read to see if it does happen. When you wonder what will happen, you read to find out what does happen. Sometimes, your ideas about what will happen are confirmed, and sometimes you are surprised by the text. Regardless of how accurate your predictions are, predicting/questioning keeps you reading and actively engaged in reading.

Summarizing

As you read, you constantly accumulate information, and you keep this information in mind by turning smaller facts into larger generalizations. You summarize the information based on the structure of the text. This magazine article presents information about Mia Hamm sequentially.

You sum up the most significant information about her childhood.

> *She was born with a club foot but became a star soccer player in high school.*

You gather information about her college years and "file" the big ideas.

> *She led the University of North Carolina Tar Heels to four NCAA national soccer championships.*

You sum up her amazing career after college.

> *She led the U.S. soccer team in several summer Olympic Games. The team won gold in the 2004 Olympic Summer Games in Athens, Greece.*

Finally, your brain files her current status.

> *She retired from soccer in 2004 to raise a family with her husband, retired baseball player Nomar Garciaparra. They have twin girls.*

Inferring

As you read, your brain synthesizes information from words to comprehend sentences, information from sentences to comprehend paragraphs, information from paragraphs to comprehend sections, and so on, as you move through the text. In addition to understanding what the text says, your brain figures out many things that are not directly stated in the text. You read about Mia's early years in Italy, how she played soccer with her older brother and in childhood soccer leagues, and you figure out the following:

She had the right early experiences and the personality to become a great soccer player.

The text did not say this. You read about those early experiences and about Mia's personality, and you used those clues to figure out that she had what it takes to play soccer at a high level. Later, you read about her leaving school for a year to compete in China and about the hours she practiced, and you infer that,

Mia Hamm was a hardworking, focused, and determined competitor, and she had to be in order to become a world champion.

Again, the text told you some things about her, and you used the information you read and what you knew from your life experiences to make inferences and draw conclusions.

Monitoring

As you read, your brain monitors your comprehension. When something does not make sense, you ask yourself questions: *What does that word mean? How can that happen? What are they talking about here?* The more complex the topic, the more monitoring your brain does. Even in familiar text, you may misread a word and have to reread when you realize that something is not right. While reading about Mia Hamm, you may ask yourself questions about soccer.

What's a shutout?

You may be able to guess at what a shutout is when you see that the final score was 2–0. Later, you may learn that Mia's brother suffered from aplastic anemia.

How is that different from regular anemia?

You won't find a definitive answer to this question in the text, but you might conclude that aplastic anemia is a more serious disease when you learn that her brother died from it.

As you read, your brain is constantly monitoring whether what you are reading makes sense. As long as it seems to make sense, you are not aware of this monitoring function, but when something—an unknown word, a misread word, or an apparent contradiction—disrupts the meaning, your brain raises a red flag. Once you realize that something is not working, you try some strategies to fix it— rereading, continuing to read while looking for clarification, or asking someone. Sometimes, you may decide that the confusion is not worth the trouble, and you forget about it while reading on. If your brain raises too many red flags, and there is too much you can't understand, you may decide to stop reading.

Your brain not only monitors whether your reading of a text makes sense but also whether you are achieving your purpose for reading it. If you expect that someone will ask you to summarize the article about Mia Hamm after you finish reading it, you are likely to exercise your summarizing thinking process more than usual. As you read, you will also monitor how well you believe you will be able to summarize the article. Because you are monitoring your thinking process, you may reread one or more parts or pause at different points and review your mental summary.

The brain's self-monitoring function works best when you encounter some—but not too many—comprehension red flags. This is one major reason all students need to read materials at just the right instructional level and be given appropriate support when reading material that is too hard for them to comprehend on their own. Before- and after-reading activities help students improve their monitoring thinking process, because the lessons give students a specific purpose to monitor for while they read.

Visualizing/Imagining

When you read, you use all of your senses. You see things in your mind's eye and hear sounds that you connect to what you are reading. When you become engaged in what you are reading, you can almost taste, smell, and feel the physical sensations you would actually have if you were in that situation. You get lost in the book and may be startled if someone interrupts your reading. While reading about Mia Hamm's Olympic victory in Atlanta, Georgia, you might see the soccer field and hear the roars of the fans in the crowd. You might feel the heat of a summer day in Atlanta. Your mouth might water as you imagine people eating pralines at the victory celebration.

As you read, you imagine the situation about which you are reading. You create a movie in your mind and enter the world created by the author. To create this movie, you use all of the other thinking strategies. You make connections to your life, to the world, and sometimes to other things you have read. Your predictions and questions keep you actively engaged and anticipating what will happen next. You summarize and make inferences using your prior knowledge and clues to figure out many things the author does not directly tell you.

Evaluating/Applying

Perhaps the most lasting traces you have of the multitude of things you have read through the years are the opinions you form and the actions you take based on what you have read. As you are reading about Mia Hamm and her soccer and life successes, you might think this:

That's the kind of woman I hope my daughter will become—not necessarily that she will be an Olympic champion but that she will believe that she can do whatever she sets her mind to, will work hard toward her goals, and will reach out to other young women.

That kind of thought is an inference, but it is also your personal opinion. Reading about Mia has helped shape the way you look at the world, and this opinion of Mia and of the role you want your daughter to play in the world will become a part of you.

Not all of your opinions and evaluations will be this momentous. You also form smaller opinions as you read.

She made exactly the right decision.

Soccer is a much more interesting sport than I thought.

Sometimes you act on your evaluations, and sometimes you don't. If after reading the article about Mia Hamm, you suggest that your daughter read it, tell her about it, or initiate some kind of discussion based on it, you have applied some of your reading to your life. If you have an opportunity to go to a soccer game and you go (when you never would have considered going before reading about Mia), you have applied something from the reading experience to your life.

How much you evaluate and apply what you read depends on many factors: what you are reading, why you are reading it, the mood you are in while reading it, the life challenges and opportunities facing you at the moment you read it, etc. Evaluating/applying is a strategy that your brain uses while you read to understand, enjoy, and learn. Most of you can name a book or two that you absolutely love or that have helped you in some way. These books are proof that you evaluate and apply some of what you read.

Thinking is something you do all of the time. You daydream, worry, plan, and ponder. As you think, you use a variety of thinking strategies. To comprehend what you read, you think as you are reading. The seven strategies described previously are some of the components of thinking that are the most useful while reading. To help you think about thinking, each strategy has been described separately, but in reality, your brain often employs several strategies simultaneously. You make a connection that leads you to predict something. You summarize, infer, and form an opinion or decide to use the information in some way. You use your senses to make mind movies and imagine yourself in the world about which you are reading. While your incredible brain performs all of these functions, the monitor in your brain is on guard, ensuring that you are able to connect, predict, summarize, infer, imagine, and evaluate. Your brain is more awesome than the most advanced computer!

Text Structures

The seven thinking strategies—connecting, predicting/questioning, summarizing, inferring, monitoring, visualizing/imagining, and evaluating/applying—are used to help you comprehend, enjoy, and remember what you read, regardless of what you are reading. In fact, these strategies are also used when you are not reading. While texts can challenge your mind more than your daily activities do, you engage in these thinking strategies as you shop for groceries, watch a movie, and have a conversation with a friend.

In addition to thinking, you must do specific text-related things to make sense of reading. For all text, you must be able to understand meaning at the sentence and paragraph level. If you are reading fiction, you must follow the story structure. Informational text requires that you understand a variety of text structures and read and interpret special informational text features, including pictures, maps, charts, and graphs.

Following Sentence and Paragraph Structure

You construct meaning as you read by identifying and understanding words and by using the words to make sense of sentences and the sentences to comprehend paragraphs. Sentences and paragraphs are the basic meaning units, yet little attention is given to helping students make sense of them. Think about how meaning accumulates in the first paragraph of a familiar tale:

> *Once upon a time, there were three pigs who lived with their mother in a little house in the woods. One day, their mother told them that they needed to go out and build their own houses. They headed out, and the first little pig met a man with some sticks. The pig asked the man for some sticks so that he could build a house for himself. He got the sticks, stopped right there, and began building it.*

In order to understand this paragraph, you must follow the sequence of words in each sentence and think about how they are related. You must also see how the sentences relate to each other. You must notice where sentences begin and end. If you ignored the ending punctuation and beginning uppercase letters, the paragraph would be much harder to follow and would look like this:

> *once upon a time, there were three pigs who lived with their mother in a little house in the woods one day, their mother told them that they needed to go out and build their own houses they headed out, and the first little pig met a man with some sticks the pig asked the man for some sticks so that he could build a house for himself he got the sticks, stopped right there, and began building it*

You must also realize to whom and what the pronouns refer. When you read "their mother" and "their own houses," you must realize that "their" refers to the pigs (the pigs' mother and the pigs' own houses). You must realize that in the last sentence, the "he" who gets the sticks is the first little pig and the "it" that he begins building is his house.

In addition to paying attention to sentence boundaries and understanding the pronouns, you must follow the logic and the sequence and keep one idea in mind as you read the next. In Chapter 20, you will find four activities that you can do with students before they read a passage. These activities introduce some words in that selection and help them focus on sentence and paragraph structure.

Following Story Structure

You have certain expectations of what you will find when you pick up a John Grisham novel. You know that there will be main characters who will be present throughout the book and other characters who will come and go. You expect that the story will take place somewhere and in a particular time period. You also know that the settings—both place and time—may change and that you need to keep up with when and where the action is happening. Speaking of action, you are expecting some! Things will happen, and problems that need to be resolved will arise. You don't know the plot, but you know that a good novel has one.

In addition to the normal expectations you have for any novel—characters, settings, plot, and resolution—you probably have more specific expectations if you are a John Grisham fan. Some characters are apt to be lawyers, and courtrooms and jails are apt to be some of the many settings. The plot will require a crime to be solved and will have twists and turns that may keep you reading late into the night to discover what happens.

Good readers have expectations in their minds about what stories include. If they are readers of particular authors or types of stories—mystery, science fiction, fantasy, etc.—they have specific expectations. Following story structure is a comprehension strategy that helps students learn what to expect and increases their understanding and enjoyment of story reading.

Following Informational Structure

Imagine that you are reading a magazine and that the first article you read is about South Africa. You are not expecting characters, settings, plots, and resolution, but you still have expectations. You expect to learn about South Africa—its geography, history, economy, people, animals, politics, etc. You also expect to find some things in the article other than a lot of words. You expect to see illustrations and photos with some accompanying quicktext labels or captions. You may also expect to find webs or charts like the ones on pages 26 and 27.

Idea Web

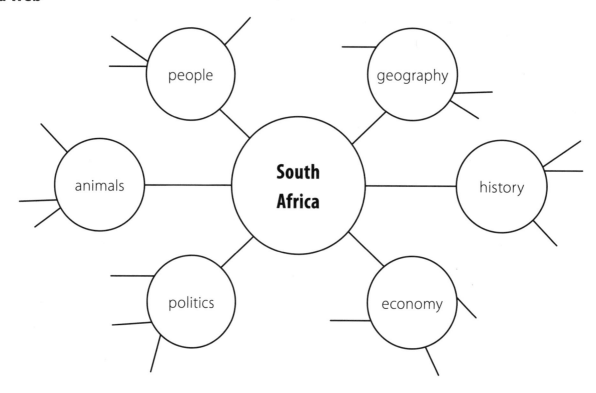

As you begin to read, you connect what you are reading to what you already know about South Africa. If there is a lot of new information, you begin to construct in your mind a web of South Africa facts and to place the information you find interesting on the appropriate spokes of the web. When you finish reading, you have a lot of information in your South Africa brain site, and it is probably organized with the interesting facts (details) connected to the main ideas.

Imagine that the next article you read in the magazine is about spiders. In this article, you find a lot of captioned illustrations, some diagrams showing various body parts, and a chart that shows a spiderweb being spun in various stages. Different kinds of spiders are described, and you learn that while spiders share certain features—eight legs, spinnerets, etc.—other features are specific to each particular spider. When you realize that the types of spiders are being compared and contrasted, you begin to construct in your mind a chart with features on the side and spider types across the top. As you read about the different kinds of spiders, you place their contrasting features in the appropriate categories.

Compare and Contrast Chart

	Tarantulas	**Crab Spiders**	**Jumping Spiders**
How They Look	Large and hairy	Short, wide, crab-like bodies	Colorful, with brightly colored hair on their legs
Where They Live	Burrow into the ground		
How They Move	Crawl	Sideways, like a crab	Jump more than 40 times their body length

Next, you read the article about Mia Hamm mentioned earlier in this chapter and, realizing that sequence is important to biography, you begin to construct an internal time line for Mia.

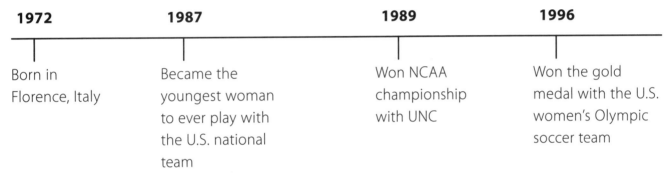

1972	1987	1989	1996
Born in Florence, Italy	Became the youngest woman to ever play with the U.S. national team	Won NCAA championship with UNC	Won the gold medal with the U.S. women's Olympic soccer team

Finally, you read an article about the effects of inflation on the stock and bond markets, and your brain starts constructing a causal chain of events.

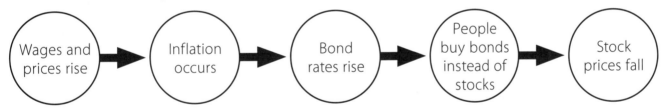

Wages and prices rise → Inflation occurs → Bond rates rise → People buy bonds instead of stocks → Stock prices fall

The previous examples are included to illustrate the most common expository text structures: main idea/details, compare/contrast, sequence, and cause/effect. Many informational pieces include two or more of these structures. Because informational pieces are structured in different ways and because the brain stores information in intricately networked and interconnected ways, it is believed that graphic organizers are excellent devices for helping students learn to follow the structures of informational text. Chapter 10 provides graphic organizers and suggestions for using these lesson frameworks to help your students make sense of different kinds of informational text.

Helping Students Use Comprehension Strategies Independently

It is much easier to teach strategies than it is to get students to use strategies when they need them. Many students can pick out the main idea from a list of four possible choices but do not sort out the main ideas from the details when reading on their own. Many students can put story events in order if you give them the events but cannot retell a story and include the important events in the right order. Many students can fill in the details on the spokes of a web if you tell them to, but they do not construct internal webs to help them follow the informational text structure as they read.

In the next chapter, you will discover a variety of materials you can use with students. In the remainder of this book, you will find powerful activities that will help your students learn to use thinking strategies (connecting, predicting/questioning, summarizing, inferring, monitoring, visualizing/imagining, and evaluating/applying) and follow text structures (sentence and paragraph structure, story structure, and informational structure). As your students participate in these varied comprehension activities every day, they will learn to use the comprehension strategies independently.

Chapter 3

Materials for Teaching Guided Reading

Teachers who are the happiest and most successful with Guided Reading use the widest variety of materials possible. In fact, meeting all of the Guided Reading goals is impossible if you stick with just one or two things for students to read every day. Here are the goals for Guided Reading:

- To teach students how to read all types of literature
- To teach comprehension strategies
- To develop students' prior knowledge, meaning vocabulary, and oral language
- To provide instructional-level reading material
- To maintain the motivation and confidence of struggling readers

If you are going to teach students how to read all types of literature, you must include instruction with all types. Why? The different types of literature require different comprehension strategies. When you read stories, you must follow the story structure and think about the characters, settings, events, and conclusions. Your comprehension will be greater if you imagine yourself in the same situations as the characters, predict what the characters will do, and evaluate the choices the characters make based on what you think they should do. You will also comprehend the story better if you think about why things happen and why characters behave the way they do.

Even different types of fiction require different comprehension strategies. When reading a mystery, you must watch for clues and draw conclusions to solve the mystery before the author solves it for you. When reading a fantasy, you must imagine a different world and infer by what rules the characters in that world live.

Informational reading requires different comprehension strategies from fictional reading. To remember and learn from nonfiction, you must determine and remember the sequence in which specific events occurred. Events that follow other events are often caused by the previous events, and you must think about which events caused which events to happen. Often, several things—animals, people, events, places, etc.—are compared and contrasted, and you must summarize and draw conclusions about their similarities and differences. Informational text contains special features, such as headings, bold print, maps, charts, and glossaries. These special features help comprehension only if you know how to read and interpret them. Poetry, plays, and directions have their own structures. With poetry, plays, and directions, you must use different comprehension strategies from the strategies you use with stories and informational text.

To meet the goal of teaching the comprehension strategies needed to read, enjoy, and learn from different kinds of texts, you must provide students with instruction and practice in reading all types of text. A variety of materials is also essential for meeting the goal of developing students' prior knowledge, meaning vocabulary, and oral language. Since students require a lot of encounters with particular words and concepts to begin using them, you should integrate the teaching of Guided Reading with science and social studies themes and topics. Read both informational and story selections that relate to what you are teaching in science and social studies. Keep charts and lists of words that students are learning in these subjects.

Finally, having a variety of materials is critical for achieving the last two goals of Guided Reading: providing instructional-level reading material and maintaining the motivation and confidence of struggling readers. Read both grade-level and easier materials. When you do Book Club Groups, choose four books and ensure that one book is easier and one is harder than the others. In the elementary grades, many teachers form a Reading for Fun Club or an After-Lunch Bunch and read short, easy selections with a small group of struggling readers several times a week. In *What Really Matters in Response to Intervention: Research-Based Designs*, Richard Allington states that working with a small group in the classroom is the best Type 2 Intervention. Allington also mentions that it is beneficial to provide many opportunities for struggling readers to receive instruction in materials at their instructional levels.

By using a wide variety of materials and grouping patterns, students will never think that they are in the "dumb group" or are reading "baby books"! The best teachers do not place students in ability groups for Guided Reading and are very good at creating ways to ensure that every student gets what she needs and feels terrific!

To achieve the goals of Guided Reading, you must collect and use the widest range of materials possible. You may be thinking, *Easy for you to say! I don't have much to work with. I'm stuck with what I have.* In this chapter, you will become convinced that you have—and can get—more than you think and that using more than just the reading textbook, text sets, or book packs is crucial for students to learn how to comprehend what they read.

Fiction, Nonfiction, Plays, Poetry, and Directions

Fiction is made up—it didn't happen! Some kinds of fiction—realistic fiction, historical fiction, and mysteries—could have happened but didn't. Other types of fiction, such as folktales, fairy tales, science fiction, and fantasy, are made up and probably could not have happened. Animals don't talk, fairy godmothers don't turn pumpkins into chariots, and there is no technology (as of today) for beaming people to faraway places. Fiction is almost always a story. It has a setting and characters. The characters interact and have goals or solve problems. There is action, plot, and drama!

Nonfiction did happen. Nonfiction includes informational books about animals, sports, places, art, cooking, gardening, health, and a host of other topics you can learn about through reading. Nonfiction also includes biographies and autobiographies.

According to a national survey, bookstores sell 80 percent of their fiction titles to women and 80 percent of their nonfiction titles to men. Those statistics are astonishing! This may indicate that females have a clear preference for fiction, and males prefer nonfiction in the U.S. adult reading population.

Now, consider the types of reading material that elementary teachers, who are overwhelmingly female, provide students and the generally less-positive attitudes boys have toward reading. Ask yourself whether there might be a connection. Could these boys have negative attitudes toward reading because most of what students are given to read is fiction, and most boys prefer nonfiction?

Regardless of gender, people have different preferences for what they read. Adult readers tend to favor one or two types of books and do most of their reading in those types. During Guided Reading, try to have students read from all of the sections of a bookstore. That way, you know that every student has the opportunity to discover the type of book that grabs him.

In addition to story and informational text, plays, poetry, and directions are included in Guided Reading. Each has its own form, and each requires particular comprehension strategies. Students enjoy the change of pace that plays, poetry, and directions provide and the special activities that you do with these types of text. You can read plays aloud, do Echo and Choral Reading of poetry with the class, and draw and make things from directions.

Your Guided Reading Materials

Look at the materials you use for Guided Reading and try to separate them into categories. If you use a reading textbook, look at the table of contents and try to fit each selection into the chart on page 32. If you use text sets or book packs, try to classify them. Conclude how balanced your Guided Reading is with text types and imagine how different students will view reading, given how much time is spent with each type.

Text Type	Two Examples Found	Total Number of Type
Realistic Fiction		
Historical Fiction		
Mystery		
Fairy Tale/Folktale		
Modern Fantasy		
Science Fiction		
Information–Science		
Information–Social Studies		
Information–Other		
Biography		
Plays		
Poetry		
Directions		
None of the Above		

What did you discover? When this chart was completed by one teacher with the typical materials used for Guided Reading, a huge amount of realistic fiction, folktales, fairy tales, and fantasy; some poetry and informational science (mostly about animals); and very little or none of the other types of material were found. The teacher began "begging, borrowing, and contriving" so that her Guided Reading time provided a more balanced reading diet. You can do the same for your class when you find out what you have and what you need. Variety is more important in grades three, four, and five than it is in first and second grade, but having a variety of fiction and nonfiction is important at all grade levels.

Finding a Variety of Materials for Guided Reading

In some schools, there is a limited amount of materials being used for Guided Reading. Some schools have basal readers or literature anthologies and rely primarily on them. Other schools have text sets or sets of six books and rely primarily on them. With the amount of materials available for purchase, classrooms and schools should offer more variety to enrich Guided Reading lessons. Following are some materials you may want to use and some suggestions for how to acquire them.

Reading Textbooks

Most elementary schools have reading textbooks, which are sometimes called basal readers or literature anthologies. In some schools, the adopted reading textbook is the core text for Guided Reading. Teachers use most of the selections in the textbook and supplement as needed to achieve the necessary variety and to integrate easier reading. In other schools, the use of the reading textbook is optional, and teachers pick and choose what they use and the order in which they read selections.

Most teachers have strong feelings about adopted reading textbooks. Some teachers feel hemmed in by them and can't make their Guided Reading work well because they are giving equal time to each selection and trying to follow all of the suggestions in the accompanying manual. Other teachers hardly use the adopted reading textbook and are constantly scrounging for Guided Reading material, even though many selections contained in their reading textbook would be useful if used appropriately. The most successful teachers use everything they can for Guided Reading, including the reading textbook if they have one. They look at the adopted reading textbook and older texts as sources of multiple copies of reading material that they can use to their best advantage. Here are two tips for using and obtaining reading textbooks:

1. **Evaluate the selections.** Go through your textbook and rank each selection. Use the categories in the chart on page 32 to determine what type of text the selection is. Decide how difficult each selection will be for most of your students and rate it as *easy*, *hard*, or *just right*. Next, consider the delight factor. How much will your students like the selection? Finally, think about the rest of your curriculum. Does the selection link to what you will be teaching in math, science, or social studies? You may want to create a chart like the one below to record your opinions.

Title, Pages	Type	Easy/Hard/Just Right	♥/OK/YUK!	Curriculum Link

2. **Decide which selections you will use and when and how you will use them.** Once you have evaluated all of the selections in your reading textbook, you can begin to use the textbook instead of letting it use you! How much control you have depends on the flexibility (or rigidity) of your school or district rules, but most teachers have more freedom than they think. Perhaps a selection that is too hard, that would hold no interest for your students, and that does not link to anything deserves only a day of your Guided Reading time. If a selection would be of interest but is hard, maybe you could skip it and do it later in the school year when students will be better readers. If you find a selection that links to another part of your curriculum, perhaps you could read it when you get to the unit, or if you must follow the reading textbook order, you could do the unit early.

Reading textbooks vary in how useful they will be to you. Some are harder than others, and some have a better balance of text types. They all have some wonderful and useful selections, some pretty good selections, and some clunkers. The activities they propose are not all wonderful; look carefully at the teacher's manual and ask yourself, *Does my class need this*? The teacher's manual is like a buffet at a restaurant. For a balanced diet, you don't need to take some of everything! Deciding what your reading textbook can do for you will put you in control and tell you what else you need to find.

Old Textbooks

If your school uses reading textbooks, there are probably old books stored somewhere. They may be in your cabinets, the grade-level chair's cabinets, or another teacher's cabinets. Perhaps they are located in a storeroom or on the back shelves in the library. Sometimes, old textbooks are stored at the central office or in a no-longer-used school. Schools that adopt reading textbooks rarely discard them. They put them somewhere. You should find out where and retrieve them.

In many school systems, you can cut apart these old texts and make skinny books with the selections you deem worthy. (This is a wonderful project for a parent or homebound volunteer who wants to help but can't commit to a big project.) If you can cut apart the books, be selective and take only the selections that will help you meet your goals. Think about when you can use them and pair some of them with selections from your adopted reading textbook so that you will have grade-level text and easier text for one week. If you can't cut apart the old textbooks, still decide which selections you will use and when you will use them.

Make a master book for yourself with paper clips and sticky notes marking the selections you will use and when they will best fit. When looking at old basals, be even pickier about which selections you will use. Make the selections you choose earn the days you and your students will spend reading them. Selections that are easy, delightful, of a text type not well represented in your current

34

textbook, and uniquely able to link to another part of your curriculum get a perfect 10! Hard, boring, same-type-as-the-others, and not-linked-to-anything selections get a goose egg. (If you are cutting apart books, recycle these.)

Reading Textbooks from Earlier Grades

When looking for easier selections, the reading textbooks from previous grades are a good place to start. Early in the year, first- and second-grade teachers use the early-grade materials and are usually willing to loan their later-grade books to a responsible second- or third-grade teacher who promises to return them in mint condition. But, how can you ask students to read these easier books without undermining their confidence and motivation? Here is what one enterprising second-grade teacher did.

After realizing that the selections in her reading textbook were too hard for most of her students at the beginning of the year, the teacher borrowed the mid-first-grade book from a first-grade teacher. She typed a table of contents that listed the title and page numbers for all of the full-length selections. She distributed copies of the table of contents to students and told them that she had heard that there were a lot of great stories in the book they had read last year. She made a big deal about how she had borrowed one of the books from the first-grade teacher, taken it home the previous night, and discovered some funny stories and selections with interesting information. As the teacher said this, she pointed to a couple of titles on the table of contents and invited students to share what they remembered about the selections.

Next, she explained that after a long summer of not reading much, everyone needed to warm up and get ready to move ahead. She said that she thought that rereading some of their favorite selections would be a good warm-up. "But," the teacher explained, "I need your help! I don't know what your favorites are, and we don't have time to reread them all." (Students are always more cooperative when they think that their help is needed!)

The teacher explained that she would give them each a book and 20 minutes to look through the book before voting on the best selections. She explained that each student could vote for four selections and that the selections that received the most votes would be the ones they would read. She also told students that they had to make up their own minds but that they could look at the books with friends if they liked.

The teacher handed each student a book and set the timer for 20 minutes. Students quickly settled down with the books and the table of contents. Most students huddled with friends and skimmed the book, remembering favorites, enjoying the pictures, rereading a little, and lobbying each other to vote the way they intended to vote.

When the timer sounded, students voted. The teacher tallied the votes and ranked the selections from favorite to least favorite. Six selections received a lot of votes, and the teacher decided that they would reread all six, beginning with the one that received the most votes and working down the list.

They spent 18 days, 3 days on each selection, reading and rereading the selections. During this time, the teacher used several before- and after-reading activities (KWL, Beach Ball, Picture Walks, etc.) to which she wanted students to become accustomed. She also taught students some of the during-reading formats that she wanted them to learn, such as Partner Reading, Play-School Groups that she renamed Reading Teams, Three-Ring Circus, and You'se Choose.

At the end of the first month of school, these second-graders were becoming better readers. Reading and rereading easy selections in a variety of formats will bring most classes back up to speed. Students had also become comfortable with some of the before- and after-reading activities and during-reading formats that they would use throughout the year.

At the suggestion of one student, echoed by the rest, the teacher borrowed the late-first-grade book and used the same procedure of having students select the best six from it. By the end of the second month of school, many students were able to read most of the selections in the grade-level text and, by combining it with easier selections from different sources using the Book Club and other formats, the Guided Reading time was off to a successful start!

Of course, there are other ways to use reading textbooks from an earlier grade. If your school has a new adoption, and your students haven't read the earlier texts yet, you can still use the choice procedure. Have students decide which selections they would have liked best last year and read the top choices. You might also institute a community service reading project and appoint all of your students as reading tutors. Students must practice reading easier materials so that they can teach them to students at a lower grade level. When making skinny books, you can include worthy selections from easier texts without having to make an excuse for them.

Sometimes in teaching children, as in cooking meals, it's all in the presentation! When clever teachers present easier reading in ways that whet students' appetites and let students make some choices, they read and reread happily.

Leveled Book Sets

Years ago, it was nearly impossible to find leveled books—books that become a little bit harder as you move through the levels—except in basal readers. Now, they are everywhere! Leveled books are controlled in several ways. Some leveled books move from very predictable to less predictable text. Some books provide sight word practice with high-frequency words. Other books are controlled by phonics elements (decodable readers) and provide practice in applying decoding to the reading of text. Leveled books are often sold in sets of six and provide a lot of materials for intervention groups, coaching groups, After-Lunch Bunches, and Reading for Fun Clubs. Some teachers use leveled books to provide easier selections for Guided Reading. If you share with another teacher from your grade level, or if your school purchases a second package, you can probably create sets of 12 books, enough for Partner Reading in most elementary classrooms.

Many leveled books give levels based on the Reading Recovery leveling system. Reading Recovery levels go from 1 to 20 for first and second grades. The books leveled 1–16 are first-grade selections, and levels 17–20 are early second-grade books. Additional levels were added later to include books through third grade. *Matching Books to Readers: Using Leveled Books in Guided Reading, K–3* by Irene C. Fountas and Gay Su Pinnell includes 7,500 titles leveled from kindergarten through third grade. These grade levels are indicated by letters, with level A being kindergarten and level P being third grade. All of the major leveled book publishers offer search by subject area and reading level.

Science and Social Studies Textbooks

Science and social studies textbooks are materials you can use for Guided Reading, but again, you have to be choosy. Often, the reading level of these books is higher than the grade level you are teaching. Because science and social studies textbooks have to cover so much information, they sometimes include the bare bones without the fascinating facts and examples that make informational text intriguing to young students. Sometimes, textbook companies add leveled readers and other sets of small books about the subject to their materials.

In spite of readability and motivational concerns, every science and social studies textbook includes something that your students can read and will enjoy reading—the pictures and graphics and the quicktext (labels, captions, etc.) that accompany them. Look through your science and social studies textbooks and ignore everything but the visuals. Imagine how you could guide your students' comprehension as you taught them the skills of picture interpretation and graph, chart, and map reading. In Part Two of this book, you will learn about some before- and after-reading activities, including KWL charts and graphic organizers, that you can use to organize and summarize the information students learn from the visuals.

As you are looking at the visuals, you might find some text to include in Guided Reading. Many science textbooks contain experiments with step-by-step directions. Social studies textbooks often contain directions for doing an interview or a simulation activity. Sometimes, you may even find a poem or two from which to learn.

Many teachers avoid science and social studies textbooks because they are hard to read and are often boring. But, the visuals—pictures, charts, graphs, maps, accompanying labels, and quicktext— are easy to read. Students, particularly struggling readers, enjoy the success they experience as they read the visuals and explain what they are learning. The directions and informational poetry found in these textbooks are a bonus. Look with a fresh eye at your science and social studies textbooks, and you may find that they will majorly help you meet the goals of Guided Reading. The informational text broadens the variety of materials students are learning how to read. You can teach the specific skills needed to interpret pictures, graphs, charts, and maps. You will be helping students increase their prior knowledge, meaning vocabulary, and oral language. The reading of the visuals is more apt to be at the instructional level of your struggling readers, and the experience will enhance their motivation and confidence. The benefits aren't bad for something you probably already have!

Don't forget to look for old textbooks, and remember that the units you are teaching may be found in old textbooks for earlier or later grade levels. If you can cut up the old textbooks, you may want to write some simple text and have students make their own books by cutting and pasting some of the visuals from the textbooks and adding them to the text you provide.

Class Sets of "Real" Books
Some schools have a central storeroom with class sets of popular books for each grade level. A teacher of grades two or three might check out the pack of *Frog and Toad Together* by Arnold Lobel, *Penguins* by Gail Gibbons, or a set of books in The Magic School Bus series by Joanna Cole. A teacher of grades four or five might check out a set of *Maniac Magee, Loser, The Library Card*, or *Stargirl* by Jerry Spinelli (or six of each for Book Club Groups) or a set of *Because of Winn-Dixie* by Kate DiCamillo for the class. Many teachers use the points they get from book fairs when students order books to accumulate class sets of books. Regardless of what material you favor for Guided Reading, it is important that you acquire some class sets of popular books so that you can guide students' reading through whole books. Many teachers worry because their students can't sustain their reading during Self-Selected Reading or independent reading long enough to read entire books, yet the teachers never guide the students through entire books during Guided Reading! Learning how to read a whole book across several days is a comprehension strategy that can be learned only with whole books!

Everyone should include some whole books in his Guided Reading lessons. So, what do you do if you don't have any? First, consider how many books you need. Having a book for everyone would be nice, but you can get by with half as many books as you have students. Students can share books during an Everyone Read To lesson, and they can share books when they read in partners, Play-School Groups, and Reading Teams. (For some reason, who holds the book is the biggest issue for students, so specify who has the first turn and alternate on different days or halfway through the reading.)

Next, consider popular books of which you may already have a few copies in your room and of which the school and public libraries have copies. In many schools, there are enough copies spread throughout the school to put together a class set, particularly if students share books. List the books you want to use and circulate it to other teachers, including special teachers and reading teachers. If some of your students' parents buy books for them or if your students order from book clubs, you may suggest to parents that they buy the books their children will read in class, and then their children will get to keep them. What about the students you taught in past years? If you are choosing popular books, they may have some at home that they would be willing to loan you for a few weeks. Some students (and some parents) don't care about keeping books once they have read them and are willing to donate them to the classroom library if you put a sticky label inside the book that states: "Donated to Mrs. Hall's Classroom Library by _____ on _____." Gathering the class sets of a few books for Guided Reading is a hassle, but the payoff in terms of students' delight in reading real books, their sense of community in enjoying the same book, and their increased ability to read longer texts makes it worth the trouble.

If you plan ahead—and particularly if your grade level or school plans together—it should be less of a hassle in future years. Teachers need each class set for only a few weeks, and they don't need too many sets because the more variety of materials used during Guided Reading, the better. Most schools can and will purchase a few class sets for each grade level if the teachers get together and take a solid stand!

Be sure to include both fiction and informational books in your class sets. Some teachers read a fiction and informational book on the same topic. Second-grade teachers might choose to have their students read *Tacky the Penguin* by Helen Lester and *Penguins* by Gail Gibbons. Third graders might read *Owl Moon* by Jane Yolen and *Owls* by Gail Gibbons. Fifth graders might read *Pink and Say* by Patricia Polacco while reading about the American Civil War in their social studies textbooks. Pair-It Books, published by Steck-Vaughn, offer thematic pairs of books on the same level—one fiction and one informational. For example, *How Spiders Got Eight Legs* by Katherine Mead is paired with *A Look at Spiders* by Jerald Halpern. *My Prairie Summer* by Sarah Glasscock is paired with *Laura Ingalls Wilder: An Author's Story* also by Sarah Glasscock. These books are available in stages from Foundation Stage (kindergarten) through Proficiency Stage 6 (grade 6) with appropriate titles for each stage/grade level.

Book Club Sets

One of the most popular and multilevel formats for Guided Reading is Book Club Groups. To prepare for Book Club Groups, find four books tied together by author, text type, theme, or topic. In choosing the books, find one that is a little easier than the others and one that is a little harder. Gathering books for Book Club Groups is easy because you need only six to eight copies of each book (depending on how many students you have). Two students in a group could share a book, so you could get away with having as few as three or four of each title.

When considering which book is easier and which is harder, depend on what you know about reading comprehension and your students. Prior knowledge is the biggest determinant of comprehension. If students know a lot about a topic, they will understand text about the topic easily. They will also have many of the words in their listening vocabularies and thus be able to identify the words more easily when they see them in the book. Topics about which students know little are harder for them to understand, and they are apt to have fewer words related to the topic in their listening vocabularies. Other factors that make books easier or harder relate to the amount of text on each page and the size of the print.

Even books by the same author can vary in difficulty. Gail Gibbons writes wonderful informational books about animals. Topic familiarity makes *Dogs* and *Cats* easier than most of her books, and *Sea Turtles* is more difficult than most. Looking at the amount of text and the complexity of the text on different pages will help you see that some of The Magic School Bus books by Joanna Cole are easier or harder than the others. Don't forget to take into consideration familiarity. *The Magic School Bus in the Time of Dinosaurs* is easy for many young students because they are interested in dinosaurs and have a lot of prior knowledge about them.

Try to find four books on four different levels that your students will find interesting and will want to read. Books by authors like Dr. Seuss, Arnold Lobel, Kevin Henkes, Gail Gibbons, Eve Bunting, David Adler, and Patricia Polacco are excellent choices for Book Club Groups. For example, the whole class could read the award-winning *The Keeping Quilt* by Patricia Polacco (GRL: M, RL: 5.3), and you could follow it up with Book Club Groups using Patricia Polacco's *Just Plain Fancy* (GRL: O, RL 3.8), *Chicken Sunday* (GRL: N, RL: 4.8), and *Applemando's Dreams* (GRL: M, RL: 5.4).

You can also use Book Club Groups to review a strategy you have taught the class. After using a whole-class book to teach Preview-Predict-Confirm, you might use Book Club Groups to review this strategy with four books by four different authors. For example, read *Suddenly* by Colin McNaughton with the whole class (GRL: J, RL: 2.5) and follow it up with Book Club Groups using *Click, Clack, Moo: Cows That Type* by Doreen Cronin (GRL: K RL 1.3), *The Monster at the End of This Book* by Jon Stone (RL 2.3), *Purple, Green and Yellow* by Robert Munsch (RL 2.4), and *The Sweetest Fig* by Chris Van Allsburg (RL 3.9). Book Club Groups have the advantage of introducing four books to the class that they might want to read during Self-Selected Reading.

Several publishers list reading levels for their books, which makes it easier to select books for Book Club Groups and to include one book that is a little easier and one that is a little harder. When selecting books for Book Club Groups, compare the levels given by the publisher with what you know about your students, particularly their prior knowledge of the topics.

Big Books

The major advantage of big books is that you can gather your class around you and focus students' attention on whatever you want. When you do Shared Reading using big books with beginning readers, you can share the lap experience some students have at home while pointing to the pictures and print. You can point to the text features and talk about the important things you want students to notice. Show students important words, ending marks, and the first word in each sentence. Shared Reading with big books helps beginners learn how to track print. Big books are not just for little kids! Big books can be incredibly helpful in teaching comprehension strategies to older students. (If you use a big book for a comprehension lesson at any grade level, students should be close enough to the book that when the teacher points to a feature, they can follow along; read the quicktext under the pictures; read the print on the pages; and see the charts, graphs, and maps. When using an interactive whiteboard, you can use a pointer to show these features.)

As students get older, less Shared Reading with big books is done and more Guided Reading in which students look at their own copies of normal-sized books takes place. But, there continues to be a place for big books—even with students in intermediate grades. Big books are helpful when you want to focus on a particular strategy. Predicting/questioning, for example, is a strategy that all good readers use to think about what they are reading. When students are reading their own books and you are encouraging them to predict and question, some students are always tempted to look ahead so that they can make a brilliant prediction. This ruins the strategy lesson for everyone! If you are using a big book, you get to turn the pages, and everyone must use their brains and prior knowledge to predict. The big book keeps students honest! Big books for older students are harder to find, but you may have access to document cameras that you can use with any size book. Project the text on an interactive whiteboard and point out the features as you read the pages together in a Shared Reading format.

Reading big books or using a document camera to project a regular-sized book on a large screen benefits older students most by helping them learn how to read informational text. Informational text has many features that are not found in story text. It often has a table of contents, an index, and a glossary. The glossary often contains the phonetic pronunciation of difficult words. Informational text has captioned illustrations and photographs, maps with symbols and a symbol key, graphs, and charts. To understand informational text, students must understand how the headings work and what bold print and bullets signify. Reading science and social studies texts is a challenge for many students, including students who read stories well. Students should be taught the specific comprehension strategies required by informational text. Using big books and projecting regular text onto a large screen allow you to focus students' attention on the unique features of informational text.

Most early elementary teachers have several big books from which to choose. Although not promoted as much as they once were, big books are still an excellent source of comprehension material for kindergarten and first-grade classrooms. If you have the right big books, the whole class will enjoy the familiar and not-so-familiar stories. Young students never tire of reading *Brown Bear, Brown Bear, What Do You See?* by Bill Martin Jr., *Little Red Hen* by Byron Barton, *Mrs. Wishy-Washy* by Joy Cowley, *Zoo-Looking* by Mem Fox, and *The Door Bell Rang* by Pat Hutchins.

Teachers of older students will have a harder time finding big books than in the past. They may need to look to their content areas for these books. Many publishers once produced big books to accompany their science and social studies textbooks. Even if these big books are not in your room, they may be in your school. Many schools buy one set of the supplementary materials that ends up sitting in the closet of the science coordinator, the grade-level chair, or the assistant principal. Find out if your current textbooks have big books available or if a past adoption with the same topics had them and start looking. If you cannot find any big books, think about using your text or a regular-sized informational book with a document camera to introduce students to features and topics.

Weekly Magazines

Magazines such as *Weekly Reader* and *Scholastic News* can be wonderful sources of material to include in Guided Reading one day each week. Most selections in these magazines are informational, but there are also some plays and poems. Often, the magazines include directions for making something or performing an experiment. Adding these magazines weekly can take you a long way toward meeting your Guided Reading goals as you teach the comprehension strategies needed for these text types. The reading, accompanied by a lot of visuals, is usually easier, and being able to read and comprehend this highly motivating material enhances the confidence of struggling readers. Because each issue has a topic, reading these selections helps students increase their prior knowledge, meaning vocabularies, and oral language. When you come across a grade-level subject in a weekly magazine, save a copy to project with your document camera and to use as you would use a big book when teaching this subject.

What if your school has limited funds and cannot afford the cost per student per year of most subscriptions? Your school might have a business partner who would want to sponsor these weekly subscriptions for your class. A few parents might want to organize a fund-raiser so that everyone could have some weekly material to call his own. Or, you might be able to raise funds by collecting something and recycling it. Sometimes when the need is apparent, the benefits are obvious, and the cost is not outrageous, you can acquire the needed funds. These weekly magazines are also available online and could be shown on an interactive whiteboard for all students to see. But, this does not take the place of a magazine in a student's hand and reading material for a student to take home and keep!

Ideally, all of your students could use weekly magazines to learn how to read during Guided Reading and could take them home to show everyone what they know and can do. But, even when you think creatively, that may not be possible. Consider this possibility: What if you could partner with three or four other teachers and order 10–12 copies of the weekly magazines that best fit your curriculum, reading levels, and text needs? Each teacher would have the magazines for one day's Guided Reading. Students could share the magazines in Partner Reading, Play-School Groups, Everyone Read To, or whatever format you decided to use. (If possible, you would laminate the copies. If not, you would have to be strict about their care and handling.) At the end of each week, each teacher would receive two or three copies to keep in the room. These copies could go in a special place and would be available for Self-Selected Reading. As the school year progressed, your supply of interesting informational material for Self-Selected Reading would grow rapidly. Students' fluency would grow as they chose some of their favorite pieces for rereading.

Local Newspaper's Kids' Section
Many local newspapers have a kids' section or mini-page supplement one day a week. Does your paper have one? If so, you have found another accessible source for Guided Reading material. Most mini-pages include a variety of text types: a preponderance of short informational pieces, visuals—maps, charts, and graphs—and some puzzles and riddle-like activities. If you can get enough copies for all of your students, let students take them home to share with their parents. If you need to share the copies in class, let each student take a copy home every other week.

Many teachers ask students whose parents receive the paper at home to bring in the mini-page the next day. They also ask everyone they know (friends, neighbors, teachers of upper grades and special subjects, custodians, secretaries, etc.) to save the mini-page supplement for them. Some newspapers print extra copies of the mini-page each week and will give them to you for use in your classroom.

In addition to helping you meet your Guided Reading goals, using the mini-page has some fringe benefits. Many students will begin to read other parts of the paper, which will increase the amount of at-home reading they do and broaden the types of text they can read. This reading is often done with parents or older siblings, and family members talk and interact around the reading stimulus. Students who look forward to the daily newspaper begin to see themselves as readers and to see reading as a real-world source of entertainment and information.

Poetry

If you find the right kind of poetry, students will love it! Poems are usually short and unintimidating. They speak to all five senses. They appeal to and stimulate the imagination. Many poems have rhythm or rhyme, and poems can be silly or informational. There are poems to fit all themes and topics. There are poems with which older, struggling readers and English Language Learners can experience success and enjoyment. You can build concepts with poems and help students understand figurative language. You can do Echo and Choral Reading to improve students' reading fluency. Poetry should be part of every teacher's Guided Reading time.

You probably have in mind many sources of poetry, and you have probably found poetry in your reading, science, and social studies textbooks (old and new). Poetry is often found in weekly student magazines and on newspaper mini-pages. In addition, you can find poetry in anthologies and at various Web sites and can use it with your class by writing it on a chart. Some teachers have students create poetry notebooks in which they write their favorite poems.

The biggest problem with poetry, once you start to look for and use it, is that you can overdo it. Remember that a goal of Guided Reading is for students to learn the strategies needed to read all kinds of text. Including poetry often—but not too often—will help you achieve that goal.

These are some of the most popular poets for children:

Lucille Clifton	Aileen Fisher	Eloise Greenfield
Karla Kuskin	Myra Cohn Livingston	David McCord
Eve Merriam	Kenn Nesbitt	Jack Prelutsky
Christina Rosetti	Shel Silverstein	Robert Louis Stevenson

Plays

Plays are another type of reading material that students enjoy enormously. Plays have a particular style, and while students are learning to read them, they practice reading their lines several times until they can read them expressively. (Don't ask students to memorize plays; it would take a very long time, and it would not help increase students' reading fluency, which is one reason to use plays with students.) There are usually some plays in textbooks and student magazines, but plays are perhaps the most difficult material to find. Many teachers resort to writing simple plays for their students or letting students help them turn stories into scripts for plays. Older students enjoy doing Readers' Theater. They write the scripts as a focused-writing activity and practice reading and performing them during Guided Reading.

Many publishers offer sets of tales and plays that are particularly useful. In some books, a story is told in the traditional tale format and as a play. These tales and plays are written on many different reading levels.

A set of plays that is perfect for Echo Reading is the Speak Out! Readers' Theater series. Different parts of these plays are written on different reading levels. The multilevel scripts are ideal for grouping students with different reading levels and providing the repeated oral reading practice students need to improve fluency. Each script focuses on a different content area, exposing students to a variety of engaging topics.

Other publishers offer plays with multilevel scripts. Their plays include fables, legends, myths, and a wide variety of science and social studies topics. Using these scripts, you can group students who read on different reading levels and assign parts to students that match their levels.

There are many books of reproducible plays for the elementary grades. Carol Pugliano-Martin has written a number of these books. Some of her titles include the following:

- *25 Just-Right Books for Emergent Readers*
- *Folk and Fairy Tale Plays for Building Fluency: 8 Engaging, Read-Aloud Plays Based on Favorite Tales to Help Boost Students' Word Recognition, Comprehension, and Fluency*
- *Just-Right Plays: 25 Emergent Reader Plays for Around the Year*
- *Greek Myth Plays: 10 Readers Theater Scripts Based on Favorite Greek Myths That Students Can Read and Reread to Develop Their Fluency*
- *25 Spanish Plays for Emergent Readers*
- *15 Plays for Beginning Readers: Famous Americans*
- *Read-Aloud Plays: Tall Tales*

Anthony D. Fredericks has also written several books of plays for elementary teachers. His titles include the following:

- *African Legends, Myths, and Folktales for Readers Theatre*
- *Silly Salamanders and Other Slightly Stupid Stuff for Readers Theatre*
- *Mother Goose: Readers Theatre for Beginning Readers*
- *Nonfiction Readers Theatre for Beginning Readers*
- *Fairy Tales Readers Theatre*

Directions

You have probably already found some directions in the books, magazines, and newspaper mini-pages you have scrounged. There are also some wonderful books full of directions. *Drawing Book of Animals* by Ed Emberley is one of many books that help students draw objects by following step-by-step directions that are given in words and pictures. Some books give directions for making things, for science experiments, and for recipes.

Learning how to read and follow directions requires specific comprehension strategies that are not required by any other kind of reading. Including direction reading during Guided Reading will allow you to teach these strategies and will motivate struggling readers who do not particularly like to read but do like to do and make things.

Duplicated Blackline Masters

Many companies produce blackline masters of little books that you can duplicate and use occasionally for Guided Reading. Many reading series provide these masters that can be used to create take-home books connected to the selection read in class. Often, these take-home books are easier to read than the selections in the reading text, and you may use them as the easier selections you include in Guided Reading every week. Advantages of the blackline masters are that they are economical, and students can take them home to show them off.

Reading A–Z (*www.readinga-z.com*) is an online source of inexpensive books to read in class and take home. The cost for a license to download these books is determined by the number of classes that will download and use the books. Science A–Z (*www.sciencea-z.com*) is a Web site by the same company with books about life science, earth science, physical science, and process science. There are not as many books available on this site, but the cost is less per class than the cost of the reading books. Many reading textbook publishers have reproducible pages from which students can construct mini-books. If your students don't have many books at home, you might use these mini-books one day a week during Guided Reading and suggest that students take them home to create their own reading libraries.

Teacher-Created Text

Another advantage of making copies for your students is that you can contrive some material. You can write out or type some simple text—fiction, informational text, poetry, plays, directions, etc.—and copy it for students to use during Guided Reading and to take home. When you write the text, you are in control and can make it as easy or hard and as predictable or unpredictable as you like.

If you are intimidated by the idea of writing something for your students to read, perhaps you are not giving yourself enough credit or you are trying to be too literary.

You should force yourself to write simple text, particularly if you are trying to include some easier text to provide fluency practice for all of your students and instructional-level reading for your struggling readers. Many teachers take something they have read to students or a selection that the class read during Guided Reading and write a similar improvised text. For example, imagine that you have read *The Little Red Hen* by Paul Galdone. You could write an improvisation, making yourself the little red hen and including students in the story as in the following example:

> *Once upon a time, there was a teacher named Mrs. Cunningham. She taught first grade at Brown School. She wanted to make some cookies. She wanted some help. She asked students for help: "Who will help me sift the flour?" "Not I," said Brandon and Joshua. "Not I," said Cerise and Rasheed. "Not I," said Pablo and Jasmine. "Then, I will do it myself," said Mrs. Cunningham, and she did.*

The improvised story continues and includes all of the students. At the end, the students help the teacher eat the cookies after promising to help her make the cookies next time. You can also write some simple text, summarizing what you have learned from reading an informational book.

Here is a summary about sharks:

> *Some sharks are short. Some sharks are long.*
>
> *Some sharks are thin. Some sharks are fat.*
>
> *Some sharks are as big as an 18-wheeler truck. Some sharks are as small as your hand.*
>
> *Sharks eat clams, crabs, turtles, fish, and other sharks.*
>
> *Sharks don't usually eat people, but they might if they think you are a fish!*
>
> *Sharks have many teeth. When one tooth falls out, another one grows in.*
>
> *Most sharks live in deep, warm water.*
>
> *Most sharks can swim 20 to 30 miles per hour, and they can live for 20 to 30 years.*

These two samples of teacher-created text show you that you can create text for students (probably much better than these examples)! Teachers who do not usually use a lot of copy paper should not feel guilty about copying some blackline masters—either commercially produced or teacher created—to provide students with the types and levels of materials that they need and deserve during Guided Reading.

Hopefully, you are feeling empowered by this chapter and have discovered that you have more materials than you thought you did and that you know how to beg, borrow, and contrive what you still need. There is just one more piece to this puzzle, before you will be ready to sample the before- and after-reading activities and during-reading formats that you can mix and match for an endless variety of Guided Reading lessons. The next section describes what to do before and after reading a selection to help you understand what the important comprehension strategies are and suggests how to decide what to teach when, with which materials, and to whom.

Part Two

Lesson Frameworks for Teaching Reading Comprehension

You teach comprehension lessons for two reasons. First, you want students to learn how to comprehend text so that they will be better readers. Second, you want students to gain prior knowledge and meaning vocabulary, especially during their reading of informational text and some kinds of stories, such as historical fiction. Comprehension lesson frameworks help you achieve both goals.

In Chapter 2, you learned that comprehension is thinking that is guided by the words and ideas in the text that you are reading. The thinking strategies most commonly used to comprehend are connecting, predicting/questioning, summarizing, inferring, monitoring, visualizing/imagining, and evaluating/applying. Often, your brain is using several thinking strategies simultaneously. In addition, your brain must follow the organization of different texts. When reading a story, your brain uses its knowledge of story structure to anticipate and make sense of characters, settings, problems, and solutions. When reading informational text, your brain must recognize the structure of the text in order to make sense of the ideas. The most common text structures found in informational text are main ideas/details, compare/contrast, sequence, and cause/effect.

In Part Two, you will learn a variety of comprehension lesson frameworks. This variety helps students learn to apply the thinking strategies when reading increasingly difficult texts and to comprehend different kinds of text structures as texts gradually become harder.

The comprehension lesson frameworks in Part Two provide you with opportunities to develop students' prior knowledge and meaning vocabulary. When you use an informational text or a science fiction or historical story, knowledge of the information, science, or history plays an important role. For example, when the before-reading activity has students predict what they will learn, they must access their prior knowledge and meaning vocabulary. Then, as students work together in the after-reading activity to determine which of their predictions were confirmed by the text, they add to and correct their prior knowledge and meaning vocabulary.

Even though there are several different comprehension lesson frameworks, effective comprehension lessons have two things in common. First, they have a before-reading activity that previews the after-reading activity and sets the purpose for reading the selection. For example, consider a comprehension lesson framework in which the after-reading activity involves completing a graphic organizer, such as a web. Because you want your students to be successful with the after-reading task, you show them the skeleton of the web before they begin reading and make sure that they understand it. This before-reading activity focuses students' attention on the information in the text that will help them complete the web after they read.

Second, effective comprehension lessons increase the likelihood of students' success by *fading to independence*. This means that students will be more successful if you do not immediately expect them to complete the after-reading task independently. Instead, you or a scribe in each small group does the writing while students work together to complete the after-reading comprehension task. After students have had collaborative success with a particular comprehension lesson framework several times, they will be prepared to complete that particular after-reading task alone.

The following lesson frameworks are covered in Part Two:

Chapter 4

Picture Walks

Do you look at the pictures before you begin reading a magazine article? Pictures are engaging, and they help you begin your reading using an important thinking strategy. When you look at pictures, your brain makes connections. The pictures trigger your brain to access certain information, and you connect what you know to the selection you will read. If the text students will read has a lot of pictures, precede your comprehension lesson with a Picture Walk. Page through the book, looking at and talking about the pictures. (If the story has a surprise ending, either do not do a Picture Walk or walk only partway through the book.) Pose simple questions that will help students connect what they know to the information that they will read.

- What do you see in these pictures?
- What is the boy (girl, woman, man, shark, cat, etc.) doing?
- Where is this happening?
- Where are they now?
- What do you think this is?

In addition to encouraging students to talk about what they see and what they think is happening, these questions ask them to name items in the pictures—particularly the items for which some students probably don't know the names. If you are teaching beginning readers who need help decoding some words, you can lead students to stretch out the words, identify the letters in the words, and point to the words in the text.

A Picture Walk Example for a Story

Here is an example of a Picture Walk using the popular book *There's an Alligator Under My Bed* by Mercer Mayer. (The bold type indicates what the teacher says.)

"Let's look at the cover of the book. What do you see here?" Students talk about the boy and the alligator.

"Where is the boy?" "In bed," students reply.

"Where is the alligator?" Students respond, "Under the bed."

"Now, let's see if we can read the title." Students read the title, "*There's an Alligator Under My Bed.*"

The teacher leads students to talk about the next several pages. He helps them understand that the boy's mom and dad cannot see the alligator, who appears only when the boy is alone in his bedroom.

"Look at this page. What is the boy doing?" "Getting something out of the refrigerator," respond students.

"The boy isn't in his bedroom anymore. What room do you think he is in?" "The kitchen," students reply.

"Let's stretch out the word *kitchen* and decide what letters kitchen has." Students stretch out *kitchen* and decide that they hear a *k*, an *n*, and the /ch/ sound in between.

"Look for the word *kitchen* and put your finger on it." Students point to the word *kitchen*, and the Picture Walk continues.

A few pages later, the teacher asks about the setting again.

"Where do you think the boy is now?" "In the garage," students say.

"Yes, the car is parked here, so this is probably the garage. Let's stretch out the word *garage*. We hear a *g*, an *r*, and a /j/ sound."

"See if you can point to the word *garage*." Students point to the word *garage*.

"Yes, that word is *garage*. We don't see a *j*. What letter do you think has the /j/ sound in *garage*?"

Students decide that garage has two *g*'s and that the last *g* has the same /j/ sound that it has in *gerbil*.

The teacher leads students to talk about several more pages and asks them to stretch out and identify a few more key words, such as *stairs* and *crawled*.

A Picture Walk Example for Informational Text

Picture Walks are an effective way to help older students begin to connect and predict/anticipate, particularly when they read informational text. Here is an example using the first third of *Amazing Fish* by Mary Ling.

The book has bold captions beside each picture and labels that go with some pictures. As you do the Picture Walk with informational text, read the quicktext (labels, captions, etc.) but move fast enough that students must wait to read the actual text. You want to whet their appetites for the feast of amazing facts that they will learn when they read.

"These two pages are called *What Is a Fish*? Let's look at the pictures and the labels and see what the pages tell us about how to decide whether an animal is a fish."

"What do you see next to the label *Our Wet Home?*" Students respond, "It is a picture of Earth."

"Look at the diagram next to the label about how fish breathe underwater. Who can explain what we see in the diagram?" "The water goes in through the gills," reply students, "and the fish get oxygen from the water." **"Say *oxygen* and point to the word *oxygen* in the text when you find it."**

"In the next diagram, you see a fish's fins with a label naming each fin. Point to the dorsal fin, the tail fin, and the pectoral fin."

The teacher continues to help students preview the pictures and labels that accompany the text. Each two-page spread is discussed quickly, but not every picture and label is discussed. The teacher introduces a few words that will probably cause difficulty in the students' reading. He uses the labels and pictures to build meaning and has students point to the words as they locate them in the text.

"Look at the two pictures of this fish. In the first picture, the fish is relaxed, and in the second one, it is disturbed. What animal does the disturbed fish resemble? It looks kind of like a porcupine, doesn't it? It is actually called a porcupine fish. Say *porcupine*, and find the word *porcupine* in the text.

"The stripes on this fish help it blend in with the coral reef. What do we call it when an animal can hide because it is the same color as its surroundings? Yes, we call it *camouflage*. Say the word *camouflage*. What letters do you hear? Find the word *camouflage* in the text and point to it."

Picture Walks

Picture Walks help students make connections and arouse their curiosity. Students do a lot of wondering as they try to make connections to the pictures.

- I wonder what that is.
- I wonder why he looks so unhappy.
- I wonder how that happened.
- I wonder how they can do that.

Because a Picture Walk is only a before-reading activity, it is not a comprehension lesson framework. It is included because it is a marvelous way to help students access prior knowledge and meaning vocabulary for any text with pictures. It also motivates students to read the text in order to discover more about what the pictures illustrate.

When using a Picture Walk, you will need another before-reading activity that previews whatever your after-reading comprehension task is. The remaining chapters in Part Two detail a number of comprehension lesson frameworks each comprised of a before- and after-reading activity. Any of the comprehension lesson frameworks described in the following chapters can follow up the connections and wonderings prompted by your Picture Walk.

1. Walk students through the text, looking at some of the visuals.
2. Ask questions about the visuals and let students share their connections with each other.
3. Use the visuals to introduce key vocabulary. Ask questions that might elicit the word, and if students do not come up with the word, say something like, "We call this a . . ."
4. For difficult-to-decode words, have students say the word, decide which letters they would expect to find in that word, and locate and point to that word in the text.
5. Take no more than a few minutes to picture walk the text. Give students enough time to peruse the pictures but not enough time to read the text. A Picture Walk should whet their appetites for what is to come when they read.
6. Follow up the Picture Walk with whatever comprehension lesson framework best suits the text and your instructional goals.

Chapter 5

Prove It!

Helping students make predictions before they read is a powerful strategy because instead of setting purposes and telling students what to read for, students are learning to set their own purposes. This is what readers do. Your brain begins making predictions the minute you see the title and cover of a book. As you read the first several pages, your brain thinks ahead about what might happen. Sometimes, you have a specific prediction:

If Clifford goes in there, he'll get stuck!

Other times, you anticipate the direction the text will take:

Clifford will get into trouble!

As you read, your predictions are sometimes proven true, and other times you are surprised. When helping students make predictions, don't emphasize whether their predictions are right or wrong. Rather, put your emphasis on whether the predictions make sense and are things that could happen. If a student makes a particularly good prediction that does not happen, assure the student that it was a wonderful prediction and that the author might have written a more interesting story if that prediction had actually happened.

The important part about predictions is not whether they are right or wrong, but that they are made. Once a student has made a prediction, her attention is engaged and comprehension is enhanced. You produce motivated, active, engaged readers when you regularly help students make predictions based on the cover, title, first few pages of text, illustrations, etc., and when you follow up the reading by discussing which predictions really happen and what surprises the author had in store for the readers. Prove It! is a lesson framework that guides students through text by having them make predictions and read to find out whether their predictions are confirmed. Students must also point to the text that proves their predictions were right.

An Example of Prove It!

For this lesson, the teacher chooses the book *Wagon Wheels* by Barbara Brenner. *Wagon Wheels* is a fairly easy, four-chapter historical fiction novel. In addition to learning to use pictures to make predictions, students learn how to sustain their reading in a simple, short chapter book. The teacher begins the Prove It! lesson by having students look at the book cover and the title and predict what the book will be about based on just these two factors. She numbers each prediction so that she can talk about the predictions more easily later. Here are some students' predictions based on the cover illustration and title of *Wagon Wheels*.

1. It is about a man and three boys.
2. The man is the boys' father.
3. They are traveling west in a wagon.
4. It happens in the old days.

Next, students look at the table of contents, read the titles of the four chapters, and make more predictions.

5. There are some Indians.
6. They move somewhere.
7. They get a letter.
8. There is a dugout, like in baseball.

Vague predictions are fine. Remember that the comprehension strategy you work on in Prove It! is predicting/questioning. Students do not yet know how the American Indians, letter, and dugout fit into the story. They are wondering, and the questions they are posing will lead to more engagement and comprehension.

Next, the teacher gives students two minutes to look at the pictures in the first chapter and come up with more predictions. After exactly two minutes, she has them close their books and make predictions. It is very important that the teacher gives them only two minutes and insists that they all close their books while the new predictions are being made. She does not want the fast readers to have time to read all of the text so that they can make the "right" predictions. This ruins the activity for everyone and gives the fast readers an unfair advantage. After looking at the pictures for two minutes, students make the following predictions with their books closed:

Chapter 1: The Dugout

9. They cross the river in a wagon.
10. They meet another man.
11. They dig a huge hole.
12. They get in the hole.
13. The man can play the banjo.

Now, students read the chapter. Their purpose for reading is to decide which predictions happen and to prepare to "prove it" by reading aloud the part that helped them figure out whether each prediction happens.

After reading, the teacher asks, "Who has a prediction they think is right and can read the part of the text that proves it?" Students respond enthusiastically:

"Number 9 is right. The book says, *We crossed the river, wagon and all.*"

"Number 10 is right. It says, *A man was waiting on the other side. 'I am Sam Hickman,' he said.*"

"Number 8 is not right. The dugout is not like a baseball dugout. It is where they live. The book says, *We got our shovels and we dug us a dugout.* And, later it says, *Pretty soon the dugout felt like home.*"

Students continue to prove and disprove the predictions. The teacher draws a check next to each prediction that happens, and she crosses out the others or changes them to make them right if only a small change is necessary. She changes the eighth prediction to this:

8. There is a dugout that they live in.

When students finish, all of the predictions for this chapter are marked with a check, crossed through, or changed into true statements. Some overall predictions are checked or changed, but several are left for the remaining chapters.

Next, the teacher asks students what they learned from the text that they had not been able to predict from the pictures. Students share some of the important events:

"Their mama died on the trip from Kentucky."

"They moved from Kentucky to someplace in Kansas."

The teacher then leads students to find the name of that "someplace in Kansas" and to pronounce Nicodemus. Students continue to add what they discovered from their reading, and the teacher leads them to the text to clarify as needed. The lesson ends with the teacher and students tracing the characters' probable route from Kentucky to Kansas on a map. Students marvel that the family traveled all that way in a wagon without any motels or restaurants!

On subsequent days, students read the remaining chapters using the "two-minute look, close book, predict" procedure. By the fourth chapter, students are much faster at making predictions, and their predictions are more precise.

14. The letter is from the daddy.
15. The three boys went out to be with their daddy.
16. They sleep outside at night and build a fire.
17. They see wolves and snakes out there.
18. They find their daddy.
19. They have a real house to live in, not a dugout.
20. They grow corn to eat.

Prove It!

Prove It! is a wonderful prediction activity that engages students' minds and helps students use the visuals in a text to make connections and predictions.

1. Ask students to make predictions based on the title, book cover, and table of contents (if there is one). Number their predictions.

2. Decide which section of the book you will read first. Have students make predictions for that section based on the pictures, including any labels, captions, charts, and maps. Limit the time students can look at the chosen section to two minutes and have them close their books before they make predictions.

3. Have students read the text in whatever format you choose.

4. After reading, have students tell which predictions happen and have them read parts of the text aloud that prove them.

5. Draw a check next to any predictions that are correct and cross out or modify any predictions that do not happen.

6. Ask students what they learned that could not be predicted based on the visuals. Discuss this information and refer students back to the text to clarify words or meanings as necessary.

7. If you are reading a longer piece, continue Steps 2–6 for each section.

Chapter 6

Rivet

Rivet is another lesson format that helps students make predictions for stories. In Rivet, students' predictions are based on key vocabulary. To prepare for a Rivet lesson, pick seven or eight vocabulary words. Include the names of characters and words that will likely be difficult for students to decode. An important two-word phrase can also be included.

An Example of Rivet

For this lesson, the teacher chooses the book *Arturo's Baton* by Syd Hoff. The teacher begins the activity by drawing lines on the board to indicate how many letters are in each vocabulary word. The board at the beginning of this Rivet activity looks like this:

1. ___ ___ ___ ___ ___ ___ ___ ___ ___ ___

2. ___ ___ ___ ___ ___ ___ ___ ___ ___

3. ___ ___ ___ ___ ___ ___ ___ ___ ___

4. ___ ___ ___ ___ ___ ___

5. ___ ___ ___ ___ ___

6. ___ ___ ___ ___ ___   ___ ___ ___ ___

7. ___ ___ ___ ___ ___ ___ ___

8. ___ ___ ___ ___ ___ ___

As students watch, the teacher fills in the letters of the first word one at a time and stops briefly after each letter to see if anyone can guess the word. Students do not guess letters but try to guess each word as soon as they think they know what it is. No students guess the first word when the board looks like this:

1. c o n __ __ __ __ __ __ __
2. __ __ __ __ __ __ __ __ __
3. __ __ __ __ __ __ __ __ __
4. __ __ __ __ __ __
5. __ __ __ __ __
6. __ __ __ __ __ __ __ __ __ __
7. __ __ __ __ __ __ __
8. __ __ __ __ __ __

Many students guess the word when a few more letters are written:

1. c o n d u c __ __ __
2. __ __ __ __ __ __ __ __ __
3. __ __ __ __ __ __ __ __ __
4. __ __ __ __ __ __
5. __ __ __ __ __
6. __ __ __ __ __ __ __ __ __
7. __ __ __ __ __ __ __
8. __ __ __ __ __ __

When a student guesses the correct word, the teacher finishes writing the word and helps students talk about the word's meaning. Some students think that a conductor is the person who drives a train. When asked if they know any other meanings for *conductor*, one student says that a conductor conducts a band. Another student asks if a conductor has anything to do with electricity. The teacher accepts all of these possibilities, knowing that the meaning of the word as it is used in *Arturo's Baton* will become clear when the other key vocabulary words are introduced.

1. c o n d u c t o r
2. ___ ___ ___ ___ ___ ___ ___ ___ ___
3. ___ ___ ___ ___ ___ ___ ___ ___ ___
4. ___ ___ ___ ___ ___ ___
5. ___ ___ ___ ___ ___
6. ___ ___ ___ ___ ___ ___ ___ ___ ___
7. ___ ___ ___ ___ ___ ___ ___
8. ___ ___ ___ ___ ___ ___

The teacher writes the letters in the second word. When four letters are written, several students guess *orchestra*. The teacher finishes writing *orchestra*, and students conclude that the conductor in the story probably conducts the orchestra.

1. c o n d u c t o r
2. o r c h ___ ___ ___ ___ ___
3. ___ ___ ___ ___ ___ ___ ___ ___ ___
4. ___ ___ ___ ___ ___ ___
5. ___ ___ ___ ___ ___
6. ___ ___ ___ ___ ___ ___ ___ ___ ___
7. ___ ___ ___ ___ ___ ___ ___
8. ___ ___ ___ ___ ___ ___

The teacher continues writing the letters of each word. As each word is guessed and completed, the teacher and students talk about possible meanings of the words.

1. c o n d u c t o r
2. o r c h e s t r a
3. T o s c a n i n i
4. A r t u r o
5. b a t o n
6. w o r l d   t o u r
7. p a j a m a s
8. c a n c e l

Once all of the vocabulary words are introduced, the teacher shows students the cover of the book. Based on information from the title, cover illustration, and key vocabulary, students predict some events that might happen in the story. Each prediction must use at least two key vocabulary words.

Arturo Toscanini is the conductor of the orchestra.

The orchestra goes on a world tour.

The conductor gets sick, so he must cancel the world tour.

Arturo must cancel the concert because the orchestra members wore their pajamas.

Toscanini forgets his pajamas when he takes the orchestra on a world tour.

When no students use the word *baton* in their predictions, the teacher prompts students to think how the baton might fit into the story. Students then suggest two additional predictions.

Toscanini uses the baton to conduct the orchestra.

Toscanini gets mad and throws the baton at the orchestra, so they have to cancel the show.

Students enjoy trying to combine the vocabulary words to make predictions—some serious and some silly. How serious the predictions are or whether the predictions turn out to be right is not important. What matters is that students are using key vocabulary words and anticipating how these words might come together to make a story.

After students make six to eight predictions using each key vocabulary word at least once, they read the story to see whether any of their predictions are right. After reading the selection, students tell which predictions actually happen and read aloud parts of the story to support this. Finally, the teacher asks students to use the vocabulary words to write some things that happen in the story. Each sentence must use at least two key vocabulary words. Students' sentences after reading include these:

Arturo wants to cancel the concert because he loses his baton.

Toscanini is Arturo's dog, and he finds the baton.

Arturo decides that he does not need a baton, and he goes on a world tour.

Rivet

Rivet is a lesson framework that combines key vocabulary introduction and prediction. Students' eyes are riveted to the words as vocabulary is introduced. Once students have used the key vocabulary to predict what might happen, they are eager to read and discover whether any of their predictions are right.

1. Choose seven or eight important words, including names and words likely to be difficult for students to decode.
2. Draw lines on the board to indicate the number of letters in each word.
3. Write the letters in each word, one at a time, pausing after you write each letter and encouraging students to guess the word. When a student guesses the word, finish writing it. (Unlike Hangman, students do not guess letters. Their eyes are riveted to the board as you write the letters, and they try to guess the word based on the letters you have written and on the number of remaining blanks.)
4. When all of the words are written, have students write predictions about what might happen in the story. Each sentence must use at least two key vocabulary words.
5. Have students read the selection and determine which predictions happen.
6. Have students write sentences summarizing what happens in the story. Each sentence must use at least two key vocabulary words.

Chapter 7

Guess Yes or No

Guess Yes or No (also called an anticipation guide) is a lesson framework in which students predict whether some statements are true or false. Unlike Prove It! and Rivet, which are lesson frameworks used primarily with stories, Guess Yes or No is used when students read informational text. As you present each statement, students talk about it and share why they think it is true or false.

When preparing the statements for Guess Yes or No, include some key vocabulary words that students will need in order to read and make sense of the selection. Have students read each statement aloud and build vocabulary knowledge as needed. Before students begin reading, have students write the statements on scratch paper and write *yes* beside each statement they believe is true and *no* beside each statement they believe is false. After reading the selection, ask students to return to the statements and decide which are true and which are false. Just as in Prove It!, have students read the part from the selection that tells them that each statement is true or false. At the end of the lesson, have students use information gained from their reading to turn false statements into true statements.

An Example of Guess Yes or No

For this lesson, the teacher chooses an article about Haiti written just after the 2010 earthquake.

> "Today, we will read about Haiti. I am sure that you have heard a lot about the earthquake that devastated Haiti in 2010. Before we read, I will show you some statements I wrote about Haiti. Some of these statements are true, and some are not true. Your job is to guess which are true and which are false. When you read the article, you will find out how well you guessed. Let's all read the first sentence together and talk about what it means."

1. Haiti is located on the island of Hispaniola in the Caribbean.

The teacher and students read the sentence and talk about it. One student says that she went on a cruise to the Caribbean, but she did not go to Haiti. The teacher probes for students' knowledge about the Caribbean. She helps students determine that the Caribbean is between the Caribbean Sea and the North Atlantic Ocean and is southeast of Florida and north of South America. There are many islands in the Caribbean, including Hispaniola. One student suggests looking at a map to see if Haiti is on Hispaniola in the Caribbean, but the teacher tells her that they will look at the map and find Haiti on it after they read.

"Now, I will show you the second sentence. Read it with me and think about what you know that will help you decide whether it is true or false."

2. The average daily wage in Haiti is five dollars.

Again, the teacher and students discuss this statement. They agree that the average daily wage is the amount that someone would get paid for a day's work. One student remarks that his brother works at the grocery store and he makes more than five dollars per hour. "That can't be true," he asserts. Other students chime in that they heard that Haiti is the poorest country in its area, so it might be true. As the discussion ends, students maintain different opinions and are eager to read to discover whether the statement is true or false.

The remaining statements are read aloud, and the teacher leads students to use their prior knowledge to guess whether each statement is true or false. The teacher draws attention to unfamiliar vocabulary (*official, independent, Caribbean, claimed, deforestation, peacekeepers, United Nations,* and *envoy*) and helps students access and build meanings for these words.

3. Spanish and Creole are the two official languages of Haiti.
4. Haiti was the last independent nation in the Caribbean.
5. Christopher Columbus landed in Haiti in 1492 and claimed it for Spain.
6. Jean-Bertrand Aristide is the president of Haiti.
7. Earthquakes are a common occurrence in Haiti.
8. Haiti faces the environmental issue of extensive deforestation.
9. Peacekeepers have been carrying out the United Nations Stabilization Mission in Haiti since 2004.
10. Former U.S. President Bill Clinton is the United Nations Deputy Special Envoy to Haiti.

Before students read the selection, they reread all of the statements and indicate which ones they believe are true and which they believe are false. Next, the teacher asks them to read the article to determine which statements are true and which are false. She gives students small sticky notes to mark the information in the text that they think proves or disproves each statement. She tells them to write the number of the statement that they think is proven or disproven on the sticky note before marking the section.

After students read, their attention comes back to the statements. Students read each statement, and a volunteer reads aloud parts of the text that prove or disprove the statement. For the false statements, students decide how to turn them into true statements. They are most amazed to learn that the average daily wage in Haiti is considerably less than five dollars.

Here are the statements, all now true:

1. Haiti is located on the island of Hispaniola in the Caribbean.
2. The average daily wage in Haiti is ~~five~~ two dollars.
3. ~~Spanish~~ French and Creole are the two official languages of Haiti.
4. Haiti was the ~~last~~ first independent nation in the Caribbean.
5. Christopher Columbus landed in Haiti in 1492 and claimed it for Spain.
6. Jean-Bertrand Aristide is the *former* president of Haiti.
7. Earthquakes are a ~~common~~ rare occurrence in Haiti.
8. Haiti faces the environmental issue of extensive deforestation.
9. Peacekeepers have been carrying out the United Nations Stabilization Mission in Haiti since 2004.
10. Former U.S. President Bill Clinton is the United Nations Deputy Special Envoy to Haiti.

Guess Yes or No

Guess Yes or No is a lesson framework that allows you to introduce key vocabulary for an informational selection and engages students by having them predict which statements are true and which are false. Once students have made predictions, they will want to read to find out how they did.

1. Write some statements concerning the topic about which students will be reading. If you have an even number of statements, half should be true and half false. If you have an odd number, use only one more or one less true statement than you have false statements. You do not want students to just guess *true* for most of the statements or *false* for most of the statements without actually thinking about each one carefully.
2. Read each statement with students and talk about what it means. Emphasize difficult names and key vocabulary.
3. Have students write *yes* or *no* for each statement. Encourage risk taking and guessing for students who are reluctant to participate by saying, "You have a 50-50 chance. Take a guess!"
4. After students read the selection, go through each statement and have the class decide whether it is true or false. When there is disagreement, require students to read supporting information from the text and to explain their reasoning.
5. When possible, have students help you reword false statements to make them true.

Chapter 8

Preview-Predict-Confirm (PPC)

Preview-Predict-Confirm (Yopp and Yopp 2004) is another lesson framework that involves students predicting what they will learn before reading an informational text. In PPC, students work in groups of three or four. Students quickly view the pictures in the text, and then, with the books closed, they predict the words that will appear in the text. Each group writes the words they think will occur. Then, the groups choose words that they think will be unique, common, and interesting. After previewing the pictures and predicting what words will be in the text, students cannot wait to read the text and confirm their predictions.

To prepare for PPC, copy only the pictures from the informational text students will read or cover all of the words in the text so that only the pictures are visible. You do not want students to see the words they will try to predict! Next, cut enough slips of paper that each group would receive 20–30 slips. You will also need three large index cards for each group.

An Example of PPC

For this lesson, the teacher chooses a selection on polar bears. The teacher divides the class into groups of three or four and shows students pictures from the polar bear article they will read. She shows pictures of polar bears swimming, cubs play fighting, etc., one at a time, giving the groups 30 seconds to talk with each other as they look at each image. (Alternately, you can gather students close to you and show them pictures from the actual text, making sure to cover all words on the pages so that only the pictures are visible.) After students have viewed all of the images and have had 30 seconds to talk about each, the teacher gives each group 25 slips of paper and tells them to write a word on each slip that they think will occur in the selection about polar bears. She hands the small slips of paper and a pen to the most fluent writer (scribe) in each group and sends the groups to far corners of the room. She asks students to use their "secret" voices so that other groups cannot hear the words their group is predicting. Groups have 10 minutes to record words and the teacher asks them to lay out their word slips and organize them into categories. They have five minutes to discuss and cluster the words.

When students have had five minutes to discuss and cluster the words, the teacher gives each group three large index cards. She asks the scribe in each group to label one index card C for common, one card U for unique, and one card I for interesting. The groups have three minutes to talk about their words and choose one common word that they think all of the other groups will have predicted, one unique word that they think no other group will have predicted, and one interesting word that they hope to learn more about when reading the text. The scribe writes these words on large index cards big enough for everyone to see.

When three minutes have passed, the teacher gathers students and has each group show the words they have chosen as common, unique, and interesting. As each group shows the words, the teacher asks students to explain how they decided which words were common to many other groups and unique to their group. Students also explain their reasoning for which word was interesting.

Finally, students read the text. As they read, the scribe in each group draws a star by each predicted word that actually occurs. When students finish reading, the teacher hands each group 6 more slips of paper and asks them to write words from the text that they should have predicted. The lesson ends with a whole-class discussion about polar bears. They also discuss how students can predict a lot of what they will learn if they think about the ideas being conveyed by the pictures.

Here are some words guessed by one group after viewing pictures of polar bears.

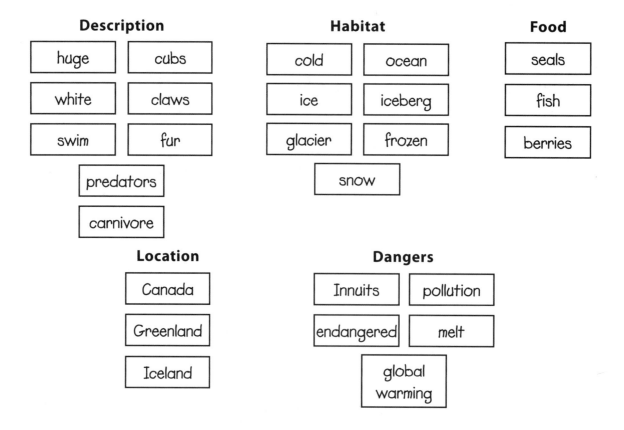

Preview-Predict-Confirm

If you have an informational text with several pictures, PPC is a good lesson framework for encouraging students to talk and think about the topic before they read about it. After a few PPC lessons, students pay much more attention to the details in pictures. After writing the words on slips of paper, grouping the words, and choosing the words they believe are common, unique, and interesting, students cannot wait to read the text and see how many of their words actually occur.

1. Divide the class into groups of three or four.

2. Show several pictures and give students 30 seconds to talk after each picture.

3. Distribute 20–30 slips of paper to each group. Ask students to use their "secret" voices while they write words that they expect to be in the text, one to a slip.

4. After 10 minutes, stop the groups and ask students to categorize their words and to label each category.

5. After five minutes, stop the groups and give each group three large index cards and a marker. Ask the group to choose three different words: one word that they think is common to all groups, one unique word, and the word about which they are most interested in learning more. The group should write these words on the index cards large enough for everyone to see. Let groups hold up the cards and share their words.

6. Have students read the text and ask the scribe to draw a star beside each word their group found in the text.

7. Give each group six more slips and ask them to write words they wished they had thought of before reading the text.

8. Have a whole-class discussion about what students learned about the topic and how studying the pictures allowed students to predict what they would learn about that topic.

Chapter 9

KWL Charts

One of the most popular ways of helping students connect prior knowledge to make predictions for informational text is by creating KWL charts (Ogle 1986). KWL stands for what you Know, what you Want to find out, and what you have Learned.

Before students begin reading, lead them to brainstorm what they already know about the topic (the K part). Then, have students talk about what they want to know and ask them to brainstorm questions that might be answered by the text that they will read (the W part). Next, have students read the text. After they read and close their books, ask students to share what they have learned (the L part). Record this information in a three-column KWL chart. Fill in the first two columns before students read and the third column after students read.

An Example of KWL

For this lesson, the teacher chooses the book *Bats* by Gail Gibbons. The lesson begins with the teacher holding up a copy of *Bats* and drawing students' attention to the pictures of bats flying at night on the cover. He lets students discuss bats for a few minutes, telling whatever they know. Students say that they have never seen a bat but that they have heard a lot about bats—and some of it is scary!

On a large sheet of chart paper, the teacher has labeled three columns *K*, *W*, and *L*. He writes what students know under the K column. They know that bats can fly at night. They know that bats have large wings and small bodies. They know that bats live in caves. One student says that bats eat fruit but others do not agree, so the teacher writes *What do bats eat?* as the first question in the W column.

Next, the teacher tells students that they will read *Bats* and that this book has a lot of information about bats. "We will learn a lot about bats, but let's list the questions about bats that we really want to be answered in the W column." One student says that she wants to know if bats live near the school. The teacher writes a more general question, *Where do bats live?* Another student wants to know if bats bite people. Several other questions follow: How do bats see at night? Are there different kinds of bats? Are bats a type of bird? Can bats hurt people? Are there really vampire bats?

Bats		
K	**W**	**L**
Bats can fly at night. Bats have large wings and small bodies. Bats live in caves. Bats eat fruit.	What do bats eat? Where do bats live? Do bats bite people? How do bats see at night? Are there different kinds of bats? Are bats a type of bird? Can bats hurt people? Are there really vampire bats?	

Next, the teacher tells the class that they will read the book across two days. In order to keep students from reading ahead of everyone else in the class, the teacher has put a large paper clip in each copy of the book to indicate how far they should read. Their purpose for reading is to discover which questions are answered in the text and what new information from the text can be added to the L column of the KWL chart. If students finish reading before the time is up, they should write information they want to add to the L column. The teacher reminds the class that they have learned how to read informational books. He shows them a few pages of the book and asks them what they will read and talk about first on each page. Students tell him that they will read and discuss the pictures, charts, diagrams, and quicktext first, and then the text to see what else they can learn.

Students read the book in whichever format the teacher decides will provide the right amount of support for everyone. They have a limited amount of time, and they know what to do if they finish reading before that time is up. When the time is up, students close their books, and the teacher gathers students to begin the after-reading part of the lesson. (If a few students are not finished reading, they can join the group anyway or they can continue reading and join the group when they finish.)

When the class is reconvened, students first look at the questions and decide if they found any answers in the reading. Answers are recorded in the L column. Then, students tell other things they learned. These things are also recorded in the L column. This activity is done with the book closed so that students have to summarize what they learned and not just read the facts from the book. If there is disagreement about what was learned, the teacher writes it in the form of a question in the W column and tells students that they can try to resolve this dispute when they read the next day.

Bats		
K	**W**	**L**
Bats can fly at night. Bats have large wings and small bodies. Bats live in caves. Bats eat fruit.	What do bats eat? Where do bats live? Do bats bite people? How do bats see at night? Are there different kinds of bats? Are bats a type of bird? Can bats hurt people? Are there really vampire bats?	Bats eat insects, fruit, nectar, and small animals. Bats live together in caves, attics, barns, and tall trees. Bats live almost everywhere, except Antarctica. Bats are shy, gentle animals. Bats are nocturnal; they come out at night. Bats are mammals.

The next day, the teacher and class review the information in the W and L columns. A few more questions have occurred to students and are added to the W column. Students finish reading the book using the same format as the day before and complete the chart.

Here is the KWL chart the class completed after reading:

Bats		
K	**W**	**L**
Bats can fly at night. Bats have large wings and small bodies. Bats live in caves. Bats eat fruit.	What do bats eat? Where do bats live? Do bats bite people? How do bats see at night? Are there different kinds of bats? Are bats a type of bird? Can bats hurt people? Are there really vampire bats?	Bats eat insects, fruit, nectar, and small animals. Bats live together in caves, attics, barns, and tall trees. Bats live almost everywhere, except Antarctica. Bats are shy, gentle animals. Bats are nocturnal; they come out at night. Bats are mammals. Vampire bats like to sip blood from animals Bats are good hunters. Today, bats have trouble finding places to roost and are endangered.

Some students notice that all of their "want to learn" questions have been answered. This does not usually happen. When the text does not answer all of the students' questions, it leads some students to read more about the topic or search the Internet to answer the unanswered question(s).

A second example for KWL uses the book *Tornado Alert* by Franklyn M. Branley. The lesson begins with the teacher using the cover of *Tornado Alert* to spark the discussion. The picture on the cover shows a large, black, funnel-shaped cloud. The teacher encourages students to tell about their experiences with tornadoes before asking them to add specific things they know to the chart. Two students have experienced tornadoes. One student, whose house was in the path of a tornado, tells how he sat in a closet and heard a strange noise as the storm passed. He concluded, "Tornadoes are scary!" Two other students have relatives who experienced tornadoes. Other students talk about what they have heard at school, how they have practiced tornado drills in the spring, and what they have seen and heard about tornadoes on the news.

When students have talked about their tornado experiences, the teacher tells them that they know a lot about tornadoes, and he begins to record what they know under the K column of a KWL chart. Students know that tornadoes have powerful winds. They know that tornadoes can cause a lot of damage. They know that tornadoes usually happen in the spring because that is when they practice tornado drills at school.

Next, the teacher asks students what they want to learn about tornadoes. One student says that she wants to know what causes tornadoes. Another student wants to know why some homes get ruined by tornadoes and others do not. Several other questions follow: How do weather forecasters know that a tornado is coming? What should you do if you are at home or outside and you see or hear a tornado coming? Do tornadoes happen everywhere? How fast can the winds blow?

Tornadoes		
K	**W**	**L**
Tornadoes have powerful winds. Tornadoes can cause a lot of damage. Tornadoes usually happen in the spring. Schools have tornado drills in the spring.	What causes tornadoes? Why do some homes get ruined and others do not? How do weather forecasters know that tornadoes are coming? What should you do at home or outside if a tornado is coming? Do tornadoes happen everywhere? How fast can the winds blow?	

Students read *Tornado Alert* in whichever format the teacher chooses. Before reading, the teacher reminds students that they should read all of the visuals and quicktext first, and then the text to see what else they can learn. She also asks students what they should do if they finish reading before the time is up. Students respond that they should begin writing things that they think should be added to the L column.

Here is the KWL chart the class completed after reading:

Tornadoes		
K	**W**	**L**
Tornadoes have powerful winds. Tornadoes can cause a lot of damage. Tornadoes usually happen in the spring. Schools have tornado drills in the spring.	What causes tornadoes? Why do some homes get ruined and others do not? How do weather forecasters know that tornadoes are coming? What should you do at home or outside if a tornado is coming? Do tornadoes happen everywhere? How fast can the winds blow?	When warm air and cold air meet, tornadoes can start. Some tornadoes are big; they can ruin houses and kill people. Small tornadoes don't travel far or cause much damage. Weather forecasters watch closely for signs of tornadoes during tornado season. At home during a tornado, find a safe place away from windows, then crouch and cover your head. If you are outside, find a ditch and lie in it. Tornadoes usually happen where there is a lot of flat land. Some people call tornadoes twisters or cyclones because they spin around and twist.

In this KWL chart, as in most, a question was not answered by the book students read. The teacher leads students to think about the question (why one house gets ruined by a tornado but the house next to it does not), and students decide that probably no one knows the answer. If it were likely that an unanswered question did have an answer somewhere, the teacher would encourage the most interested students to do additional research.

KWL is an excellent format for helping students connect prior knowledge and predict/question what they will learn. "K-W-L Plus" (Carr and Ogle 1987) includes a variation that helps students learn to summarize. Teachers help students write a summary of the facts that they have learned. Depending on the levels of your students, you might model summary writing and have students write summaries. You may also want to write a summary together in a shared-writing format or give students a simple summary-writing frame (like the example below) that they can use to organize important information.

Bats are interesting animals. Bats have _____. Bats eat

_____. Bats live in _____.

The most fascinating thing about bats is _____.

KWL Charts

When students engage in KWL lessons, they use the connecting thinking strategy as they list what they know in the first column. They predict what they might learn as they list questions in the second column. They summarize the important facts as they list information learned in the last column. To further develop students' summarizing abilities, have students use the information from the last column to construct a summary.

1. Before beginning the chart, lead a general discussion about students' experiences with the topic. By allowing a student to tell about how her aunt was in a tornado or how another student saw a bat at the zoo, you avoid having students want to list these experiences in the K column.

2. After the general discussion, ask students what they know about the topic. List the facts. (If a student tells you again that her aunt was in a tornado, accept that but don't write it because it is not a fact about tornadoes.)

3. If students disagree about a fact, turn the fact into a question and write it in the W column. (A dispute about whether bats eat fruit is recorded as *What do bats eat?* on the chart.)

4. When you have recorded all of the facts that students know about the topic in the K column, show students what they will read and ask them to come up with questions that they think the text will answer. If their questions are too specific, help students broaden their questions. "We are trying to come up with questions that might be answered in this book. I doubt that this book will tell us if Gibsonville has had a tornado, but it might tell us where tornadoes happen. Let's write *Where do tornadoes happen?* instead."

5. After reading, make sure students' books are closed. Have students tell what answers they found to the W questions. Write them in the L column. Then, add other important facts to the L column.

6. If students will continue reading about the topic another day, ask them if they have any questions that might be answered in the remaining part of the text. Add these additional questions to the W column.

7. To focus on the summarizing thinking strategy, have students use the information in the L column to write a summary about the topic.

Chapter 10

Graphic Organizers

You learned in Chapter 2 that there are four common informational text structures. Reading comprehension lessons built around graphic organizers help make these relationships among textual ideas concrete and visible to students. When students read to fill in the spokes of a web, they must decide which details go with which main idea. When they read so that they will be able to complete a data chart or a Venn diagram, they must compare and contrast information. When they read in order to be able to complete a time line, they attend more carefully and thoughtfully to the sequence of ideas in the text. Reading to fill in a causal chain helps them focus on and understand some of the cause-and-effect relationships in the selection. From repeated comprehension lessons in which the after-reading tasks are to complete different graphic organizers, students will learn one of the most important comprehension strategies: how to follow different text structures.

Webs

To decide which graphic organizer to use for a particular book, read the book and determine what the important information is and how it can best be organized and displayed. One teacher wanted his class to read *Sarah Morton's Day: A Day in the Life of a Pilgrim Girl* by Kate Waters, which has many facts and details. While looking through this book, the teacher noticed important information about Sarah Morton and her life as a pilgrim girl. There are descriptions of Sarah's clothes, her house, her chores, her meals, the games she plays, and her lessons. The teacher decided that this information could best be organized and displayed with a web.

The lesson began with the teacher writing *Sarah Morton, pilgrim girl* in a large circle in the center of the board and drawing six spokes to six smaller circles. Next, he labeled the small circles with the words *home, clothes, food, chores, studies,* and *games.* As the teacher labeled them, he invited students to connect (access their prior knowledge) by asking questions.

"What kinds of clothes are you wearing today? What do you wear when you get dressed up?"

"Do you live in a house, an apartment, or a mobile home? What rooms are in your home? What is in each room?"

"What kinds of chores do you do?"

"What kinds of food do you eat for breakfast? Lunch? Dinner?"

"What games do you play at recess and at home?"

"What do we study at school?"

Next, the teacher showed students the cover of the book and explained that pilgrim children wore clothes, had homes, did chores, ate food, played games, and studied things in school but that many of these items and activities were different from what we have and do today.

To help students focus while they read, the teacher displayed the skeleton (the lines with the major labels) of the web and said, "When you are reading today, your job is to find information about these topics and to help decide which details we should write next to each spoke of our web."

After students finished reading, the class reconvened to complete the web. Students worked with their books closed, but the teacher let them open them when there was a disagreement to settle. (Having students use bookmarks helps them if the text they read is only part of a large book.)

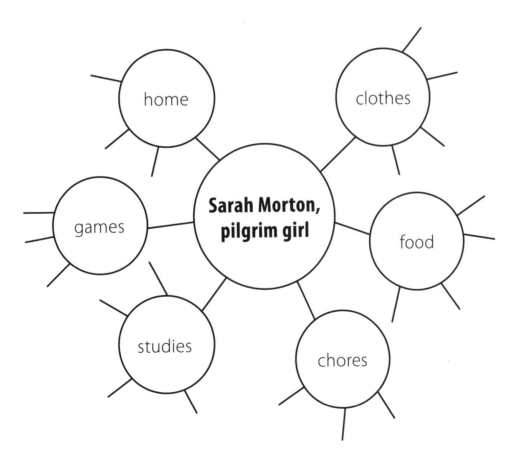

Data Charts

Another way to organize this information is with a two-column chart. The first column is labeled *Pilgrims*. The second column is labeled *Us*. The headings beneath the columns are *Clothes*, *Food*, *Chores*, *Home*, *Games*, and *Studies*. The teacher showed students the data chart with the labeled columns and rows and told them to read so that when they finished, they could help fill in the cells of the chart with the information they had learned.

	Pilgrims	Us
Clothes		
Food		
Chores		
Home		
Games		
Studies		

Venn Diagrams

Another graphic organizer you can use to help students compare and contrast two subjects is a Venn diagram. After students read, information shared by the two subjects is written by you or each small-group scribe in the space where the two circles intersect. The information unique to each subject is written in the remainder of each circle. This way, it is easy for students to see which information is the same and which information is different between the two subjects.

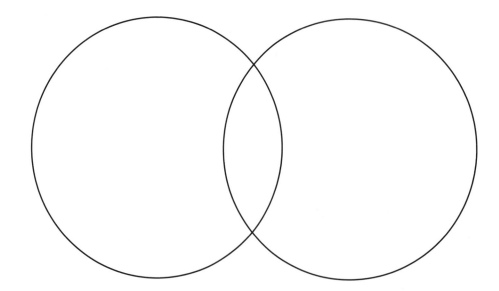

In one classroom, after reading some Frog and Toad books by Arnold Lobel, students became curious about the differences between frogs and toads. The teacher constructed a Venn diagram to compare the two amphibians. Then, she had students read an informational book about frogs and toads with the purpose of learning information to use to complete the Venn diagram.

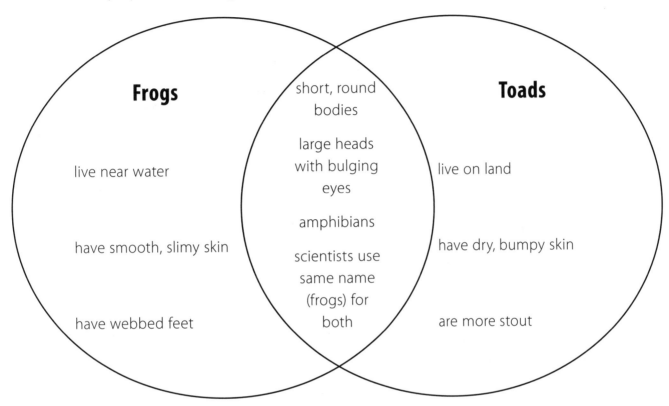

Time Lines

Requiring students to complete a time line after reading a text in which the sequence of events is important helps students concentrate on and understand the events in the text and the order in which the events happened. The essential feature of a time line is that events are labeled and represented in order on a linear chart. After reading *Caterpillar Diary* by David Drew, one class created a time line to show the stages caterpillars go through from eggs to moths.

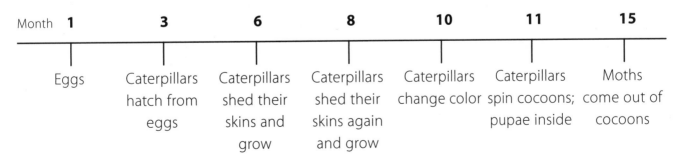

Time lines are usually used with informational text, but they can also be used with stories and novels. Time lines can be especially helpful when fiction or fantasy includes flashbacks and flash-forwards that can confuse some students.

Causal Chains

A causal chain is a graphic organizer that helps students see the relationship between causes and effects. Students also see how there is often a chain reaction when one thing causes something to happen. That, in turn, causes something else to happen (an effect of something becomes a cause of something else). Much of the text students read in science and social studies has cause-and-effect structures, and students can understand this kind of text better if they graphically depict the causes and effects.

Showing students a skeleton of the causal chain based on the text before they begin reading it makes the cause-and-effect relationships in the text obvious to them. After reading about how cars and trucks discharge gases from their exhausts and the effects these gases have on the environment, a class created this causal chain.

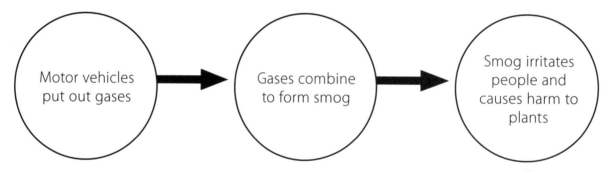

Promoting Independence with Graphic Organizers

As students become familiar with the four common text structures and how graphic organizers can show the relationships between ideas, they need to learn how to construct their own graphic organizers. In order to use graphic organizers to organize ideas when they are reading on their own, students must be able to decide which graphic organizer they should use to organize particular information. Once students are familiar with webs, data charts, Venn diagrams, time lines, and causal chains, you may want to create a reminder with all of the skeletons. When students will read informational text, have them preview the text and use the visuals and headings to decide which graphic organizer will best show the relationships between ideas. They can then work in groups to create the skeleton and read to complete it with information they have learned.

Turning Graphic Organizers into Summaries

Once students have a completed graphic organizer, you have an excellent opportunity to teach them how to summarize informational text. Here is a summary comparing frogs and toads, created in one classroom:

Frogs and toads are a lot alike. They are both amphibians, which are cold-blooded animals that hatch from eggs. They have short, round bodies and large heads with bulging eyes.

One difference between frogs and toads is where they live. Toads live on land. Frogs live in water. Frogs have webbed feet that help them swim. Another difference is how their skin feels. Frogs have smooth, slimy skin. Toads have dry, bumpy skin.

Graphic Organizers

Reading to prepare to complete graphic organizers helps students learn to follow the structure of a text in order to organize and summarize its information. Repeated use of graphic organizers is a powerful tool to teach students how to comprehend and learn from informational text.

1. Look at the text and decide how the information can be organized graphically. If the text structure is topic/subtopic/details, you will probably want to use a web or a data chart. If the text compares two or more things, a data chart or a Venn diagram works well. Time lines help students focus on chronological sequence. Causal chains direct students' attention to cause-and-effect relationships.
2. Let students watch as you construct the graphic organizer skeleton (the lines with the major labels). Use this time to discuss the meanings of words you are writing on the skeleton, since these are apt to be key vocabulary words from the selection.
3. Have students read to find information to add to the organizer.
4. After they finish reading, guide students to complete the organizer with their books closed.
5. Have students open their books to check any information they think might not be correct and to fill in the parts they could not complete from memory.
6. When students understand and can complete the various organizers, teach them to preview a text and decide which graphic organizer would work best. Then, let them help you construct that graphic organizer's skeleton before they read.
7. Teach students how to summarize important information by showing them how to turn the information on the graphic organizer into a summary or report.

Chapter 11

Ten Important Words

Many students, even older students, have difficulty determining what the most important words in a selection are, and thus, they have difficulty determining the main ideas. Ten Important Words (Yopp and Yopp 2007) is a comprehension lesson framework that helps students learn to determine which words in an informational text are the most important ones. When students have chosen the most important words, they have simultaneously identified most of the main ideas.

Unlike some of the other lesson frameworks described in this book, you should not introduce key vocabulary to students before they read. Rather, you want students, working in small groups, to choose the key words and decide what these words mean. The selection students read should be relatively short, such as three or four pages of a textbook or a two-page spread in an issue of *Weekly Reader*, *Scholastic News*, or *Time for Kids*.

An Example of Ten Important Words

For this lesson, the teacher chooses an informational selection on Ecuador. The teacher begins the lesson by dividing the class into groups of three or four students, including a range of abilities in each group. She gives each group 10 small sticky notes and tells them that their job is to read the text together and place the sticky notes on what they think are the most important words. The piece they are reading should be relatively short.

As they read, if students decide other words are more important than the ones they have already marked with sticky notes, they may move the notes. When the reading time is almost up, the teacher stops students and tells them that they must make their final decisions and write each of the 10 words on a sticky note.

Once the groups have made their choices, the teacher gathers students and creates a class tally. She asks each group to tell her one word and finds out how many other groups included this word. The teacher writes that word and the number of groups who chose it on her list. Then, she asks a second group for one word and counts the number of groups who included the word. The teacher continues with each group until all of the groups' words are tallied.

Here is the completed tally for the selection on Ecuador. This class of 25 students was divided into seven trios and one quartet, so the largest number of votes a word could get was eight.

Ecuador Word Tally

South America	⊦⊦⊦ |||	independence	|||
equator	⊦⊦⊦ ||	Spanish	⊦⊦⊦	
rain forests	||||	Pacific Ocean	⊦⊦⊦	
bananas	⊦⊦⊦ ||	mountains	⊦⊦⊦
coffee	⊦⊦⊦ ||	Quito	⊦⊦⊦
giant tortoise	⊦⊦⊦		fish	||
Galapagos Islands	⊦⊦⊦		iguanas	||
volcanoes	|||	penguins	||

The top 10 words chosen by the class from the article on Ecuador are *South America, equator, bananas, coffee, giant tortoise, Galapagos Islands, Spanish, Pacific Ocean, mountains,* and *Quito.*

Once the class tally is established, each student writes one to three sentences (depending on the grade level and how many times you have used this lesson framework with students) summarizing important information. Each sentence uses at least two of the class's top 10 words and includes other information from the text. Here are some sentences students write to summarize information from the article on Ecuador:

Quito, the capital of Ecuador, is located only about 15 miles from the equator.

Ecuador grows a lot of coffee and bananas.

The giant tortoise lives on the Galapagos Islands, which are in Ecuador.

Ecuador is in South America on the equator.

People speak Spanish in Ecuador and in South America.

Ecuador has mountains and beaches along the Pacific Ocean.

Ecuador exports bananas, coffee, and fish.

Ten Important Words

Most students are not very good at determining the most important words in an informational text. Often, they choose words that are the most interesting to them but not necessarily the most important. (This explains choices like *volcanoes* and *penguins* in the Ecuador example.) If you regularly use Ten Important Words, students will develop the ability to determine important words as they see which words make the class's final cut for the top 10 words. Having each student write one or more sentences using at least two of the important words helps students learn to summarize important textual information.

1. Form groups of three or four students, including some good and some struggling readers in each group.

2. Give each group 10 sticky notes. Ask students to read the informational selection and decide what they think the 10 most important words are. They should place sticky notes on candidates as they read.

3. When students finish reading, they should move the sticky notes to reflect their consensus about which 10 words are the most important. When each group has agreed on their top 10, they should write each word on a sticky note.

4. Create a class tally by asking each group to share one word and having the other groups indicate whether they also had that word. Continue the tally until all possibilities are included in the list.

5. Use the tally to create the class's top 10 list.

6. Have each student write one or more sentences (depending on the grade level and how many times you have used this lesson framework with students) using at least two of the top 10 words.

Chapter 12

Story Map and the Beach Ball

What comes immediately to mind when someone begins reading to you with the words *Once upon a time . . .*?

Most people expect to hear a story with characters, a setting, a problem or goal, and a solution. People expect a beginning that sets the stage, a middle where events occur, and an end in which things are resolved. Some psychologists say that humans have a story schema. A *schema* is a set of expectations, and these expectations allow us to anticipate and interpret. Students who are lucky enough to have had someone read or tell stories to them have already begun to develop a story schema (a sense of how stories are structured). All students need to develop a story schema. Story Map and the Beach Ball are two comprehension lesson frameworks that help students develop a story schema.

Story Map

A story map is a graphic organizer that helps students organize information from stories. Before students begin reading, present them with the skeleton of a story map. Then, working together, students fill in the information on the story map after reading. There are many different story maps. This simple one works well for all stories:

Title: _____
Author: _____

Setting: _____

Characters: _____

Beginning: _____
_____
Middle: _____
_____
End: _____
_____

Conclusion: _____

A story map can be used to set the purpose and help students organize information from a story or a chapter book. If each chapter of a book has most of the elements listed on the story map, students might fill in the map together after reading each chapter. Here is an example based on the popular mystery character Cam Jansen. There are many mysteries in the series. This lesson uses *Cam Jansen: The Chocolate Fudge Mystery* by David A. Adler.

This mystery has eight chapters that are each approximately six pages long. There are one or two pictures in each chapter. The teacher decides that he will read the first chapter to the class and they will fill out the story map together. The class will then read the remaining chapters and complete the story map together or in small groups.

The teacher begins by showing students the story map skeleton and explaining how they can help him complete the story map after they listen to the first chapter. The teacher then tells students that he will read the chapter without stopping and that they should listen for and think about what they can contribute to the story map. Students listen attentively, and their eyes dart back and forth to the story map. When the teacher finishes reading, he turns to the story map and asks questions that help students formulate concise answers. At the end of the first chapter, the story map looks like this:

Title: *Cam Jansen: The Chocolate Fudge Mystery* (Chapter One)
Author: David A. Adler

Setting: A street in town

Characters: Cam Jansen; Cam's father, Eric Shelton; Mr. and Mrs. Miller; a man and a woman running; a "suspicious-looking" woman

Beginning: Cam and Eric are going to houses selling chocolate and rice cakes to raise money for Ride and Read.

Middle: A man and a woman run past them and won't stop.

End: The suspicious-looking woman rushes past, wearing a raincoat when it isn't raining and dark glasses when it isn't sunny.

Conclusion: Cam thinks the woman has something dangerous in the bag and decides to follow her.

Next, students read the second chapter and complete a second story map. The reading continues until the mystery is solved. The information for each chapter is summarized in a story map.

The Beach Ball

The Beach Ball accomplishes the same goals as Story Map, but most students think that it is more fun! The Beach Ball uses a real beach ball that has a question written in black permanent marker on each colorful stripe. Here are the questions one teacher writes on her ball:

- *Who are the characters?*
- *What is the setting?*
- *What happens in the beginning?*
- *What happens in the middle?*
- *How does it end?*
- *What is your favorite part?*

The teacher could also phrase her questions as sentence starters:

- *The characters are . . .*
- *The settings are . . .*
- *In the beginning . . .*
- *In the middle . . .*
- *At the end . . .*
- *My favorite part is . . .*

Before reading, the teacher ensures that students know that after reading they will do the Beach Ball. This knowledge helps students set their purpose for reading. While students read, the teacher notices that many students glance at the ball. They are gathering ideas from the story that they want to use to answer the Beach Ball questions. This is active, purposeful reading!

After reading, the teacher and students form a large circle. The teacher begins by naming a student and tossing the ball to that student. The student catches the ball and can answer any question on the ball. That student tosses the

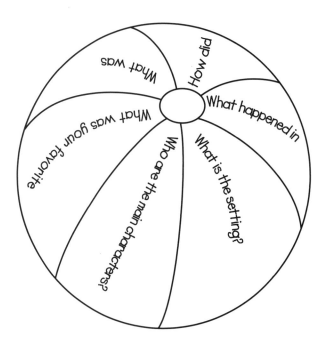

ball back to the teacher, and she names another student and tosses the ball to him. This student can add to the answer given by the first student or answer another question. The ball is thrown to different students until all of the questions have been thoroughly answered.

Story Map and the Beach Ball

The goal of comprehension instruction is for students to learn how to independently use strategies as they read. Following story structure and summarizing stories are important comprehension strategies. Both Story Map and the Beach Ball help students develop their understanding of story structure and learn to summarize stories.

Story Map

1. Decide on a story map skeleton that will work best for your students.
2. Talk about the story map and make sure that students understand that their purpose for reading is to prepare to complete the story map.
3. Have students read the story or chapter of a book.
4. Have students complete the story map as a class or in small groups with their books closed.
5. Tell students to open their books to correct mistakes and fill in gaps.
6. If you are reading a longer selection, have students complete the story map for each section or chapter.

The Beach Ball

1. Decide how to phrase the questions (or sentence starters) and write them with permanent marker on a beach ball.

2. Talk about the questions and make sure that students understand that they should read to find answers to all of the questions.

3. Have students read in whichever format you choose.

4. Have students form a large circle and then toss the ball to a student. That student answers any question and tosses the ball back to you.

5. Toss the ball to a second student. Remind the student that she can answer any question and can answer the same question as the first student only if she has something to add or has a different answer. (You may want to toss the ball first to struggling readers, who will have some answers but perhaps not as many as some of your more able readers.)

6. Continue to toss the ball to students until all questions have been thoroughly answered. Remind students as needed that they cannot give the same answer as someone else.

7. Alternate Story Map with the Beach Ball.

Chapter 13

Doing the Book

Children love to read and pretend! When they pretend, they are imagining. When a child acts out a story by portraying a character, he feels as if he is that character in that setting and in those circumstances. He moves like the character, talks like the character, and for a brief moment, becomes the character. Having students "do the book" is one of the best ways to work on the thinking strategies of inferring and visualizing. This chapter describes three ways of doing the book: plays, Readers' Theater, and pantomiming.

Plays

Children love plays, and in many classrooms, the whole school year passes without students performing a single play. Why does this happen? Here are four reasons teachers say they do not do more plays, as well as ways to combat each reason.

  1. "Plays require too much preparation."

When most teachers think of plays, they imagine productions with costumes, scenery, rehearsals, and lines to be memorized. Many teachers have lived through working on these plays and never want to work on one again! The plays you do with students to help them develop their inferring and visualizing strategies are not productions. You do not make costumes or scenery. You never have students memorize lines. Instead, students always read the plays. Reading and rereading builds fluency; memorizing does not. When students are doing the play, it means that they stand up, move around, gesture, make faces, and read their lines. They practice a few times. Then, they do the play for the rest of the class. These plays are not productions; they are more like happenings.

  2. "Plays don't have enough parts for all of my students."

Many plays require only four or five characters, which makes them perfect for small groups.

When the class is doing a play with few parts, put students into Play-School Groups (heterogeneous groups) and designate one student as the "Teacher" in each group. Either assign the parts or let students choose parts. Then, have the four groups simultaneously read and practice the same play. The next day, combine the groups and do the play twice. Two groups are combined into one cast, with one group reading the first half of the play and the other group reading the second half. When the first two groups read the play, the other groups are the audience. Then, the remaining two groups combine and read the play while the first two groups become the audience.

Plays are also a wonderful lesson framework for Book Club Groups in which the groups read different plays. Students read and practice the plays in groups. When it is time to do the plays, each group reads their play for the rest of the class. If the number of group members does not work out quite right for the number of parts in a play, members from other groups can be drafted to read bit parts.

3. "I don't have time to do plays!"

When you use the play framework for your reading lesson, it is not something extra; it *is* the reading lesson. The play framework focuses on the inferring and visualizing strategies, which are both underemphasized in most elementary classrooms. To produce a class full of students who excel at comprehending, you don't have time *not* to do some plays!

4. "I'd do some plays, but I don't have any!"

Are you sure that you don't have any plays? Look at Chapter 3 and think about the suggestions for begging, borrowing, and contriving materials. There are many plays out there. Most reading textbooks have one or two plays per grade. Most magazines include several plays over a year's time that often fit into holiday or seasonal themes. Many sets of leveled readers include plays. There are also books of reproducible plays for readers at different levels.

If you teach younger students, you can take some of your students' favorite stories and turn them into plays. It is not hard to write a play based on *The Little Red Hen* or *The Gingerbread Man*. If you teach older students, you can have them turn stories into plays using a writing activity called Readers' Theater.

Readers' Theater

In Readers' Theater, students turn a story into a play script and read and act out the play. In Chapter 17, you will find an example of Readers' Theater in which the class and the teacher create a script for *The Doorbell Rang* by Pat Hutchins. In this example, the script is written in a shared-writing format in which students and the teacher share the process of coming up with ideas. The teacher does the writing, but students can also learn to write scripts. Readers' Theater is an excellent activity to integrate reading and writing.

An Example of Readers' Theater
For this lesson, the teacher chooses the book *Frog and Toad Are Friends* by Arnold Lobel. *Frog and Toad Are Friends* has five chapters. The teacher tells the class that they will work together to turn the first chapter into a play script. Students will then work in groups to write scripts for the other chapters. Each group will read and write the script for one chapter.

The teacher reminds students of plays they have read and how these plays are written. She tells students that they will help her write a play based on the first chapter of *Frog and Toad Are Friends*. She leads students to talk about the pictures in the chapter before they read it. Students decide that Frog visits Toad, and Toad does not want to get out of bed. At the end of the chapter, Frog and Toad are outside. Students do not see other characters in the pictures, but there may be some. The teacher takes out paper and three colorful markers. She explains that she will write the narrator's part in black, Frog's part in green, and Toad's part in red.

The teacher leads students in an Echo Reading of the first two pages. After they have echo read the pages, students decide what Frog says, what Toad says, and what the narrator explains. The teacher tapes each page on the board in order. The play script for the first two pages of the chapter looks like this:

Frog and Toad Are Friends

N: Frog is knocking at Toad's door.

F: Toad, Toad. Wake up. It is spring.

T: Blah!

1

F: Toad, Toad! The sun is shining. The snow is melting. Wake up!

T: I am not here!

2

Students echo read the next two pages and write the script.

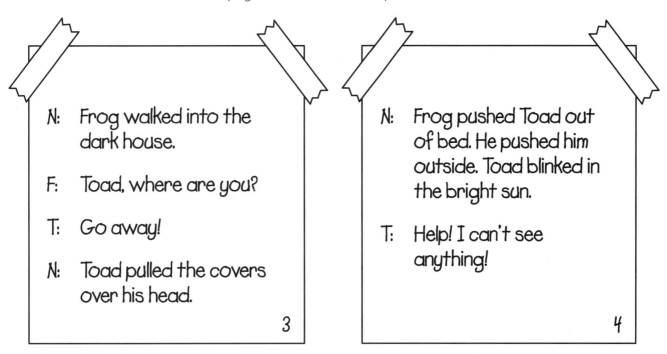

N: Frog walked into the dark house.

F: Toad, where are you?

T: Go away!

N: Toad pulled the covers over his head.

3

N: Frog pushed Toad out of bed. He pushed him outside. Toad blinked in the bright sun.

T: Help! I can't see anything!

4

The teacher and students continue to echo read each two-page spread, and they write the lines and tape them to the board in order until the script is written for the whole chapter. Next, the teacher divides the class into thirds, and each third chorally reads the part of the narrator, Frog, or Toad.

For the next several days, students work in Play-School Groups to read one chapter and write the script. In each group, there is a "Teacher" who is the first voice in the Echo Reading, a student with a black marker who writes the narrator's lines, a student with a green marker who writes Frog's lines, and a student with a red marker who writes Toad's lines. The third chapter has a sparrow and a raccoon also, so the teacher assigns six students to this group and gives blue and orange markers to the students who will write the sparrow's and the raccoon's lines. The fifth chapter has a snail, so that group has five people. The fourth chapter absorbs everyone else because it has a turtle, a snake, a field mouse, two dragonflies, and some lizards. Because the group for the fourth chapter is larger, the teacher assumes the Teacher role in the group and keeps everyone on track. The teacher includes students who need the most help and structure in this group.

As the groups are writing, they number the pages in the order in which people speak. When the script is complete, students practice reading it with the Teacher assuming the role of director and the other students reading the lines they wrote. The groups read and act their parts for each other, and *Frog and Toad Are Friends* comes to life.

Writing and reading this Readers' Theater for *Frog and Toad Are Friends* takes several days, but a lot is accomplished. As students echo read and reread to determine lines, write lines, practice lines, and do Readers' Theater, they develop reading fluency. Determining exactly what Frog, Toad, and the other characters say and what the narrator explains requires students to pay attention to detail and to read each page carefully. As they read and act out their parts, students infer and imagine what the characters sound like and how they move and look.

Pantomiming (with a Little Speaking)

Pantomiming is an acting out of a selection, with various students playing different parts as the rest of the class reads the story. You can organize your class into Play-School Groups or Book Club Groups or do pantomiming with the whole class. If you are pantomiming with the whole class, try to find selections that have enough characters for at least half of the class to be actors while the other half reads. Then, switch the cast and the audience. Unlike in plays and Readers' Theater, you do not have a script, and the actors are not reading. They are pantomiming the actions about which the readers are reading, and you prompt the actors to say occasional ad-libbed lines.

An Example of Pantomiming

For this lesson, the teacher chooses P. D. Eastman's *Are You My Mother?* The first time the class reads this book, they read it to do the Beach Ball. For the second reading, the class is divided into halves. The halves take turns chorally reading the pages and listening to determine who the characters are and what they do.

The designated half of the class reads the first page.

> *"A mother bird sat on her egg."*

Volunteers from the other half of the class report that there is one character so far, the mother bird, and she has not said anything—she's just sitting there. The teacher helps students realize that the egg is also a character—or will be soon.

The teacher writes *mother bird* and *egg* on two laminated index cards that each have the ends of a piece of yarn attached at two corners.

The reading half of the class continues to read the next several pages, and the listening half of the class determines that there are no new characters. The mother bird says that her baby will soon be here, so she flies away to get food. While the mother is away, the egg jumps, and a baby bird comes out. He looks for his mother and says,

> *"Where is my mother? I will go and look for her."*

The teacher adds another character card, *baby bird*, and switches the roles of the readers and the listeners. Students who had been listeners do the Choral Reading for the next several pages, and students who had been readers listen for new characters and what those characters say and do. The teacher does not write dialogue because the book will be pantomimed by students while other students read. The teacher continues to write characters' names on the character cards and has students tell her what the characters are saying and doing. When they finish reading the book, the teacher has these character cards:

Next, the teacher shuffles index cards labeled with students' names and begins calling out names as she draws their cards. As each student's name is called, the student selects the part he wants to play. Each student picks up the card that designates which character he is and puts the yarn around his neck. Now, the reading of the play can begin. The teacher and students who do not have parts read the play, while the students with parts come "onstage" when their characters are mentioned in the reading. They do not read any lines, but they are encouraged to say appropriate things after the class reads the text. The class might read this:

"He could not fly, but he could walk. 'Now I will go and find my mother,' he said."

The baby bird character would pantomime being able to walk but not being able to fly, and the character might say something like this:

"I need to find my mother."

This activity is much harder to explain than it is to do. Basically, the teacher and students without parts read everything, including the dialogue, and the students with parts perform and say things with the same meaning but not necessarily the same words.

When the book is read, the teacher collects the character cards from the actors and goes through the shuffling of names and choosing of parts for students who have not been actors. Some actors from the first cast fill in as needed, and the entire book is read and pantomimed again.

Pantomiming the story with ad-libbed speech is the easiest way to do the book. No script or practice is required. Students become good at identifying characters and what these characters say and do. They infer and visualize the actions of the characters and actually perform them. Reading fluency develops as students participate in an initial reading to summarize the story, a second reading to determine who the characters are and what they do, and a third reading as the story is acted out.

Doing the Book

When students do the book, they think about the important story elements—characters, settings, actions, and sequence. They use the thinking strategies of inferring and visualizing to imagine what the characters look and sound like and how they move and talk. Doing the book is especially helpful for English Language Learners. Watching and being part of the enactment helps build vocabulary and gives students who are learning English a nonthreatening way to practice reading and speaking.

Plays

1. Choose a play with many characters or several plays with fewer characters.
2. Have students read the plays first. Then, assign parts and have students practice reading their parts until they can read them fluently.
3. If you have one play with many characters, have two casts read it and alternate the cast and audience roles. If you have groups reading different plays, let each group read their play for the class.

Readers' Theater

1. Choose a book with a lot of dialogue.
2. Work together as a class to turn the first chapter (or section) into a script.
3. Have students work in groups to write the scripts for the remaining chapters. Determine how many students should work together according to the parts needed and give students in the groups specific roles. If necessary, work with one group to help them succeed.
4. Have groups read the scripts and watch the story come to life.

Pantomiming

1. Choose a story with a lot of characters and dialogue.

2. Have students read the story first to figure out what is happening. You may want to focus their attention on characters, settings, and events by using Story Map or the Beach Ball.

3. Read the story as a class and decide who the characters are and what they are saying and doing.

4. Make character cards and let students choose the characters they want to play.

5. Have the readers chorally read the story while the actors pantomime and ad-lib a few lines.

6. Switch roles and do the book again so that all students can be actors at least once.

Chapter 14

Figuring Out How and Why

Many teachers find inferring to be the hardest thinking strategy to teach students. Inferring is figuring out something the author does not tell you by paying attention to what the author does tell you. Students make inferences in their lives all of the time. They figure out how others are feeling by paying attention to facial expressions and tones of voice. They figure out why something happened by thinking about the events that preceded it. But when they read, many students pay attention to the details without thinking beyond the literal information. The comprehension lesson framework that teaches students to make inferences while reading is called Figuring Out How and Why because most inferences are answers to *how* and *why* questions.

In a Figuring Out How and Why lesson, students are given questions that begin with *how* and *why* and have to use the clues in the text to figure out probable answers. It is important, however, for the *how* and *why* questions to not be directly answered in the text. Read the following story and the *how* and *why* questions. Which *how* and *why* questions require you to use clues to figure them out?

> *Without warning, a genie appears during a faculty meeting at an elementary school and tells the principal that he wants to reward her unselfish and outstanding leadership. She is given her choice of unlimited wealth, beauty, or wisdom. Without hesitating, the principal selects unlimited wisdom.*
>
> *"Done!" says the genie as he disappears in a flash of light and a puff of smoke.*
>
> *Everyone turns to the principal, who is now surrounded by a faint halo of light. One of the teachers whispers, "Say something."*
>
> *The principal sighs and says, "I should have taken the money!"*
>
> *Questions:*
>
> *1. Why is the principal chosen for this reward?*
>
> *2. How is she rewarded?*
>
> *3. Why does the principal change her mind?*
>
> *4. How does the principal feel about the choice she made?*

The answers to the first two questions are found in the text. The principal is chosen because of her unselfish and outstanding leadership. Her reward is the choice of unlimited wealth, beauty, or wisdom.

The answers to the other questions, however, are not found in the story. You have to figure them out. Why does the principal change her mind? She probably changes her mind because she is wiser now that she has unlimited wisdom! How does she feel about her choice? Since she sighs and says, "I should have taken the money," she probably regrets her choice and feels disappointed.

The most crucial step in planning a Figuring Out How and Why lesson is constructing questions that require inferring—questions that your students will not be able to answer just by understanding the information stated in the text.

An Example of Figuring Out How and Why

For this lesson, the teacher chooses *Commander Toad in Space*, a fantasy by Jane Yolen. Students have recently read the book and filled out a story map. Today, they will meet in small groups to discuss the following how and why questions:

1. How does Jake Skyjumper feel when he is told that he has to stay on board while the others go to the planet?

2. Why does Deep Wader roar, "I am Deep Wader, and this planet belongs to me"?

3. How does the landing crew of Commander Toad, Mr. Hop, and Lieutenant Lily feel when Deep Wader first appears?

4. How does the landing crew feel when they lose their sky skimmer, and Deep Wader is getting closer?

5. How does Deep Wader feel when the landing crew floats away?

6. How could the lily pad float all the way to the mother ship?

Before sending students to their groups, the teacher uses the completed story map to help them review and summarize what happens in the story. He explains that the story map contains the facts about what happens, but today they will go beyond the facts and figure out things that the author does not say.

The teacher says, "Your job today is to be detectives. You will try to figure out some things that the author doesn't tell you. Some things that the author tells you give you clues to help you figure out things that the author doesn't tell you. You also need to use your own experiences to come up with logical answers. When your group agrees on an answer, you should decide why you think that answer is correct. What clues do you get from the story and from your own experiences? For some questions, your group may not agree on the answers. If you don't agree with your group, explain why you believe your answer is more logical."

The teacher assigns students to groups of three or four and appoints a leader in each group. The leader should direct everyone's attention to each question and make sure that everyone has a chance to talk. In addition, the leader should make sure that everyone tells the reasons for thinking her answer is correct. The teacher tells the class that they will have 15 minutes to discuss the six questions and that he will alert them to move to the next question every few minutes.

As the groups discuss the questions, the teacher walks around and listens. He resists the natural teacher inclination to take over the discussion and rarely inserts himself into the conversation. He notes particularly insightful comments and writes each comment and the initials of the student who made it so that he can discuss it when the class reconvenes. Every few minutes, he tells the class to wrap up their discussions and move to the next question.

When the time is up, the teacher gives the groups two more minutes to summarize their answers, reminding them that it is fine if they do not agree on every answer as long as they have reasons to support their ideas.

The class reconvenes, and the teacher conducts a class discussion of each question. He uses his notes to ask particular students to share their reasoning. Students are pleased that he has taken note of their ideas, and even the shy students are willing to share. They spend a lot of time talking about the last question:

How could the lily pad float all the way to the mother ship?

Students have different ideas about how this could happen. The teacher makes sure that students explain their reasoning and compliments them on their clever, logical thinking. Of course, students want him to decide which inference is correct. He tells them that sometimes there are several possible answers to a *how* or *why* question, and they may not be able to decide which is correct. The lesson ends with the teacher congratulating students on their good detective work and expressing pleasure with how well the groups stayed focused and how the leaders made sure that everyone had a chance to talk and explain their ideas. Students enjoyed this discussion, and the teacher promises that they will do more Figuring Out How and Why lessons in future weeks.

Constructing *How* and *Why* Questions

Constructing *how* and *why* questions that require students to figure things out is critical to the success of the lesson. Remember to not include any questions that have answers that can be found in the text. The *how* question often probes how characters feel about something that happens or the way things are. These *how* question frames will help you construct good *how* questions:

How could [an explicit action, event, or state occur]?

How does [a character] feel when [an action, event, or state occurs]?

For both story and informational text, the *why* question often asks students to speculate about the cause of an action or event—why something happens or why something is the way it is. In constructing *why* questions, you might find these question frames helpful:

Why does [a character] [take a particular intentional action]?

Why does [an explicit action, event, or state occur]?

Look at the six questions in the example with Jane Yolen's *Commander Toad in Space*. You will see that every question fits one of the four question frames.

1. How does Jake Skyjumper feel when he is told that he has to stay on board while the others go to the planet?

2. Why does Deep Wader roar, "I am Deep Wader, and this planet belongs to me"?

3. How does the landing crew of Commander Toad, Mr. Hop, and Lieutenant Lily feel when Deep Wader first appears?

4. How does the landing crew feel when they lose their sky skimmer, and Deep Wader is getting closer?

5. How does Deep Wader feel when the landing crew floats away?

6. How could the lily pad float all the way to the mother ship?

To construct those six questions, the teacher read through the story looking for any action, event, or state described by the author. When he found one, he constructed a question of each type that the author does not answer.

Discussion Skills

Figuring Out How and Why lessons can help students develop good discussion skills. When having students discuss questions with groups, it is important that you make clear to students that you want them to spend a few minutes on each question. By listening in, taking notes, and signaling students to move to the next question, you help them keep their discussion focused and on task. Choosing a leader in each group who can keep everyone focused and can ask students to explain their reasoning will also make for better discussions. In some classrooms, students may need to learn how to listen to each other and how to disagree politely. If your students' discussion skills are not well developed, you may want to role-play the discussion of the first question with a few students as everyone else watches. Some teachers find that posting sentence starters, such as the following, and role-playing and rehearsing them with students before they get into their discussion groups improves the discussions.

- *I agree with [name of another student in the group] when [he or she] says . . .*

- *Let me put in my own words what I think I heard you say.*

- *So, don't we agree that . . .*

- *What did you mean when you said . . .?*

- *I agree with the part about . . . but I disagree with the part about . . .*

Figuring Out How and Why

All of us, children included, make inferences as we go through our daily lives. We see the clouds thickening, and we infer that a storm may be coming and the softball game might be canceled. We notice a neighbor running through the yard looking around frantically, and we infer that something bad may have happened. Making inferences pervades our daily life experiences and decisions. Reading also requires us to infer when we must figure out many things that the author does not tell us. Most of the inferences that we make in life and in reading relate to how and why certain things happen and how people feel about what happens. Figuring Out How and Why is a lesson framework that you can use to help students make inferring as natural a part of their reading experience as it is their life experience.

1. Prepare for your Figuring Out How and Why lesson by constructing five to seven *how* and *why* questions that are not directly answered in the text.

2. Use this lesson framework after students have read the text and completed a lesson focused on the textual information (Story Map, the Beach Ball, Ten Important Words, or any lesson framework from previous chapters).

3. Have students read your *how* and *why* questions and make sure that they understand that these questions can be answered only if they use their "figuring out" skills.

4. Divide the class into groups of three or four. Appoint a leader in each group who will keep everyone focused, make sure that all students are included, and ask students to explain the reasoning behind their answers.

5. Give students a limited amount of time—15 minutes for six questions—to discuss their answers to the questions.

6. Circulate and listen to the discussions. Write comments that demonstrate good thinking and the initials of the students who make the comments. Remind students when they need to move to the next question.

7. When the time is up, give groups two minutes to summarize their answers and reasoning.

8. Gather the class and share answers to the questions. Ask students whose comments you noted to share their ideas. Spend more time on questions for which students have different ideas. Make sure students know that there are often several possibilities when figuring things out. A good answer is one that can be supported with good reasoning.

9. If students' discussion skills are less than stellar, assemble a small group and role-play the discussion of the first question as everyone else watches. Include some of your best thinkers in this group and model good listening strategies. Post a list of discussion sentence starters to help students learn to listen and respect the ideas of their classmates.

Chapter 15

What Do You Think?

Although thinking involves different processes, when someone asks you, "What do you think?" that person is most likely asking for your opinion.

>Your teenage daughter walks down the stairs in a new outfit and asks, "Well, what do you think?"

>A speaker makes a presentation at a faculty meeting, and as you and a friend are walking to the parking lot, your friend asks, "What do you think?"

>Your spouse hands you a travel brochure about Alaska and asks, "What do you think?"

When you and the person you are talking with are present in the same room with the event, "What do you think?" is all that needs to be said to communicate. You know that your daughter wants your opinion about her clothes, your friend wants to know your opinion about the ideas presented at the faculty meeting, and your spouse wants to know if you are interested in visiting Alaska.

Sometimes, when you and the person who wants your opinion are not both present when the event occurs, the question needs more elaboration.

>You are talking with co-workers at lunch and someone asks, "What do you think about the budget cuts the board made last night?"

>You meet a friend for dinner and he asks, "What do you think we could do to help the earthquake victims?"

>You are talking with your sister on the phone and she asks, "What do you think I should do about selling the house?"

In Chapter 2, evaluating was described as one of the seven thinking strategies that readers use to comprehend. When you evaluate, you give your opinion.

>"I like the style of that dress, but I'm not sure that it's the right color for you."

>"I think that my students would respond well to the vocabulary ideas."

>"This Alaska trip looks like it would be really fun."

>"Elementary schools always suffer the most when the budget is cut."

"I think that the Red Cross has the most efficient system for disaster relief."

"This is not the time to sell a house. I think that you need to wait at least a year."

Sometimes, you act on your opinions and apply them to the situation.

"Let's shop this weekend to see if we can find a similar dress in red or blue."

"I am going to use some of the vocabulary ideas in math and science next week."

"Let's go to Alaska as soon as the school year ends."

"I am going to donate money to the Red Cross effort."

What Do You Think? is a lesson framework that teaches students that their opinions matter. It also teaches them how to support their opinions with information from the text and from their prior knowledge.

Teaching a What Do You Think? Lesson

You can use the What Do You Think? lesson framework when you want students to connect their beliefs and values to the information they learn from the text. Before you ask students to make evaluations and form opinions, make sure that they understand the facts about what they are reading. What Do You Think? always follows lessons in which you have made sure that students understand what is happening in the text. All of the lesson frameworks described previously in the book teach students to make sense of the text. If the text you want students to form opinions about is a story, you can use Prove It!, Rivet, Story Map, the Beach Ball, or Doing the Book as your lesson framework for the first reading of the text. If the text is informational, having students read using Guess Yes or No, Preview-Predict-Confirm, KWL, Graphic Organizers, or Ten Important Words will ensure that your students have the information on which to base their opinions. In What Do You Think? lessons, students reread parts of a text they have already read to decide what they think and to justify their opinions with facts and examples from the text.

The most important part of planning a What Do You Think? lesson is constructing a good question. Constructing this question is not hard if you consider what students care about. In some stories, the ending is emotional, and students enjoy thinking about whether the story ends the way it should. Charlotte's Web by E. B. White is a classic example of a story with a controversial ending. After reading Charlotte's Web, lively discussions will ensue if you pose these questions:

What do you think about the way the story ends? How else could the story end, and would that be a better ending?

© Carson-Dellosa

Some stories—particularly traditional tales—have two versions with the biggest difference being how they end. After reading the version of *The Three Little Pigs* in which the wolf falls in the pot and dies and the version in which the wolf runs into the forest and is never seen again, students could participate in a discussion prompted by these questions:

> Which ending for *The Three Little Pigs* do you think is best? Why do you think so?

When you read stories, you often have opinions about what the characters do and what their actions tell you about them.

> Frog and Toad in *Days with Frog and Toad* by Arnold Lobel solve many problems. Do you think Frog or Toad is the better problem solver? Explain your decision with examples from the story.

> Many characters in *The Butterfly* by Patricia Polacco show that they are brave and courageous. Which character do you think shows the most courage? Give examples to support your choice.

> In *Lilly's Purple Plastic Purse* by Kevin Henkes, Lilly gets in trouble at school with her new purple purse. Do you think she deserves to be in trouble? Explain why or why not.

> In *Missing: One Stuffed Rabbit* by Maryann Cocca-Leffler, Janine decides to let the girl with the broken leg keep Coco. Do you think Janine makes the right decision? What would you do? Explain why you think as you do.

Students should also have opinions when they read informational text. In some texts, students learn about life in other times and places. They could compare these settings with a Venn diagram or a data chart and think about the advantages and disadvantages of life in the different settings.

> You have read *Sarah Morton's Day: A Day in the Life of a Pilgrim Girl* by Kate Waters. Imagine that you were a pilgrim who lived where and when Sarah Morton did. What do you think you would have liked about being a pilgrim? What would you have disliked?

> You have read about Japan and learned that some things are the same there as in the United States and some things are different. What do you think you would like better about living in Japan? What do you like better about living in the United States?

> We have been reading about many kinds of pets. Which animal do you think would be the best pet for you? Why did you choose that pet?

After you construct your opinion-forming question, separate students into small mixed-ability groups and give each group the question. Appoint a referee in each group and explain that the referee's job is to make sure that everyone has a chance to state an opinion and to ask each student

108

to explain the reasons for her opinion. Give the groups 10–12 minutes to share and support their opinions. Poll each student to see what his opinion is. Emphasize that there is not a right or a wrong answer and that people will have different opinions.

What Do You Think?

Think back to the educational psychology course you took in college. Do you remember learning about Bloom's Taxonomy? Can you visualize the pyramid with *knowledge* and *understanding* at the bottom and *evaluating* and *applying* at the top? Evaluating and applying is a higher-level thinking process. The lower levels of knowledge and understanding are required in order to move to higher levels, but thinking should not stop there. Unlike questions at lower levels, questions that require higher-level thinking do not have right or wrong answers. The focus in a What Do You Think? lesson is not on whether the answer is correct but rather on the reasoning that students go through to come up with their answers.

1. Have students read the selection for knowledge and understanding first. Use a lesson framework that focuses on the facts to make sure that all students have sufficient information on which to base their opinions.

2. Construct a What Do You Think? question that helps students focus on their opinions about what they have read.

3. Put students in small groups and give them the question. Appoint a referee in each group whose job is to make sure that all members of the group have the chance to give their opinions and the reasons for those opinions.

4. Poll each student and tally each opinion.

5. Compliment the class on their good thinking and remind them that What Do You Think? questions do not have a right or a wrong answer. The goal is not that everyone agrees, but rather that everyone can explain her thinking and be tolerant of others' opinions.

Chapter 16

Think-Alouds

Think-Alouds (Keene and Zimmermann 2007) are a way of modeling, or making public, the thinking that goes on inside your head as you read. To explain Think-Alouds to students, tell them that there are really two voices speaking as they read. The voice they can hear is their actual voice reading the words aloud, but there is also a voice inside their brains that tells what it thinks about what they are reading. Use Think-Alouds to demonstrate for students how you think as you read.

Thinking is the most complex act humans do, and it is risky to try to define it. Chapter 2 describes seven thinking strategies that play a large role in reading comprehension. In Think-Alouds, you demonstrate these thinking strategies. Use words for Think-Alouds that seem natural and that students will understand. Here are some examples of words that might be used to communicate each thinking strategy.

Connecting
- This reminds me of . . .
- I remember something like this happened to me when . . .
- I read another book in which the character . . .
- This is like what happens in our school when . . .
- Our country does not have that holiday, but we have . . .

Predicting/Questioning
- I wonder if . . .
- I wonder who . . .
- I think that I know what is coming next . . .
- He will be in trouble if . . .
- I think that we will learn how . . .

Summarizing
- The most important thing I have learned so far is . . .
- So far in the story, . . .
- So far, I have learned that . . .

Inferring
- It does not say why she does that, but I bet . . .
- I know that he must be feeling . . .
- The author didn't tell us that it is . . . but I can use the clues to figure out that it is . . .

Monitoring

- I wonder what it means when . . .
- I don't understand . . .
- It didn't make sense when . . .

Visualizing/Imagining

- Even though it isn't in the picture, I can see the . . .
- Mmm, I can almost taste the . . .
- It sent chills down my spine when . . .
- For a minute, I thought that I could smell . . .
- I could hear the . . .
- I can imagine what it is like to . . .
- I can picture the . . .

Evaluating/Applying

- My favorite part in this chapter is . . .
- I really like how the author . . .
- What I don't like about this part is . . .
- I don't agree that . . .
- In my opinion, . . .
- I am going to try this when . . .
- I would really like to . . .

A Think-Aloud Example

Teachers use Think-Alouds in a variety of ways, but the most efficient and effective way is to read and think aloud the first quarter or third of the selection that students will read. In addition to hearing you think your way through the text, students are introduced to the selection, including characters, setting, and important vocabulary. Next, students finish reading the selection in small groups and share their thinking.

Here is an example of a Think-Aloud based on the first third of *Aunt Flossie's Hats (and Crab Cakes Later)* by Elizabeth Fitzgerald Howard. The Think-Aloud begins with studying the cover of the book. The teacher reads aloud the title and looks at the picture, saying something like this:

> "I bet the lady in the picture is Aunt Flossie. She is a pretty lady, and she has two hats—one on her head and one on her lap. I bet she likes hats and has a lot of them. The two girls have hats too. I wonder if those are their hats. They don't really look like kids' hats. Maybe they belong to Aunt Flossie. I wonder what the girls' names are and if they are sisters. I think that I will like this book because everyone looks happy and because I love hats!"

The teacher turns the page and thinks aloud about the picture on the title page.

> "This is a nice, quiet street, and the houses are all joined together. I think that they are called row houses. They remind me of the house my great-grandmother lived in. The houses were all connected and didn't have yards. When I visited her, we played in the street."

The teacher turns the page and thinks aloud about the pictures on the next two pages before she begins reading.

> "There are the two girls. I think that they are the same girls we saw on the cover. I will look back and check. Yes, they are the same girls. It looks like they are knocking on the door. I wonder if this is Aunt Flossie's house and if she is home."

The teacher then reads the first sentence.

> *On Sunday afternoons, Sarah and I go to see Great-great-aunt Flossie.*

> "Oh, it's their great-great-aunt. She must be really old. I had a great-aunt named Aunt Hester. I wonder which girl is Sarah."

The teacher reads these two pages and comments:

> "My great-grandmother's house had a lot of stuff too. I loved playing in the attic. She didn't have a lot of hats, though."

The teacher turns the page and again thinks aloud about the picture before reading the words.

> "Mmm, those cookies look delicious. I bet she baked them. I can almost taste them."

The teacher reads the page and comments:

> "The other girl's name is Susan. I wonder which girl is Susan and which girl is Sarah. It doesn't say that they are sisters, but she is their great-aunt and they look alike, so I think that they probably are. They are going to have tea and cookies and later, crab cakes. Now, that really makes my mouth water. Crab cakes are one of my favorite foods!"

The pictures on the next page elicit these comments:

> "They are having tea and cookies, and the younger girl is trying on a hat. The older girl is opening a box. I bet it is a hatbox, and she will try on that hat."

The teacher reads the page and comments:

> "I wonder why Aunt Flossie says that the hats are her memories. That doesn't really make sense to me. Maybe we will find out as we read the rest of the story."

The next page shows hatboxes and hats everywhere.

"She has a lot of hats! On this page, she looks like she is telling Sarah and Susan something. I wonder if she is telling them about the hats."

The teacher reads the text and comments:

"It says that the green hat has a smoky smell. I wonder if you can really smell something on the hat. Sarah and Susan can't smell it."

She turns the page and comments extensively on the pictures.

"Whoa, I wonder where we are now! I think that these people are all firefighters, but horses are pulling the fire truck. This must have happened a long time ago. There is a woman holding a child. They both look very frightened. I can almost feel how afraid they are. I wonder who they are and if the fire is at their house. I wonder what this has to do with Aunt Flossie and her hats."

While reading the page, the teacher stops several times and thinks aloud.

"The book says that it was a really big fire and that everything smelled of smoke for days. I think that I can smell the smoke now."

"Oh, now I understand what it says."

Your great-grandma and I couldn't sleep. We grabbed our coats and hats and ran outside."

"The child must be Aunt Flossie, and the woman must be her sister. Aunt Flossie is wearing the green hat. That's why she thinks that she can still smell the smoke on it. It was the hat she was wearing when they had the big fire in Baltimore."

"She says that the hats are her memories because they remind her of something. I wonder what the other hats remind her of."

"I can't wait to read the rest of the book!"

When the teacher has read and shared her thoughts on the first part of the book, she leads the students in a discussion about what has happened in the story so far. Together, they summarize what has happened, and the teacher asks students what they think will happen in the rest of the story. Then, students read the rest of the story in Play-School Groups. The "Teacher" in each group stops students after each page and asks them to share what their brains are telling them.

Think-Alouds

Think-Alouds are an opportunity for you to demonstrate for students how your brain uses the thinking strategies to comprehend. It is *not* necessary to include all seven thinking strategies in every lesson. Some texts do not lend themselves to particular strategies, and you do not want to force it. Across several lessons, however, you want to make sure that you include examples for each thinking strategy.

While teachers normally invite participation while reading, it is important not to let students chime in as you are demonstrating thinking aloud for them. If you use the procedure of beginning the selection with your Think-Aloud and having students finish the selection and share their Think-Alouds, students are usually willing to let you have your turn! Some teachers tell students that they should pretend to be invisible while the teacher is reading and thinking. Students get to hear the teacher thinking, but since they are "invisible," they should not let her know that they are there! You want to signal to students when you are reading and when you are thinking. Many teachers look at the book when they are reading and look away from the book—perhaps toward the ceiling—to signal when they are thinking. Other teachers use a different voice to signal their thinking. They read in their reading voice and think in their thinking voice.

1. Choose a selection that causes you to think.

2. Decide how much of that selection you will read aloud to students.

3. Look at the pictures and read the selection to plan what you will say. Look for places where you actually use the thinking strategies—connecting, predicting/questioning, summarizing, inferring, monitoring, visualizing/imagining, and evaluating/applying. Mark these places with sticky notes and cryptic comments to help you remember what to say.

4. Do the Think-Aloud as the "invisible" students watch and listen. Comment on all pictures first. Then, read the text. Stop at appropriate places in the text and comment.

5. Do not try to force all of the thinking processes into one selection, but do try to include all seven across several lessons.

6. Have students finish reading the selection in Play-School Groups, sharing their thinking as they read each page.

Part Three

During-Reading Formats

You now know how to plan your Guided Reading lessons with a focus on comprehension, keeping thinking strategies and text structure in mind. You are using the largest variety of materials you can find and teaching students how to read all types of text. You are integrating some of the reading with your science and social studies content and themes. The final decision you must make is in which format students will read the materials during Guided Reading. This part of the book describes some formats we use to make Guided Reading as multilevel as possible for a wide range of students. These formats will help you achieve the Guided Reading goals of providing instructional-level reading (and the instruction to go with it) and maintaining the motivation and confidence of struggling readers. If the material is not at the instructional level of some students, you must decide what kind of support these students need to successfully navigate the text.

When you think about how students will read the materials you have on hand, consider teacher-led formats and collaborative formats. Teacher-led formats are Shared, Echo, and Choral Reading; Everyone Read To . . . (ERT); Sentence and Paragraph Detectives; and Coaching Groups. Teachers usually use and model teacher-led formats before moving into collaborative formats. The collaborative formats are Partner Reading; Play-School Groups/Reading Teams; Three-Ring Circus; You'se Choose; Book Club Groups; Literature Circles; and, once in a while for fun and fluency, Pick a Page. Continue using the formats that you have previously taught and perfect them as you add new formats throughout the year. Each format has a purpose, and each format will be a favorite of some students in your class.

Teacher-Led Formats

Collaborative Formats

Chapter 17

Shared Reading

Shared Reading with big books is a wonderful way to expose emergent readers to books. It also provides opportunities for you to model for and interact with students as you show them how you think as you read. By using a big book in which all students can see the pictures and print, you can focus students' attention on whichever strategy is being developed. Shared Reading of big books should not be confined to kindergarten and early first grade. Rather, teachers should try to find big books that help them "think aloud" and use them to demonstrate any comprehension strategies being introduced to students.

Shared Reading is when the teacher and students read together. Typically, a selection is read and reread several times. As students become more familiar with the book, they join in and "share" the reading. During Shared Reading, many things can be learned, depending on what students are ready to learn. Students who have had little experience with reading learn how print works, how to track print, and how the pictures and the words support each other. They also learn a few words, and they notice how the letters can help them tell which word is which. For students who are further along in reading, Shared Reading provides an opportunity to learn many words.

Most students enjoy Shared Reading, and participating in Shared Reading lessons helps them build concepts, vocabulary, and comprehension strategies. Because there is something for everyone in a good Shared Reading lesson, Shared Reading is one of the most multilevel formats. For older students, teachers can use a regular-sized book and a document camera or interactive whiteboard to do Shared Reading.

Shared Reading with Predictable Big Books

The best big books for beginning readers are predictable by pictures or print. An excellent example of a big book that is predictable by pictures is *Things I Like* by Anthony Browne. In this book, students can read the words by looking at the pictures. If students are taught to look at the pictures and stretch out the words that they expect to describe each picture, they can cross-check to see if they are correct by looking for the letters that they expect to appear in these words. When the little monkey in *Things I Like* lists the activities he likes, students can figure out the text by looking at the pictures and thinking about what the monkey is doing on each page. "What does it say on this page? Yes, it says riding my bike. In the picture, you see the monkey on a little red bike and know that he is riding his bike." *Riding my bike* makes sense with the picture, the sounds students hear, and the letters they expect to see. Predictable pictures allow young students to share the reading before they are fluent at decoding many words. Thus, books and stories that are predictable by pictures are easier for children.

In books that are predictable by print, words or phrases are repeated over and over again in the text. As soon as students hear this pattern, they begin to chime in and share the reading of the story. Two familiar big books with predictable text are *Brown Bear, Brown Bear, What Do You See?* by Bill Martin Jr. and *Mrs. Wishy-Washy* by Joy Cowley. Once students have heard the book, they pick up the pattern and want to share the reading of the book. Students enjoy chiming in, "Wishy, Washy, Wishy, Washy," every time Mrs. Wishy-Washy puts an animal in the tub.

An Example of Shared Reading

In the predictable big book *The Doorbell Rang* by Pat Hutchins, the repeated pattern is this:

> *"Nobody makes cookies like Grandma," said Ma as the doorbell rang.*

Use this book for three days during Guided Reading and include some math and snack links. One day at snack time, before the first reading of *The Doorbell Rang*, tell students that you have brought some cookies to share with them. As you say this, place 12 cookies in front of the students and ask them to estimate the number of cookies and how many cookies each person can have. After students estimate, count the number of cookies and the number of students present and conclude that you do not have enough for everyone to have one! At that point, either divide the cookies in half (Let's hope they're big cookies!) or bring out more cookies and count out enough for everyone to have at least one.

If you do this activity with students, it will provide some concrete experience with the problem in *The Doorbell Rang*. Do not mention the book when you are sharing the cookies and do not mention the cookies when you begin reading *The Doorbell Rang*. It is much more fun to let students discover the link as they are reading the book. Someone is sure to observe, "This is just like what happened to us when we had only 12 cookies!" (Caution: Before beginning any food activity, ask families' permission and inquire about students' food allergies and religious or other food restrictions.)

Shared Reading with a Predictable Big Book: Day One

The first thing the teacher does during Guided Reading when sharing a big book is gather students where they can all see the pictures and print in the book. The teacher reads the title and the author's name and asks students what they see in the picture on the cover. Students tell her that there is a woman, a cat, and a bunch of children. The "bunch of children" is counted, and there are 12 children. The woman and all 12 children are peeking out the door, and they do not look happy.

The teacher turns the page, and this time, she asks students to help her read the title and the author's name. There is a picture on the title page too. The same woman is in the picture, and she is holding a cookie sheet full of cookies. The teacher leads students in counting the cookies, and there are 12. The cat is sitting on the sink. There are no children in this picture, but both the cat and the woman are looking toward the door. The teacher inspires students to predict/anticipate by saying, "I wonder what will happen." Students make various comments:

"The doorbell just rang, and she is going to answer the door when she puts down the cookies."

"There are 12 cookies, and 12 children are at the door."

"Hey, that's like when we had 12 cookies at snack, but there were 22 of us!"

The teacher says, "Well, let's turn the page, and we will find out."

She turns the page, and they discuss the picture. Two children are sitting at a table and are about to grab some of the cookies. One student comments that those were two of the children on the cover looking out the door, and the teacher and students turn back and identify the two children on this page in the crowd of children on the cover. After discussing the picture, the teacher says, "Now, I will read the words to you. Watch and listen, and we will talk about what we learned from the words that we couldn't figure out from the picture." The teacher reads the page to students, pointing to words as she reads them. After she reads, she asks students what they learned. They tell her that the children are named Victoria and Sam, and the woman is their mother, who tells Victoria and Sam to share the cookies because she made plenty.

Before turning the page, the teacher asks students to make more predictions. She uses the names of the characters—Victoria, Sam, and Ma—to talk about them and encourages students to use the names so that they will eventually be able to read them.

"What's going to happen?"

"Will Victoria and Sam eat all 12 cookies?"

"If they share them as Ma told them to, how many cookies will Victoria get? How many will Sam get?

Students conclude that if they share the cookies, Victoria and Sam will each get six. Some students think that they should save some cookies for later. One student predicts, "All of those other kids will want cookies."

The teacher turns the page again, and the picture shows just Victoria, Sam, Ma, and the cat. After discussing the picture, the teacher asks students to watch, listen, and see what they can learn from the words that they could not learn from the picture. Students watch, listen, and tell what they learned.

"They will get six cookies each, just like we figured out."

"They have a grandma, and she makes cookies too."

"The cookies look and smell as good as the ones their grandma makes."

"The doorbell rings."

"What do you think will happen next?" the teacher asks.

The teacher continues through the rest of the book, one page at a time, using the same procedure. Each time the doorbell rings, more children arrive. Tom and Hannah arrive from next door—"That's three each." Peter and his little brother come by—"Two each." As more children arrive, students delight in going back to the cover and finding the children there. After Peter and his little brother arrive, students begin to predict which children from the cover are coming next. When Joy, Simon, and four cousins arrive, there are 12 children and 12 cookies—"One each!" The children are just about to grab their cookies, commenting that these cookies look and smell as good as Grandma's, when the doorbell rings again. Everyone looks anxiously at the door, and Ma suggests that perhaps they should eat their cookies before opening the door. Sam decides that everyone should wait, and he opens the door. Fortunately, it is Grandma with an enormous tray of cookies. The book ends:

"And no one makes cookies like Grandma," said Ma as the doorbell rang.

The teacher takes a few minutes to let students discuss what they like about the story and to make connections to their own lives. Students talk about their grandmothers, making cookies, sharing, and how it is good that it was Grandma at their door and not more kids.

Next, the teacher tells students that they will read the book again and that this time, she wants them to read with her, joining in on the refrain and any other words they can read. Quickly, they look at the cover, reading the title and author's name again. The teacher asks students why they think the author titled the book *The Doorbell Rang*, and students delight in explaining why it is a good title. They count the children again, and some students begin to identify the children in the book.

"That's Sam and his sister, Victoria"

"There's that kid and his little brother."

"Those are all of the cousins."

Students do not remember all of the characters' names, and the teacher says that they will pay more attention to that when they read this time. She asks students if anyone remembers what they call the people in a story, and someone says, "They are the characters." The teacher then asks students where the action in the story takes place, and they say that it all happens in the kitchen. The teacher helps students remember that the setting is where the story takes place.

Students read the book once more, talking about the pictures and joining the teacher as she reads some words, especially the refrain. This time, before turning each page, the teacher asks, "Does anyone remember what happens on the next page?" Students enjoy sharing what they remember, and the second reading continues in this way.

They end Shared Reading on this day with a group retelling. The teacher turns the pages again and asks students to tell the story based on the pictures. She leads them to use the names of the characters as they tell the story. By the end of the first day, students know all of the characters' names and can retell the action.

Shared Reading with a Predictable Big Book: Day Two

The teacher begins the second day of Shared Reading with *The Doorbell Rang* by displaying a laminated story map skeleton and having students help her fill it in. The finished product looks like this:

Story Map

Title: The Doorbell Rang
Author: Pat Hutchins

Setting: a kitchen

Characters: Victoria; Sam; Ma; Tom and Hannah; Peter and his brother; Joy, Simon, and four cousins; Grandma

Beginning: Ma makes some cookies for Victoria and Sam to eat.

Middle: The doorbell rings, and some friends come to see Victoria and Sam. Victoria and Sam share their cookies with their friends until there is just one cookie on each plate, and the doorbell rings again.

End: Grandma is at the door with a big batch of cookies.

Conclusion: Everyone likes Grandma's cookies best. Now Victoria and Sam have a big batch of cookies to share with their friends.

When the story map is completed, the teacher directs students' attention back to the book. They reread the first page, and the teacher asks, "Who is talking on this page?" Students conclude that Ma, Victoria, and Sam are all talking, and they decide what each character is saying. They do this for a few more pages. After looking at the first several pages, students decide that most of the words on the pages are things people are saying.

The teacher then announces that she thinks *The Doorbell Rang* would make a great play. She says that if students will help her, she will write what everyone is saying and tomorrow the class can act out *The Doorbell Rang*. Students love acting out books, so they are eager to help her write this play.

The teacher sits at her computer, which is connected to her interactive whiteboard, and prepares to type. (If you do not have an interactive whiteboard in your classroom, write the script on several sheets of paper or a transparency. If you do have the technology, it is quicker and more dramatic to type the text so that students can view it. You can show them how you copy and paste to save time. You can also make copies for students to take home!) The teacher appoints one student to turn the pages of the big book, and everyone else helps her decide who is saying what.

On the first page, students decide that Ma is talking to her children, Victoria and Sam. They notice that Ma is talking first, and she says, *"I've made cookies for tea."* Next, Victoria and Sam talk. *"Good. We're starving."* The page ends with Ma talking again. The beginning of the play looks like this:

Ma: *I've made some cookies for tea.*

Victoria and Sam: *Good. We're starving.*

Ma: *Share them between yourselves. I made plenty.*

As each page of dialogue is written, the teacher stops and has students read it. For this page, the teacher asks one student to be Ma and asks the rest of the class to be Victoria and Sam. The class reads the first page of the play and continues through the book. For each page, they first read the page chorally, then decide who is talking and what each character says. These lines are added:

Victoria and Sam: *That's six each.*

Victoria: *They look as good as Grandma's.*

When students tell the teacher that she should write that Sam says, *"They smell as good as Grandma's,"* the teacher says that she will show them a trick to add that line really fast. She then copies *"They look as good as Grandma's"* from the script and pastes the sentence into the play script where it is needed. She highlights *look* and changes it to *smell*. The page finishes with the refrain.

Ma: *No one makes cookies like Grandma.*

Students delight in telling the teacher each time they come to the refrain to copy and paste it again.

The teacher and students continue reading each page in the book chorally and deciding what the play script should say. They copy and paste with abandon. As each page of the play script is written, the teacher appoints someone to read the new parts while the rest of the class recites Ma's refrain. The play script is read as it is created.

They conclude this day by doing the Beach Ball. Students become fluent in telling about their favorite part, what happens, how it ends, and even naming the characters.

Shared Reading with a Predictable Big Book: Day Three

Students cannot wait for Guided Reading time on the third day because they know that they will act out and read the play based on *The Doorbell Rang*. The teacher has written the character names on cards and has attached yarn to two corners of each card so that students can wear the cards. She even made a card with a picture of a bell for the student who will make the doorbell sound. (She also drew bells in the appropriate places in the script.)

The teacher assigns parts by shuffling index cards with students' names on them, pulling cards from the set, and calling on students to choose which characters they want to be in the play. The first person whose card is chosen puts the card for Grandma around her neck. The next person chooses to be the doorbell. The choosing continues until the 15 character cards are around 15 necks. The teacher tells the six remaining students that she will join them as the "audience," but when the class does the play again, the six will be the first to choose parts for the second production.

Each student is given a copy of the script that the class helped the teacher write the previous day. For the most part, students read their lines and enter on cue because they are so familiar with the story by now. The "doorbell" enjoys going *ding-dong* when necessary and is the first part chosen for the next reading. The teacher decides that the four cousins should also get to choose a speaking part for the second reading since they did not get to say anything the first time. The play is read and acted out a second time, and students beg to do it a third time. The teacher tells them that they do not have time to do it again in class, but they can all take their scripts home. She says that they can recruit family or friends, or use puppets or stuffed animals, to play the parts and do the play at home.

For an after-reading activity, the teacher directs students' attention to the last page in the book.

"And no one makes cookies like Grandma," said Ma as the doorbell rang.

The teacher asks students to think about who is at the door now and what will happen next. "I don't want you to tell me aloud," she says, "I want you to tell me in writing." She gives everyone a sheet of paper and asks students to write who they think is at the door and what they think will happen. She gives students a few minutes to write and lets them share their writing with the class if they want to.

Shared Reading with Informational Big Books

There are informational big books for teaching science and social studies topics in grades K–2. In recent years, however, the number of informational big books for all grade levels, especially grades 3–6, has decreased. Many students in third through sixth grade have trouble reading content area textbooks and informational books because of the books' many features: table of contents, illustrations with quicktext, diagrams, maps, charts, glossaries, and indexes. Using each of these features requires a different skill, and students must be taught how to read each feature in order to be successful. Informational books require a different kind of reading from stories. These books require students to slow their reading pace and pay attention to more than just the words.

Shared Reading with Informational Books for Primary Grades

Books written primarily for the primary grades do not usually have table of contents or indexes. Examples of informational books written for the primary grades include *Insects* by Robin Bernard, *Pilgrims of Plymouth* by Susan E. Goodman, and *Exploring Space* by Toni Eugene. After talking about what is on the cover and doing a Picture Walk with one of these books, you could use a document camera or an interactive whiteboard to project the regular-sized book onto a screen and do a Shared Reading. With large pictures and print for the whole class to see, you read the text *to* students and discuss the pictures that accompany the print. Then, read the pages again sentence by sentence *with* students. After the Shared Reading, have students talk about what they learned and draw pictures of or write things that they learned from the book. *Apples for Everyone*; *Seed, Sprout, Pumpkin, Pie*; and *Everything Spring* by Jill Esbaum can each be read with the class in a Shared Reading format in one day. The beautiful pictures add much to the class discussion and students' knowledge.

For grades 2–3, look for an informational book that has a table of contents and/or an index to share with students. Several books in the Learn All About series—*Penguins* and *Creepy Crawlies* by Robin Bernard, *Whales* by Kath Buffington, and *Ocean Life* by Lisa Jo Rudy—are written like textbooks with tables of contents and indexes and can be used to model these features. Some informational books have some, but not all, of the features that textbooks contain. The following is an example of Shared Reading that uses a book that has some textbook features to teach students the various skills needed to successfully read informational text. The book *Bugs! Bugs! Bugs!* by Jennifer Dussling contains an index and some information boxes.

Shared Reading with an Informational Book: Day One

On the first day, the teacher projects the book on a screen with a document camera or an interactive whiteboard. The teacher begins the lesson by having students take a Picture Walk to preview the text. She tells students that she will page through the text quickly, giving them a peek at all of the pages. Then, she tells them to think about two questions:

Is what we will read today a story or information?

What will it mostly be about?

She reminds students that no one talks during the preview. Instead, they will use their eyes and brains to figure out the answers to the two questions. She turns the pages of the book *Bugs! Bugs! Bugs!* and pauses for about 5–10 seconds on each page. As she gets to the last page, all students' hands are raised. Students agree that it is not a story and has a lot of information about different bugs. "How do you know?" the teacher asks. Students explain that they saw a lot of pictures of bugs and that the bugs looked real.

Next, the teacher reminds students that informational text often has special features that are not usually found in story text. "What is this, and what does it tell us?" the teacher asks as she points to an information box and the index. The teacher identifies an information box and reads the information. Next, she identifies the index and explains how to use it to find information in the text. The teacher and students check a few entries and see that this feature is indeed a way of finding information. "Sometimes, you don't want to read the whole book," the teacher explains, "and you can use the index to quickly find the pages that have the information you need." She asks the class a couple of questions:

"Where will we find information about spiders?"

"What pages would we go to if we were interested in caterpillars?

Students identify the page of bug facts. The teacher leads students to read a fact and explains how this page helps summarize some of the things that they will learn when reading the book. Having finished the preview, the teacher and the class begin a KWL chart. On a large sheet of chart paper, the teacher writes what students know about bugs in the K column.

Bugs		
K	**W**	**L**
They are alive. They have heads. They have bodies. They have legs. They need food to live.		

The teacher then asks students, "What do you want to learn?" She records some of their questions in the W column.

Bugs		
K	**W**	**L**
They are alive. They have heads. They have bodies. They have legs. They need food to live.	Are bugs insects? What do bugs eat? Are bugs dangerous? Do all bugs change as they grow?	

Students' questions are specific and show that the preview has them thinking about what they would like to learn.

Next, the teacher turns to the title page, and they talk about the title and the author of the book. Then, she turns to pages 4 and 5 and, after discussing the pictures of four named bugs, begins a Shared Reading of the text. They continue this way until they reach page 15; half the book. On every two-page spread, they talk about all of the visuals and read any information boxes and the names that accompany pictures of bugs first. Finally, the teacher and students read the text. They talk about what they learned from the text that they had not learned from the pictures and information boxes. The teacher ends the lesson by closing the book and writing several new things they learned about bugs under the L column on the KWL chart.

Shared Reading with an Informational Book: Day Two

The next day's lesson follows the same procedure. The teacher and students begin the lesson by reviewing what they have on the KWL chart. Then, they discuss the pictures and read the information boxes for the remainder of the book and do a Shared Reading of the text. They finish their reading with the bug facts at the end of the book. They discuss that these facts sum up what they learned in the book, and they add the facts that are not already on their list to the L column of the KWL chart. The teacher ends the lesson by having students write or draw three things they learned about bugs in this book.

Shared Reading with Informational Books for Intermediate Grades

Helping students in grades 3–6 become more successful with content area textbooks and informational books is a goal of many teachers. These books often have tables of contents, illustrations with quicktext, diagrams, maps, charts, glossaries, and indexes. Using each of these features requires a different skill, and students must be taught how to read each feature in order to be successful.

Big books are one way to introduce the features of informational books to students. With a big book, you can focus students' attention on the features and guide them through the reading of the text with a Shared Reading format. If you cannot find informational big books, a textbook or regular-sized informational book with these features can be used with a document camera or an interactive whiteboard to project the book onto a screen.

Here is an example using *Dr. Seuss* by Laura Hamilton Waxman. This book begins with a table of contents. It has several chapters with illustrations and quicktext. At the back of the book, it has a time line, suggestions for other books, Web sites, and DVDs about Dr. Seuss, and an index. (If you use a big book for a comprehension lesson at any grade level, students should be close enough to the book that when you point to a feature, they can follow along.)

The teacher has just one copy of *Dr. Seuss*, so he uses a document camera or an interactive whiteboard to project the book onto a screen for all to see. He has chosen this book for two reasons. First, most of the class can read the text, so they will be able to concentrate on the information and the features in the book. Second, it is March 2 and they are celebrating Dr. Seuss's birthday. For years, these students have been reading Dr. Seuss's books. Now, they can read a book about him and learn more about his life. Since this book has five chapters, the teacher plans to spend five days with the book.

Shared Reading with an Informational Book: Day One

The first day, the class looks at the cover of *Dr. Seuss*. They discuss Dr. Seuss's photograph and the small pictures around it and read the title and the author's name together. Next, the teacher turns to the table of contents, and the class looks at the titles of the five chapters and predicts what they are about. Students realize that they know a lot about Chapter 3 but very little about the other four chapters. Next, the teacher tells students that he will page through the text quickly, giving them a peek at all of the pages. He tells them to think about two questions as they preview the book:

Is what we will read today a story or information about a real person?

When does most of this story or information happen?

When the teacher finishes paging through the text, all students raise their hands. They agree that this book is about a real person and happened long ago because it has real photographs that show life "before we were born!" Next, the teacher reminds them that informational text often has special features that are not usually found in story text. He pages through the book again and asks, "What is this, and what does it tell us?" as he points to quicktext near the pictures on some pages, the table of contents, a time line, and the index.

"Sometimes, you don't want to read the whole book," the teacher explains, "and you can use the table of contents or index to quickly find the pages that have the information you need."

"This time line tells the important events in Dr. Seuss's life."

Students notice that many pictures are photographs of things that actually happened. The teacher points to and talks about the photographs of Dr. Seuss at various ages and the drawings of him from some of his most famous books. "How do photographs help?" asks the teacher. Students explain that they can learn a lot from studying the photographs and quicktext that tells what is happening in the pictures. The quicktext is easier for students to read because it is not as long as the regular text.

Next, the teacher turns to the table of contents. He reads the titles and the pages on which they are found. He asks the class a couple of questions:

"What do you think we will find out in this chapter?"

"What chapter would we go to if we were interested in . . . ?"

Finally, the teacher and students read the introduction in a Shared Reading format and talk about what they learned. They also read the first chapter together in a Shared Reading format. They look at the pictures on each two-page spread and discuss them, read the quicktext, read the page together, and discuss what they learned after reading. After the Shared Reading and discussion of the first chapter, the teacher and the class write a short summary together about what they learned.

Shared Reading with an Informational Book: Days Two through Five
Each day, students tell the teacher what they learned about Dr. Seuss from the previous day's reading. Then, the teacher turns to the table of contents to locate the title of the chapter they will read that day and the page on which it begins. He turns to that chapter, and together they look at the pictures, read the quicktext, do a Shared Reading of the text, and discuss what they learned. Then, they write a paragraph summarizing the chapter.

When students finish the book, they are given copies of the chapter summaries the class wrote. They read the summaries silently before sharing with partners what they liked about the book. Students can take home the copies of the summaries to share with their families.

Tips for Reading Information

1. Preview the text to see what it is about and what special features it has.
2. If you are looking for something specific, use the table of contents and index.
3. See if the text has a glossary with meanings for the important words.
4. Make a KWL chart in your mind or on paper. Think about what you already know and what you want to learn.
5. Read the title first to see what the page is about.
6. Next, read the pictures and all of the quicktext.
7. Study the charts and diagrams and figure out what they tell you.
8. Read the regular text to find out what you did not learn from the visuals.
9. Stop and add things that you learn to your KWL chart.
10. If you spend several days reading, summarize what you have learned in writing each day.

Shared Reading with a Book That Has a Story and Information

Many stories contain true information. When students read *Wagon Wheels* by Barbara Brenner, a story of a family's trip across the country in a covered wagon, they learn information about what life was like then. When students read a story about a boy and his horse, they learn true information about horses. They are stories, however, and students should read them as stories, paying attention to the characters, settings, problems, events, and solutions. After reading such a story, you might discuss the true things students learned, but students must understand that they have read a story.

Sometimes, you come across a book that is primarily information but is written in story form. A popular example of this is The Magic School Bus series by Joanna Cole. There are a number of books in this series, and each one contains a lot of science information within the story. Children delight in the fantasy of going to the waterworks, to a solar system, or inside the human body on an imaginary field trip. It can be very hard for students to figure out how to read one of these books. What do they read first, and how do they keep up with the story and learn new information simultaneously? Made-to-order big books can help students learn how to read "different" text. This example of Shared Reading is based on the big book version of *The Magic School Bus: Lost in the Solar System*.

To begin the Shared Reading of this book, students are asked to decide whether the text they will read is a story or information and what it is about. The teacher turns the pages of the book, pausing briefly on each two-page spread. Students use their brains and their eyes—not their mouths—to figure out the two questions. When they have looked at all of the pages, the teacher asks students again whether they think it is a story or information.

"It's a story," many students respond.

"How do you know?" the teacher asks.

Students tell her that the text has characters (Ms. Frizzle and all of the kids in the class), that things happen, and that it has a beginning, a middle, and an end.

"It's all about the solar system, and it teaches us about the solar system by taking us on a trip through it," another student suggests. "I think that it is information."

An argument ensues about what kind of text it is, and the teacher interrupts to suggest that maybe it is both. "Let's look at the special features in this text and see what we can figure out," she suggests.

The teacher leads students to look at several pages again, and they conclude that there are pictures, charts, and four different kinds of text on most pages.

"What Ms. Frizzle and the children in this story are saying is in rectangular speech balloons. There are also irregularly shaped bubbles that show what people are thinking," the teacher explains. "The story is told in the long text on each page. The facts to be learned from each page are on the 'notebook paper' on the side of the page."

The teacher reminds the class that they had decided that when reading informational text, it was best to read all of the visuals and quicktext first, then the long text. "With a book like this," she says, "we need to decide which things on each page to read first, next, and last." The teacher then turns back to the first page and tells students that she will read everything on the page, working from left to right and top to bottom, and they need to think about the best order in which to read this book.

Because it is on the left side of the page, she reads the notebook paper text labeled *What is the solar system?* first. It explains that the solar system is made up of the sun, the planets, moons, asteroids, and comets. It also explains what asteroids and comets are.

Next, the teacher reads the regular text, which explains that it is field trip day and Ms. Frizzle's class is preparing to go to the planetarium. She then reads the speech balloon in which Ms. Frizzle explains what an orbit is. The picture shows Ms. Frizzle pointing to a diagram of the solar system. Another picture shows a boy holding a ball and orbiting a lamp labeled *the sun*.

After reading all of the text, the teacher asks, "What do you think we should read first on this page?" Students decide that it would be best to start by reading the visuals and quicktext to see what they can learn. Next, they will read the regular text that tells the story. Then, they will read the speech balloons and thought bubbles. Finally, they will read the notebook paper text that gives facts about the solar system.

The teacher leads students to try that order with two more pages. First, they read and talk about any pictures, diagrams, charts, and other visuals. Then, they read the regular text that tells the story. Next, they read the speech balloons and thought bubbles, and finally, they read the notes. This system seems to work well, so they return to the first page and the teacher gives students reading roles. She has the class count off by 3s, and tells them that they will begin reading the book again. The teacher tells them that, for the first several pages, the 1s will discuss the pictures and read any quicktext, the 2s will read the story text chorally, the 3s will read the speech balloons and thought bubbles, and she will read the notes. The class reads approximately one-third of the book in this fashion. The teacher signals to students that their reading time is up for the day. She assures them that they will finish reading the book over the next two days and that each group will get to read the different texts.

As an after-reading activity, the teacher asks students to retrieve their response logs and write two things that they learned about the solar system. In addition, she asks them whether they liked this complicated book and why or why not. She puts on some "thinking music" and gives them five minutes to write. Students know that talking and moving around are not allowed when the thinking music is playing, so everyone sits quietly, thinks, and writes something. She lets a few students tell things they learned and express their opinions about the book.

The reading on the next two days follows the same format, with the groups of students reading the three kinds of text as the teacher reads the notes. Each day, they have five musical minutes to write in their response logs and a few minutes to share what they learned and what they liked or disliked about the book. Students are almost unanimous in their enthusiasm about the book, and the teacher promises to try to acquire multiple copies of four more Magic School Bus books so that they can do Book Club Groups with the books later in the school year.

Many older students approach their science and social studies text the way they approach stories. Shared Reading is the most efficient way to teach them strategies that are more appropriate for information.

Shared Reading

Shared Reading is the most appropriate format when students are just learning to track print. It is also the most efficient format for teaching any new strategy.

1. Be on the lookout for and select big books that help teach the comprehension strategies your students need to work on. (If you have access to a document camera or an interactive whiteboard, you can also use a regular-sized book and project it on a screen for the entire class or group to see.)
2. Decide how many days you will spend with the book and what you will do with students before and after reading.
3. Plan some rereadings of the book to help students develop fluency or write a simple summary of the book or chapter for your students to read.

Chapter 18

Echo and Choral Reading

In Echo Reading, the teacher reads first and students become the echo, reading back to her. As students echo read, they match the teacher's vocal expressions. In Choral Reading, reading together "in chorus," students are often assigned parts and practice their parts several times. Teachers often combine Echo Reading and Choral Reading. After they do an Echo Reading of a selection, they assign parts from the selection for Choral Reading. The remainder of this chapter gives you separate examples for Echo and Choral Reading, but in real classrooms, they are often used together—especially if fluency is a major concern.

Echo Reading

One teacher had been doing Echo Reading for months in her classroom when a student suddenly asked, "What's an echo?" When the teacher tried to explain it, she discovered that many students in her class had never heard an echo. After some "field research," the teacher located a spot in the auditorium where sound echoed. She took students there, and they got to hear their voices echoing back to them. Echo Reading made a lot more sense to her students after that! It is sometimes easy to forget that your students do not know everything that you know. If your students have not heard an echo, take them to a place where they can have firsthand experience with echoes.

Echoes are made as sound waves hit a large object and bounce back. The large object has to be at least 30 feet (9.144 m) away. Sound travels approximately one mile (1.609 km) in five seconds. So, if you shouted from one end of a canyon and the echo came back 10 seconds later, the canyon would be one mile wide—five seconds out and five seconds back!

Echo Reading is usually done one sentence at a time with short, easy text that has only one sentence on a page. Echo Reading is more fun to do when the text has different voices. *Brown Bear, Brown Bear, What Do You See?* by Bill Martin Jr., *I Went Walking* by Sue Williams, and *Hattie and the Fox* by Mem Fox are favorites for Echo Reading. Echo Reading also works well for stories written in first person, such as *There's An Alligator Under My Bed* by Mercer Mayer. When you echo read first-person stories, you try to sound the way the character who is telling the story would sound. You read in a careful, frightened way when you read this:

When it was time to go to sleep, I had to be very careful, because I knew he was there.

You shout when you read this:

> *So, I'd call Mom and Dad.*

You whisper when you read this:

> *I followed him down the stairs.*

Children love to use different voices, and reading stories aloud using an Echo Reading format is one of students' favorite ways to read. You will be amazed by how many first-person stories there are when you start looking for them. Some favorites are *One of Three* by Angela Johnson, *My Little Sister Ate One Hare* by Bill Grossman, and *My Friends* by Taro Gomi.

Echo Reading is also appropriate for reading plays. You read the whole play in an Echo Reading format first, using different voices for the different characters. Ask students to think about which characters they would like to play when you read the play again. Move from Echo Reading into a Play-School Group format in which students read their parts in small groups. Children love plays, and many teachers say that they would use more plays if they had multiple copies of easy plays. You can easily turn your students' favorite story into a play script, and fairy tales make good, easy plays. Students love reading and doing plays of *The Little Red Hen*, *The Gingerbread Man*, *The Three Little Pigs*, and *The Three Billy Goats Gruff*. One nice thing about writing and copying simple scripts for these classic stories is that you can let students take them home. For their homework assignment, have students gather as many actors as they can and read the play at home. Families love helping with this kind of homework and some family members say that they wish they'd had homework like this when they were in school.

An Example of Echo Reading

The teacher and students have copies of *My Friends* by Taro Gomi, a popular book for beginning readers. If the teacher did not have a copy for every student, she would partner students for this Echo Reading lesson. The teacher begins the lesson by talking about the cover and taking a Picture Walk with students. (The bold type indicates what the teacher says.)

"Let's look at the cover of the book. What do you see here?" Students talk about the picture of a little girl running outside, and they point to and talk about the title of the book and the author's name.

"Let's read the title of the book. You will be my echo. I will read the title, and you will read it after me." The teacher reads the title aloud, and students echo her. (Some teachers cup a hand behind one ear to show when they expect to hear students.)

"Now, I will read the author's name, and you will be my echo and read it after me."
The teacher points to the author's name and reads it, and students echo her.

The teacher opens her book and asks students to do the same. She leads students to talk about the title page. Then, she turns to pages 4 and 5, where the story begins.

"Look at these pages. What is the girl doing here?" Students answer that she is going for a walk with the cat. Some students think that she might be following her cat.

They continue the Picture Walk through the book, talking about what is happening on each two-page spread. The teacher asks students to turn back to pages 4 and 5. She tells them that she will read each page and they will echo it. **"Listen as I read the writing on one page. Then, become my echo and read it after me."**

"I learned to walk from my friend the cat."

"I learned to walk from my friend the cat," students repeat as the teacher models it.

"Let's turn to pages 6 and 7." The teacher reads the text, **"I learned to jump from my friend the dog."** Students echo her.

"Turn the page." The teacher reads the text, **"I learned to climb from my friend the monkey."** Students echo her.

"Let's turn the page." The teacher reads the text, **"I learned to run from my friend the horse."** Students echo her. The teacher and students continue like this until they finish the book.

The teacher has students act out the book for the after-reading activity to make sure that they understand what the story is about. Students stand while the teacher reads the book again. This time, students act it out when the teacher reads lines about walking like a cat, jumping like a dog, climbing like a monkey, running like a horse, etc.

Choral Reading

Choral Reading works best for poetry, refrains, and books with a lot of conversation. The whole class can read, or you can assign groups and parts. Use old favorites for Choral Reading, such as *Itsy Bitsy Spider*, *Five Little Pumpkins*, *Rudolph the Red-Nosed Reindeer*, *Peter Cottontail*, and other nursery rhymes and finger plays. Choral Reading is a wonderful way to reread materials, such as *Brown Bear, Brown Bear, What Do You See?* by Bill Martin Jr., in which the characters talk to each other. Choral Reading should be used throughout the grades because rereading provides students with the practice needed to build fluency and confidence.

Here are a variety of Choral Reading activities with nursery rhymes and traditional poems, chants, and songs. Many of these are in the public domain, which means that the author is unknown or they are no longer copyrighted, and thus can be reproduced in this book. You can also use contemporary poetry found in poetry collections, reading texts, children's magazines, and at various Web sites. Take the following ideas and apply them to the wealth of materials you have available to you.

Nursery and Other Rhymes

Begin by reading the rhyme to students. You may want to echo read it with them once or twice. If you have the rhyme in a big book, use that. If not, reproduce the rhyme on a chart. After reading the rhyme together, students enjoy pantomiming it while other students read it aloud.

For "Humpty Dumpty," have students count off by 5s and get together by numbers. Read the rhyme five times; each time, members from a different group read a line or act out a line. Attach numbered sticky notes to the lines on the chart and change the order for each reading. The first time, put the sticky notes in sequential order. Everyone reads the title. Then, the 1s read the first line, the 2s read the second line, the 3s read the third line, the 4s read the fourth line, and the 5s act out the rhyme. Move the sticky notes five times so that everyone will read each line and act out the rhyme. This activity is quick, easy, fun, and fair!

The same count-off procedure (with one group for each line and a group for acting) works nicely for "Jack and Jill"; "Hickory Dickory Dock"; "Little Jack Horner"; "Hey Diddle Diddle"; "Hop, Hop, Hop"; and many other short rhymes. Students build fluency as they read the lines of the poems several times. In addition, you can work with students' sequencing skills and talk about what happens at the beginning, middle, and end of each rhyme.

Humpty Dumpty

Humpty Dumpty sat on a wall.
Humpty Dumpty had a great fall.
All the king's horses, and all the king's men
Couldn't put Humpty together again!

Jack and Jill

Jack and Jill went up the hill,
To fetch a pail of water.
Jack fell down and broke his crown,
And Jill came tumbling after.

Hickory Dickory Dock
Hickory, dickory, dock,
The mouse ran up the clock.
The clock struck one, and down he did run.
Hickory, dickory, dock.

With longer rhymes and poems, you may want to assign students verses rather than lines. Begin by reading the poem to students. Then, have students read it with you several times. Assign reading parts and a pantomiming group. The count-off procedure works well with most rhymes that have actions students can pantomime. Count off by 5s to read and pantomime "The Squirrel."

The Squirrel
Whisky, frisky,
Hippity hop,
Up he goes
To the tree top.

Whirly, twirly,
Round and round,
Down he scampers
To the ground.

Furly, curly
What a tail!
Tall as a feather
Broad as a sail!

Where's his supper?
In the shell,
Snappity, crackity,
Out it fell.

Once you start choreographing your Choral Readings, you will find it easy to assign parts. For "Five Little Monkeys," divide the class into groups of five. The first time you do the rhyme, call on one group to pantomime the monkeys, assign another group to say the doctor's lines, and have the rest of the class read all of the other lines. Continue until all groups have been monkeys and doctors. You may need some monkey characters from previous readings to be monkeys a second time to fill out your last group.

Five Little Monkeys

Five little monkeys jumping on the bed.
One fell off and bumped his head.
Momma called the doctor, and the doctor said,
"No more monkeys jumping on the bed!"

Four little monkeys jumping on the bed.
One fell off and bumped his head.
Momma called the doctor, and the doctor said,
"No more monkeys jumping on the bed!"

Three little monkeys jumping on the bed.
One fell off and bumped his head.
Momma called the doctor, and the doctor said,
"No more monkeys jumping on the bed!"

Two little monkeys jumping on the bed.
One fell off and bumped his head.
Momma called the doctor, and the doctor said,
"No more monkeys jumping on the bed!"

One little monkey jumping on the bed.
He fell off and bumped his head.
Momma called the doctor, and the doctor said,
"No more monkeys jumping on the bed!"

No little monkeys jumping on the bed.
None fell off and bumped his head.
Momma called the doctor, and the doctor said,
"Put those monkeys back in bed!"

For the song "The Ants Go Marching," you will need two sets of index cards numbered 1–10. One set of numbers should be written very small, and the other set should be written normal size. Students with the small numbers do the little one's action in the rhyme. So, the student with the small 1 will jump and run, the student with the small 2 will tie his shoe, and so on. Everyone reads until it is her turn to join the march. As everyone begins reading, the two "ants" with the 1s march in and the student with the small number does the appropriate action. Then, the two students with the 2s join them as everyone else reads or sings. Then, the two 3s join the others, and so on, until there are 20 marching ants and the student with the small 10 shouts, "The End!" Have students switch cards so that the marching partner is now the one with the small number and have them read the rhyme again. If you have fewer than 20 students, designate stuffed animals or puppets to be numbers that do not have an action, and let each partner number march in holding a stuffed animal. If you have more than 20 students, do the whole thing again, allowing students who did not get numbers the first time to pick their numbers and letting some students have parts again.

To save space and time in writing this, write only the first verse on a chart. Then, write the parts of the verse that change—two by two, three by three, to jump and run, to tie his shoe, etc.—on sentence strips and cut them to fit on the chart. Have students stop after each verse and wait for you to insert the appropriate words.

The Ants Go Marching
The ants go marching one by one.
　Hurrah! Hurrah!
The ants go marching one by one.
　Hurrah! Hurrah!
The ants go marching one by one;
The little one stops to jump and run,
And they all go marching down to the ground.
　Boom, boom, boom!

The ants go marching two by two.
　Hurrah! Hurrah!
The ants go marching two by two.
　Hurrah! Hurrah!
The ants go marching two by two;
The little one stops to tie his shoe,
And they all go marching down to the ground.
　Boom, boom, boom!

The ants go marching three by three.
Hurrah! Hurrah!
The ants go marching three by three.
Hurrah! Hurrah!
The ants go marching three by three;
The little one stops to catch a bee,
And they all go marching down to the ground.
Boom, boom, boom!

The ants go marching four by four.
Hurrah! Hurrah!
The ants go marching four by four.
Hurrah! Hurrah!
The ants go marching four by four;
The little one stops to jump and roar,
And they all go marching down to the ground.
Boom, boom, boom!

The ants go marching five by five.
Hurrah! Hurrah!
The ants go marching five by five.
Hurrah! Hurrah!
The ants go marching five by five;
The little one stops to jump and dive,
And they all go marching down to the ground.
Boom, boom, boom!

The ants go marching six by six.
Hurrah! Hurrah!
The ants go marching six by six.
Hurrah! Hurrah!
The ants go marching six by six;
The little one stops to pick up sticks,
And they all go marching down to the ground.
Boom, boom, boom!

The ants go marching seven by seven.
Hurrah! Hurrah!
The ants go marching seven by seven.
Hurrah! Hurrah!
The ants go marching seven by seven;
The little one stops to chase a hen,
And they all go marching down to the ground.
Boom, boom, boom!

The ants go marching eight by eight.
Hurrah! Hurrah!
The ants go marching eight by eight.
Hurrah! Hurrah!
The ants go marching eight by eight;
The little one stops to roller-skate,
And they all go marching down to the ground.
Boom, boom, boom!

The ants go marching nine by nine.
Hurrah! Hurrah!
The ants go marching nine by nine.
Hurrah! Hurrah!
The ants go marching nine by nine;
The little one stops to read a sign,
And they all go marching down to the ground.
Boom, boom, boom!

The ants go marching ten by ten.
Hurrah! Hurrah!
The ants go marching ten by ten.
Hurrah! Hurrah!
The ants go marching ten by ten;
The little one stops to shout, "THE END!"
And they all go marching down to the ground.
Boom, boom, boom!

"Over in the Meadow" can be choreographed in a similar way. Give students cards numbered 1–10 and a card labeled *Mother*. In the first verse, the student with the 1 is the turtle and does the action. In the second verse, the student with the 2 joins in, and the 1 and 2 students both do the fish's action. The Mother stays the whole time, playing all of the different mothers. When you get to the last verse, you will have all students with numbers 1–10 and Mother. Unless you have 55 students in your class, having each student who does an action also do the following actions is the only way to act this out and have the right number of animals each time. You will need to do this a few times, letting students with the high numbers take the low numbers so that they can also do all of the actions.

Over in the Meadow
(A traditional counting rhyme adapted by Patricia M. Cunningham and Dorothy P. Hall)

Over in the meadow in the sand in the sun,
Lived an old mother turtle and her little turtle one.
"Dig," said the mother. "I dig," said the one.
So he dug all day in the sand in the sun.

Over in the meadow where the stream runs blue,
Lived an old mother fish and her little fish two.
"Swim," said the mother. "We swim," said the two.
So they swam all day where the stream runs blue.

Over in the meadow in a hole in a tree,
Lived an old mother squirrel and her little
    squirrels three.
"Jump," said the mother. "We jump," said the three.
So they jumped all day in a hole in a tree.

Over in the meadow by the big barn door,
Lived an old mother mouse and her little
    mice four.
"Squeak," said the mother. "We squeak," said
    the four.
So they squeaked all day by the big barn door.

Over in the meadow in a big beehive,
Lived an old mother bee and her little bees five.
"Buzz," said the mother. "We buzz," said the five.
So they buzzed all day in a big beehive.

Over in the meadow in a nest built of sticks,
Lived an old mother bird and her little birds six.
"Sing," said the mother. "We sing," said the six.
So they sang all day in a nest built of sticks.

Over in the meadow in the house built by Kevin,
Lived an old mother cat and her little kittens seven.
"Meow," said the mother. "We meow," said
    the seven.
So they meowed all day in the house built
    by Kevin.

Over in the meadow by an old wooden gate,
Lived an old mother rabbit and her little
    bunnies eight.
"Hop," said the mother. "We hop," said the eight.
So they hopped all day by an old wooden gate.

Over in the meadow by a tall green pine,
Lived an old mother pig and her little pigs nine.
"Oink," said the mother. "We oink," said the nine.
So they oinked all day by a tall green pine.

Over in the meadow in a cozy little den,
Lived an old mother fox and her little foxes ten.
"Play," said the mother. "We play," said the ten.
So they played all day in a cozy little den.

Finally, perk up your Choral Reading lesson one day with "Little Bunny Foo Foo." Divide your class into three groups: Little Bunny Foo Foos, good fairies, and narrators. (It is prudent to let the field mice be imaginary rather than risk the heads of any of your precious students!) You may or may not want to include the "moral of the story" at the end, depending on whether you think your children will "get it," but we included it for your entertainment!

Little Bunny Foo Foo

Little Bunny Foo Foo, hopping through the forest,
Scooping up the field mice and bopping them on
the head.
Down came the good fairy, and she said:
"Little Bunny Foo Foo, I don't want to see you
Scooping up the field mice and bopping them on
the head.
Now I'll give you three chances, and if you keep it
up, I'll turn you into a goon!"

Little Bunny Foo Foo hopping through the forest,
Scooping up the field mice and bopping them on
the head.
Down came the good fairy, and she said:
"Little Bunny Foo Foo, I don't want to see you
Scooping up the field mice and bopping them on
the head.
I'll give you two more chances, and if you keep it
up, I'll turn you into a goon!"

Little Bunny Foo Foo hopping through the forest,
Scooping up the field mice and bopping them on
the head.
Down came the good fairy, and she said:
"Little Bunny Foo Foo, I don't want to see you
scooping up the field mice and bopping them on
the head.
I'll give you one more chance, and if you keep it
up, I'll turn you into a goon!"

Little Bunny Foo Foo hopping through the forest,
Scooping up the field mice and bopping them on
the head.
Down came the good fairy, and she said:
"Little Bunny Foo Foo, I don't want to see you
Scooping up the field mice and bopping them on
the head
You disobeyed me three times, so now I'm turning
you into a goon!"

And the moral of this story is: Always remember,
"Hare today, goon tomorrow!"

There is a high correlation between the number of words students read and how well they read. The more words they read, the better readers they are! You must maximize the amount of reading students do while they are in school. One reason to avoid round-robin reading during Guided Reading is that students just do not read enough when they take turns! You want everyone reading as much as possible every day during Guided Reading, and you want to send students home with things that they are motivated to read and can read fluently. Echo and Choral Reading help create fluent, eager readers.

Echo and Choral Reading

Echo and Choral Reading are most appropriate for plays, predictable text, text with refrains, and text with a lot of dialogue. Students enjoy reading in these ways, and Echo and Choral Reading help build the confidence of struggling readers.

1. Choose poems, plays, songs, predictable books, and other texts that your students will enjoy.
2. Choreograph the reading in a simple way so that students are reading different parts.
3. Reread the selection several times, letting different groups read different parts.
4. If possible, provide copies for students to take home or to store in their personal reading binders.

Chapter 19

Everyone Read To . . . (ERT)

Everyone Read To … is a way of guiding your whole class or a small group through the reading of a story or an informational selection. Use ERT when you want your students to do the initial reading on their own, but you want to keep them on the same pages so that you can provide a lot of guidance and support for that initial reading. With ERT, you tell students how much to read at a time. They read that segment, and you follow up on whatever purpose you set for the segment by asking questions like these:

"What is the author telling us?"

"What new things did you learn?"

"What is the problem in this story?"

"What is making the sky so dark?"

Asking questions is how you set the purpose for reading each segment. When the answer your students are reading for is stated directly on the page, you ask them to read to *find out* that specific answer. When they have to make inferences, you ask your students to read to *figure out* the answer.

Students tell in their own words the answer they have found or figured out, and everyone goes to the next segment. For older students, ERT is silent reading. Because students must develop some reading fluency before they can "read in their minds," this ERT time with young students is often not silent but is called whisper reading. In ERT, students are reading the text for themselves to find or figure out specific things that they will then share with the class or a small group.

An Example of ERT: Day One

The teacher passes out the book *Arthur's Pet Business* by Marc Brown. The teacher and students have already read the title, author's name, and illustrator's name. Students now do the first reading of the book, and the teacher guides them through each two-page spread using ERT to help students set purposes for reading to themselves.

For the first pair of pages, the teacher reminds students of the title and says:

"Everyone read these pages to figure out what Arthur will ask his mom and dad."

Students read the two pages to themselves, some silently and others whisper reading. As students figure out the answer to the question, they raise their hands and keep them up while they finish reading the segment. When enough time has passed for students to have read the two pages, the teacher calls on individuals with hands raised to tell what Arthur will ask his parents.

Some students explain that even though the text does not directly say it, they have figured out that Arthur wants a puppy and is waiting for the right moment to ask for one.

Now, the teacher directs students to turn the page and says:

"Everyone read to find out what Arthur's mom and dad say about Arthur getting a puppy."

The teacher reminds students that this is a "two-hander." They are reading to find two things, and they should raise one hand as soon as they find each thing. Again, students read silently or quietly, and many raise both hands while they finish reading. It is clear that they enjoy two-handers.

The teacher directs students to turn the page again and asks them to read to find out what Arthur has to do before he can have the puppy. She continues to lead students through each two-page spread. For each pair of pages, the teacher sets a purpose that she thinks good readers would want to read to find or figure out.

"Everyone read to find out what Arthur's friends suggest he can do to earn the puppy."

"Everyone read to figure out what the phone call is about."

"Everyone read to figure out who the first customer is and what Arthur's family thinks about this pet."

"Everyone read to find out what is written on the long list that Perky's owner brings."

"Everyone read to figure out what Arthur does to take care of Perky and how he feels."

This process takes the class almost to the halfway point of the book, which is a good stopping point for the first day. For their after-reading activity, students work on summarizing/concluding. The teacher has them work with partners to retell the important events that have happened so far in the story. Since this is a picture book, the teacher encourages students to use the pictures as reminders to tell what they learned on each page. The teacher walks around, listening in on their retellings, and leads the class in a quick retelling, using the pictures as prompts.

An Example of ERT: Day Two

The next day, the teacher continues ERT, leading students through each remaining two-page spread by having them read to find or figure out important events. Students raise their hands as soon as they figure out the answer—two hands for questions with two parts—and finish reading that pair of pages. As each question is answered, the teacher calls on someone to read aloud the sentences with the important information. Unless the answer is obviously stated, the teacher leads students to explain how they figured it out.

Students explain that it does not say why Arthur is under the table, but it does say that Perky is lost. Since Arthur is looking for her, he must be under the table looking for Perky. Students read to find out whether Arthur finds Perky. They say that he does, and someone reads these sentences:

> *Suddenly they heard a bark. "Everybody come quick," called Arthur.*

Students explain that the bark and Arthur's calling must mean that he finds Perky.

When the story is finished the second day, the teacher asks students to work with partners and use the pictures in the book to retell the second part of the story. This ends the two-day ERT lesson.

ERT can also be done with informational and content area books. The procedure is the same. During reading, you can ask students to read each page to find or figure out the answer to a question (raise one hand) or two (raise two hands). As you ask students to read, use the phrase "*Everyone read to . . .*" Here are examples based on a short section about communities in a social studies textbook:

"Everyone read to find out what goods and services are." (two-hand answer)

"Everyone read to find out why people work." (one-hand answer)

"Everyone read to find out what a consumer is."

"Everyone read to find out what we mean by *our economy*."

When having students read one page at a time in ERT, many teachers have students cover the right-hand page while they read the left one so that they will not be tempted to read ahead. Another book, a sheet of card stock, or a folded sheet of paper can be used as a cover. Of course, whenever you teach an ERT lesson, listen for the sound of pages turning!

Everyone Read To . . .

The Everyone Read To . . . format is used to guide students through text, a page or two at a time, and to help them understand the important information on each page. This format can be used with a small group or with the whole class. Students who struggle with reading can often read better if they have something specific for which to read. Their success motivates them to continue to try.

1. Choose a text for which you think students need page-by-page guidance in order to read to themselves with comprehension.

2. Plan before- and after-reading activities that will develop comprehension strategies.

3. Lead students through the text a page or two at a time. Have students read to find or figure out important events or information.

4. Include questions whose answers are not literally stated but can be inferred. For example, you may say, "Read to figure out how Charlie is feeling." The text may say that it has been a bad day, and Charlie is stomping down the street. Students have to infer his feeling and explain how they know. Ask students to *find out* when the answer is literal and *figure out* when it is inferential.

5. Have students raise their hands when they read the part that helps them figure out the answer and continue reading. Notify them when you are asking a "two-hander."

6. When most hands are up, ask a volunteer to give you the answer. Ask someone else to read the parts aloud that helped her figure out the answer.

7. When the answers are not literally stated, ask students to explain how they figured them out. You might say, "Yes, he is feeling bad and unhappy. It didn't say that in the text, but you figured it out. What did it say that helped you figure it out?"

Chapter 20

Sentence and Paragraph Detectives

Chapter 2, Using Thinking Strategies and Text Structures to Help Students Comprehend, explains that to construct meaning, readers must follow the sentence and paragraph structure of a book or selection. As a rule, very little instruction is devoted to teaching students this basic but essential skill. Yet, one of the differences between students who are good at comprehending and students who are not is that the better readers can handle the structure of the sentences and paragraphs that are challenging for them. While comprehending the sentences and paragraphs of a text is not as important or as interesting as understanding the text as a whole, it is just as necessary for reading.

This chapter describes four types of lessons that will help you guide students to attend to and make use of sentence and paragraph structural clues. These lesson types succeed with elementary students by encouraging them to become sentence and paragraph detectives.

All comprehension lessons that fit under the Sentence and Paragraph Detectives label share four common instructional features. First, you take the sentences or paragraph for one of these lessons from the *beginning* of a book, a story, or an article. The first sentences or paragraph of a book chapter can also be used as long as it has a clear beginning, rather than being only a continuation from the previous chapter. Second, you alter the text you have selected in a specific way to focus students' attention to one kind of clue to syntactic or paragraph structure. Third, you use an interactive whiteboard to present the sentences or paragraph that you have altered and guide students to read or restore while their books are closed. Fourth, you do each of these lessons as a group task. That is, you work with the class or small group as a whole to achieve consensus rather than having individual students give answers and telling them whether they are right or wrong.

Before working together to complete the task, have students read the sentences or paragraph to themselves, either silently or by whisper reading. You can choose to have them work together as a small group before you work with them.

Each of these lessons follows the before-and-after pattern in which you tell your students before they read the projected sentences or paragraph what they will do after they read the sentences. What makes these lessons different from the other before- and after-reading activities in Part Two is that these are *mini* comprehension lessons. They focus on a small portion (the beginning few sentences or paragraph) of a text that your students have not read because they are designed to teach students how to follow sentence and paragraph structure. They can be done as stand-alone lessons, but most teachers do them with the beginning of the text that they will teach with another comprehension lesson framework.

This chapter describes four lesson types that fit under the Sentence and Paragraph Detectives label—Who Took Our Caps?, What's the Missing Word?, Who Did What?, and Who Mixed Up Our Sentences?—and gives you two examples of each. For the first example of each lesson type, the first several sentences or the first paragraph from a version of the story *The Bremen Town Musicians* by the Brothers Grimm is used. For the second example of each type, the beginnings of four successive chapters in the book *The Summer of the Swans* by Betsy Byars are used. From these examples, you can imagine how each lesson type helps students become more sensitive to different sentence and paragraph structural clues. Ordinarily, you would not do more than one kind of Sentence and Paragraph Detectives lesson with the beginning of the same book, chapter, story, or article.

Who Took Our Caps?

Uppercase letters at the beginning of sentences are important clues to readers because—along with periods, question marks, and exclamation points—they help readers divide the text into sentences for meaningful processing. Moreover, knowing where to place beginning capitalization and ending punctuation when they write requires them to perceive the sentence as a meaningful structural unit. When readers attend to capitalization and punctuation, they must also have the sense that the sentence is a meaningful structural unit in order to comprehend the sentences in texts that are challenging for them. Who Took Our Caps? lessons help students learn to pay more attention to and make use of sentence structure when they read.

Before you teach a Who Took Our Caps? lesson to your class for the first time, read the book *Caps for Sale* by Esphyr Slobodkina to interest students in the activity. After reading the book to students, tell them that it will help them remember that books, newspapers, magazines, and handwriting have "caps" that someone can "take." The caps in print and writing are the uppercase or capital letters that start all of the sentences. Someone can take those caps by retyping or rewriting the sentences without any uppercase letters, punctuation, or other indicators of where one sentence ends and the next one begins. Later, you can refer back to the book as a reminder to students of what they do in a Who Took Our Caps? lesson.

A Sample Who Took Our Caps? Lesson

The teacher turns on the interactive whiteboard to project the following sentences that begin *The Bremen Town Musicians*:

> *once upon a time, a man owned a donkey the man had used him to carry sacks of grain to the mill for many years he was now old and worn out from all the hard work because the donkey was no longer strong enough to work, his owner was thinking about killing him he didn't want to have to feed and take care of him anymore*

The teacher tells students, "Someone took our caps, as well as our periods. We need to put them back."

Beginning with the first word, the teacher draws three lines under the first letter to indicate that it should be uppercase. Then, he asks students to figure out where the first period goes. (These sentences didn't have any question marks or exclamation points. If they did, students would have the additional challenge of deciding which ending punctuation marks to put where.) The teacher tells students that when the majority of them agree on where the uppercase letters and periods should go in the sentence, he will put them where they indicate. If there is a difference of opinion among students as to where the first period goes, he does not settle it for them. Rather, the teacher has students take turns reading the sentence aloud both (or however many) ways. Then, students vote, and the teacher places the period where the majority says to put it. The teacher starts the next word after that period with an uppercase letter and repeats the process to determine where the next period goes. The majority of students were probably right about the location of the first period, but if they were not, it will become obvious to them as they try to place the second and third periods correctly. In that case, hopefully they will figure out that they need to go back and redo the placement of the first period. If not, the teacher will suggest it. The lesson ends with the teacher asking students to open their books and then leading them as a group to evaluate and correct their performance.

Now, consider how you would teach a Who Took Our Caps? lesson by altering the beginning sentences of a chapter of *The Summer of the Swans*:

> *in the house Wanda and Aunt Willie were still arguing Sara could hear every word even out on the porch Aunt Willie, who had been taking care of them since the death of their mother six years ago, was saying loudly, "no, not on a motorcycle no motorcycle"*

For this lesson type, you never want to have more than six sentences in which students will find the beginnings and endings. Repeated use over time of Who Took Our Caps? lessons will help students learn to value and pay attention to beginning capitalization and ending punctuation as reading clues. It will also help sensitize them to seeing the sentence as a structural unit of meaning.

Link to Writing: Editor's Checklist

Another excellent way to teach students to attend to beginning capitalization and ending punctuation when they read is to teach them to begin all of their sentences with uppercase letters and to end all of their sentences with periods, questions marks, or exclamation points. During writing instructional time, teach students to use an Editor's Checklist to proofread and correct their own first drafts for the most important mechanics and usage rules. By learning to edit their writing independently and correct mechanical errors, students also learn to pay attention to mechanical clues to sentence and paragraph structure when they read.

Who Took Our Caps?

1. Select the first six or fewer sentences from a book, a book chapter, a story, or an article.

2. Write or project the selection on a whiteboard with no sentence capitalization, punctuation, or extra spaces between sentences.

3. Work to achieve student consensus of where the first sentence ends and the second one begins. Add capitalization and punctuation to mark where the majority wants the change of sentence to be.

4. Continue sentence by sentence until consensus of where all of the sentences begin and end is achieved.

What's the Missing Word?

The Cloze task has been used to assess reading comprehension and text readability for several decades. The Cloze task is rarely used for assessment, but it is a valuable group task for the Sentence and Paragraph Detectives lesson type What's the Missing Word? These What's the Missing Word? lessons help students become more sensitive to the syntactic and semantic clues in a paragraph and pay more attention to the structural clues of the words.

While there are many variations, creating the standard Cloze task means deleting every fifth word from a text and replacing that word with a blank of uniform length. Using the standard deletion pattern, a Cloze passage is likely to have more structural words than content words deleted. That is helpful for this purpose because the structural words most directly convey sentence and paragraph structure. In addition to structural words, any word with an inflected ending that is deleted becomes an occasion for students to take syntactic and cohesion cues into consideration when trying to determine what word was most likely in the original text.

Keep in mind that not all of the blanks in a standard Cloze passage can be filled in with the exact word that the author used. In fact, getting more than half of the words exactly right is doing well. Therefore, an important part of any What's the Missing Word? lesson is to guide students to decide whether the word they chose for a blank was the author's word, a different word that has the same meaning as the author's word, or an incorrect word.

A Sample What's the Missing Word? Lesson

The teacher turns on the interactive whiteboard to project the following paragraph that begins *The Bremen Town Musicians*:

> Once upon a time, _____ man owned a donkey. _____ man had used him _____ carry sacks of grain _____ the mill for many _____ . He was now old _____ worn out from all _____ hard work. Because the _____ was no longer strong _____ to work, his owner _____ thinking about killing him. _____ didn't want to have _____ feed and take care _____ him anymore. The donkey _____ smart, as donkeys go, _____ he figured out what _____ about to happen. So, _____ ran away and started _____ the road to Bremen. _____ he thought he could _____ one of the town musicians.

Beginning with the first blank, the teacher asks students to decide what word the author probably used there. She tells students that when they decide as a group, she will write the word they choose in the blank. If there is a difference of opinion among students as to what word goes in the first blank, the teacher does not tell them who is right. Rather, she has them take turns reading the sentence aloud both (or however many) ways. Then, she has students vote, and she writes the word in the blank that the majority says goes there. The majority of students probably put the right word or a synonym in the first blank, but if they did not, it will become obvious as they try to determine what word goes in the second and third blanks. In that case, hopefully they will figure out that they need to go back and redo the word they put in the first blank. If they do not figure it out and they have trouble because of a previously incorrect answer, the teacher will suggest that they may need to redo an answer they did previously. The lesson ends with the teacher asking students to open their books and leading them as a group to evaluate and correct their work.

Here is what the class agreed to put in the blanks in the first paragraph of *The Bremen Town Musicians*: (Words in the blanks that are different from the author's words are in italics.)

> Once upon a time, _a_ man owned a donkey. _The_ man had used him _to_ carry sacks of grain _to_ the mill for many _years_ . He was now old _and_ worn out from all _that_ hard work. Because the _donkey_ was no longer strong _enough_ to work, his owner _was_ thinking about killing him. _He_ didn't want to have _to_ feed and take care _of_ him anymore. The donkey _was_ smart, as donkeys go, _so_ he figured out what _was_ about

to happen. So, __he__ ran away and started __down__ the road to Bremen. __So__ he thought he could __be__ one of the town musicians.

These students chose the author's words for 15 of the 20 blanks. That is better than students can be expected to do ordinarily and is probably due to the large number of structure words that had been deleted. For the five blanks where students did not choose the author's words, the teacher has students read and reread each sentence both ways to decide if their word has the same meaning as the author's word. Students decide that four of the five mean about the same thing as the author's words and work fine in the sentences. Students also decide that *So* in the next-to-last blank, rather than the author's *There*, is incorrect. The teacher is happy with this evaluation and does not feel the need to dispute the students' evaluation of their work.

Now, consider how you would teach a What's the Missing Word? lesson by altering the beginning sentences of the next chapter of *The Summer of the Swans*:

> *"Wait, wait, you wait." Aunt* _____ *came onto the porch drying her* _____ *on a dish towel. She stood at the top of the steps until Frank, a thin boy with red* _____ *, brought the motor scooter to a* _____ *. As he kicked down the* _____ *she called out, "Frank, listen, save yourself some steps. Wanda's not going* _____ *on that motorcycle."*

For this lesson type, there should never be more than 20 blanks to be filled. At first, 10 is plenty. Repeated use of What's the Missing Word? lessons will help students learn to pay more attention to structure words. It also will help them improve their ability to follow both meaning and syntactic structure through the sentences of a paragraph.

What's the Missing Word?

1. Select the first paragraph or two from a book, a book chapter, a story, or an article.
2. Write or project the selection on a whiteboard with every fourth or fifth word deleted and replaced by a blank of uniform length, up to a maximum of 20 blanks.
3. Work to achieve student consensus of what word was probably deleted and replaced by the first blank. Write the word the majority wants in the first blank.
4. Continue blank by blank until a consensus of what words go in all of the blanks is achieved.

Who Did What?

An often forgotten challenge of reading is keeping up with the referents for all of the pronouns. One reason texts can be challenging for students, even when they can identify most of the words, is that texts use a lot of pronouns. Every pronoun requires the reader to infer to whom or to what the pronoun refers. The more pronouns are used in a paragraph, the more inferences the reader must make to understand the paragraph. Who Did What? is a lesson type that helps students learn to pay more attention to pronouns and be able to infer their referents better.

Obviously, the first paragraph you use for this lesson type must have several pronouns referring to different people and things. Here is a list of pronouns to look for:

he	her	him	his	I	it	me	my	our
she	their	them	they	us	we	you	your	

A Sample Who Did What? Lesson

The teacher turns on the interactive whiteboard to project the following paragraph that begins *The Bremen Town Musicians*:

> Once upon a time, a man owned a donkey. The man had used him to carry sacks of grain to the mill for many years. He was now old and worn out from all the hard work. Because the donkey was no longer strong enough to work, his owner was thinking about killing him. He didn't want to have to feed and take care of him anymore. The donkey was smart, as donkeys go, and he figured out what was about to happen. So, he ran away and started on the road to Bremen. There he thought he could become one of the town musicians.

The teacher tells students that the words with boxes around them (or that are circled, underlined, etc.) are pronouns and that every pronoun stands for one or more people or things. The teacher also tells students that when they are reading, they have to figure out to whom or what each pronoun refers or they will be confused about who did what.

Beginning with the first boxed pronoun, the teacher asks students to decide whom or what the pronoun stands for. He tells them that when they decide the answer as a group, he will write what they think the answer is above the pronoun. If there is a difference of opinion among students as to whom or what the first pronoun refers, the teacher does not tell them who is right. Rather, he has students take turns reading the sentence aloud both (or however many) ways. Then, the teacher has them vote, and he writes above the pronoun to whom or what it refers, according to what the majority of students say. The majority of students are probably right about the first pronoun, but if they are not, it will become obvious as they try to determine the referents of the second and third pronouns. In that case, hopefully they will figure out that they need to go back and redo the referent for the first pronoun. If not, the teacher will suggest it. The lesson ends with the teacher asking students to open their books and leading them as a group to evaluate and correct their work.

Now, consider how you would teach a Who Did What? lesson by drawing boxes around the pronouns in the beginning sentences of the next chapter of *The Summer of the Swans*:

> When [they] were out of earshot Sara said, "Aunt Willie thinks [she] knows everything. [I] get so sick of hearing how [I] am exactly like Wanda when Wanda is beautiful. [I] think [she's] just beautiful. If [I] could look like anyone in the world, [I] would want to look like [her]." [She] kicked at some high grass by the sidewalk.

For this lesson type, you never want to have more than a paragraph or more than 10 pronouns. Repeated use of Who Did What? lessons will help students learn to pay more attention to pronouns. It also will help students improve their ability to infer the referents of pronouns.

Who Did What?

1. Select the first few sentences, or at most the first paragraph, from a book, a book chapter, a story, or an article. Make sure that there are several pronouns with different referents in these sentences.
2. Write or project the selection on a whiteboard with up to the first 10 pronouns boxed, circled, or underlined.
3. Work to achieve student consensus of to whom or to what the first pronoun refers. Write the referent on which the majority agrees above that first pronoun.
4. Continue pronoun by pronoun until consensus of to whom or to what each pronoun refers is achieved.

Who Mixed Up Our Sentences?

The order of the sentences is the most important aspect of paragraph structure. The linear logic of a paragraph is like a thread sewn through the sentences, one at a time, in sequence. Taking the sentences out of order destroys the logic of most paragraphs. By mixing up the sentences from the first paragraph of a book, a chapter, a story, or an article, you can present students with a problem in paragraph logic. Presenting this problem to students as a group task helps them become more sensitive to the linear logic of paragraphs and the other meaning and structure clues that reflect that logic.

A Sample Who Mixed Up Our Sentences? Lesson

The teacher turns on the interactive whiteboard to project the following five sentences that begin *The Bremen Town Musicians*:

1. Because the donkey was no longer strong enough to work, his owner was thinking about killing him.
2. He didn't want to have to feed and take care of him anymore.
3. He was now old and worn out from all the hard work.
4. Once upon a time, a man owned a donkey.
5. The man had used him to carry sacks of grain to the mill for many years.

The teacher tells students that these are all sentences from the first paragraph of the story and that all of the sentences are correct. Then, she says, "Someone has mixed up our sentences, and it is our job to put them back in the right order."

The teacher begins by asking students to decide which of the sentences is the first one. She tells them that when they decide as a group, she will mark through the number of that sentence and replace it with a *1*. If there is a difference of opinion among students as to which sentence is first, the teacher does not tell them who is right. Rather, she has them take turns reading both (or however many) sentences aloud. Then, the teacher has students vote and renumbers the sentence that the majority says should be the first sentence. The majority of students are probably right about the first sentence, but if they are not, it will become obvious as they try to determine which sentence is the second one. In that case, hopefully they will figure out that they need to go back and renumber the sentence they thought was the first one. If not, the teacher suggests that they do so. The lesson ends with the teacher having students open their books and then leading the students as a group to evaluate and correct their performance.

Now, consider how you would teach a Who Mixed Up Our Sentences? lesson by altering the beginning sentences of the next chapter of *The Summer of the Swans*:

1. The watch was a great pleasure to him.
2. The whole world seemed to have been turned off when Sara went into the Weiceks' house, and he did not move for a long time.
3. He had no knowledge of hours or minutes, but he liked to listen to it and to watch the small red hand moving around the dial.
4. Charlie sat in the sudden stillness, hunched over his knees, on the bottom step.
5. The only sound was the ticking of his watch.

For this lesson type, you never want to have more than six sentences for students to put in order. Repeated use of Who Mixed Up Our Sentences? lessons will help students learn to follow the logic from one sentence to another when they read.

Who Mixed Up Our Sentences?

1. Select the first six or fewer sentences from a book, a book chapter, a story, or an article.
2. Print or write those sentences on a whiteboard in random order in a numbered list.
3. Work to achieve student consensus of which sentence should be first. Number the sentence that the majority of students say is first.
4. Continue sentence by sentence until consensus of the correct order of the sentences is achieved.

More Advanced Sentence and Paragraph Detectives Lessons

There are lesson types that are more advanced than the four described previously for encouraging older students to become sentence and paragraph detectives. One advanced lesson type is the GIST Procedure. In the GIST Procedure, you show only the first sentence of the first paragraph of a selection and display 15 blanks on the interactive whiteboard. You have students read this first sentence to themselves and then you hide the sentence. Working as a group, students restate the important information in that first sentence, and you type what they say in the blanks. Students may remember and repeat the entire first sentence, but they don't have to. Using synonyms or alternate word order is fine. Then, you reveal both the first and second sentences. Students read the first two sentences to themselves before you hide them. Working as a group, students direct you to modify what they already have in the blanks to include the most important information from the second sentence. Under no circumstances would you type the 16th word. If students have 16 or more words, they have to eliminate some words to make room. This process continues until your students have summarized the entire paragraph in a single sentence of 15 or fewer words.

In the Old or New? type of Sentence and Paragraph Detectives lesson, you show the first paragraph or two that you have altered from a book, a chapter, a story, or an article. Every content word or phrase is circled. For every circled word or phrase, you lead students to decide whether that word or phrase is providing new information or refers back to the same or a synonymous word or phrase used earlier. You write *old* or *new* above each circled word as students reach a consensus.

Chapter 21

Coaching Groups

In classrooms with comprehensive reading instruction, word identification is taught and practiced each day. Students learn to read and spell high-frequency words, perhaps during daily Word Wall practice. They also learn how the high-frequency words with regular spelling patterns help them decode and spell other words. They gradually come to understand how our complex vowel system works, perhaps during Making Words when they switch the vowel to change *tan* to *ten* and add a vowel to change *tap* to *tape*.

Activities for teaching decoding and word recognition should also include steps that stress transferring this knowledge to reading and writing. Some students have little difficulty applying word identification knowledge and strategies as they read. Other students need to be coached to use what they know as they read. Coaching Groups allow you to provide that coaching to students as they read text on their level.

Once students know how to read with partners, you can call together a small group of students and coach them to use their word identification strategies in text that is at their instructional reading level. Include different students on different days, but try to include students who are at just the right level with the text. With a little coaching, they will probably be able to successfully read the text.

Explain Coaching Groups to students by making analogies to sports teams. For example, students understand that you practice various basketball moves, and in a game, the coach stops you from time to time to coach you to use the skills you have practiced. Include some more advanced readers in Coaching Groups, and once they understand how to coach, let them play the role of "Word Coach." Before long, students learn how to coach and begin to use their coaching skills when reading with partners.

When reading with the whole class, use formats such as Echo and Choral Reading and Everyone Read To … to avoid round-robin reading. In Coaching Groups, have students read to themselves before you ask a student to read the page aloud. Tell students that you hope they will come to at least one word they need help with so that they can all learn how to be Word Coaches.

Coaching Steps

Before students start to read, remind them of the strategies they can use to figure out an unfamiliar word. You may want to post a chart of these steps, which you can review each time students begin reading.

How to Figure Out a Hard Word

1. Put your finger on the word and say all of the letters.
2. Use the letters and the picture clues.
3. Look for a rhyme you know.
4. Keep your finger on the word, finish the sentence, and pretend the word is the covered word.

These are the steps that students should use if they stop on a word. If they misread a word instead of stopping, let them finish the sentence and bring them back to the word they have misread. Imagine, for example, that the student reads, "There was not a cold in the sky," when the sentence is *There was not a cloud in the sky.*

When the student misreads *cold* for *cloud*, *cold* does make some sense at that point in the sentence. But by the end of the sentence, the student should realize that the sentence as a whole does not make sense, and she should go back and try to fix something. So, when a student makes an error, let her finish the sentence so that she will develop her own self-monitoring system. If, however, the student does not notice and continues reading past the end of the sentence, stop her and say this:

"That didn't make sense. Let's look at this word again. Say all of the letters in the word."

Then, take the student through Steps 2–4 as needed to help her decode the word.

Here is how you coach each step and why each step is important. (Depending on their age, share as much of this explanation with students as you think they can understand. With older, struggling readers, explain it all. They love to know how their brains work!)

1. **Put your finger on the word and say all of the letters.** When a student comes to a word he does not know, have him put his finger on the word and say all of the letters. It is very important here that the student says the letters. Saying the letters is not sounding out the word. English is not a sound-it-out-letter-by-letter language, and the worst readers are the ones who try to do it letter by letter. You want students to say all of the letters so that you know that they have looked at them all in the right order, and having students say the letters is the

only way to know for sure. You also want students to say the letters because there is strong evidence that retrieval from the brain's memory store is auditory. If students just look at letters and search in their brains for that word or a rhyming word, it is apt to be harder to find than if they say the letters that go through the brain's auditory channel.

If students are reading at the right level and say the letters of an unfamiliar word aloud, they will sometimes identify that word immediately—positive proof that they needed the auditory channel for retrieval! When students say all of the letters and successfully pronounce the word, cheer! They have scored a goal. "See, it was in there. You just had to say it so that your brain could find it!" If, after they say all of the letters, they still do not know the word, remind them of Step 2. (The exception here is strange names. If the word students are trying to decode is *Timbuktu*, *Claribel*, or *Houdini*, just pronounce it for them and let them continue reading. The decoding strategies in the remaining steps do not help with names.)

2. **Use the letters and the picture clues.** For this to work, you must be doing some Picture Walks prior to reading. Students should know that just guessing based on pictures or on letters will not get them very far but that the two make a powerful team. The student who sees the word *raccoon*, says all of the letters, and glances at the picture may see a picture of a raccoon. The picture and the letters he has seen will often allow him to decode the word. So, once the student has said all of the letters aloud, cue him by asking questions: Will the picture help? What is that animal called? If the student gets the word correct now, cheer! If not, proceed to Step 3.

3. **Look for a rhyme you know.** Like the previous step, this will be helpful only if you have been stressing that students can often figure out a word they know by looking at the pattern. *Raccoon*, for example, rhymes with *moon* and *soon*. If the student does not see this, the coach can say, "That word rhymes with *moon* and *soon*." If the student still does not get it, proceed to the final step.

4. **Keep your finger on the word, finish the sentence, and pretend the word is the covered word.** Guess the Covered Word is an activity that helps students use beginning letters and context to figure out words. Students become very good at this during word identification instructional time, but they often need to be coached to use it as they read. Have each student keep his finger on the word so that when he has read the sentence, he can quickly look back at the letters.

Most of the time, assuming students in your coaching group are reading at the right level, they will be able to figure out the word by using these four steps. Everyone should cheer and talk about how he figured out the word! If students cannot figure out the word, it is often a word that they do not have in their listening vocabularies. For example, an ostrich may be in the picture. The word *ostrich* rhymes with *rich* and makes sense, but if a student does not have the word *ostrich* in her listening vocabulary, she will not be able to decode it. When this happens, just tell her the word and say, "Good try! That was a really tough word," and move to the next page.

When to Do Coaching Groups

Coaching Groups are commonly done when using the Three-Ring Circus or You'se Choose formats (collaborative groupings). Students not in the Coaching Group are reading with partners or by themselves. Usually, the Coaching Group reads the selection that everyone else is reading and for which you are teaching comprehension strategies through your before- and after-reading activities. The Coaching Group may occasionally read something different from what the other students are reading. Imagine that you read a selection the previous day with the whole class using Echo or Choral Reading or an Everyone Read To … format. Students in the Coaching Group have read this selection once. The other students are rereading it for a different purpose. You might wish to use a different, easier text with your Coaching Group since they have already read the main selection and could benefit more from being coached in a new text.

Some teachers find time in their weekly schedules to meet with Coaching Groups outside Guided Reading time. In some classrooms, the teacher meets daily with an After-Lunch Bunch and coaches at that time. Include all students in the After-Lunch Bunch activities during the week, but make sure to include struggling readers almost every day. In some classrooms, teachers have "center time" each day and do a Coaching Group that they call the Reading for Fun Club during that time. Coaching Groups last only 10–15 minutes. Do not do before- and after-reading activities to teach comprehension with Coaching Groups if comprehension is your focus during Guided Reading time. Also do not introduce high-frequency words or teach decoding strategies if that is your focus during word identification instructional time. Simply choose some material at the instructional level of most of the students you intend to include and begin reading it. With this activity, you want to simulate what students must do during Self-Selected Reading when they tackle text on their own without any pre-teaching. As students read and encounter problems, coach them to apply what they have learned when they actually need to use it.

In some classrooms, special teachers or assistants do Coaching Groups with students. If you have help coming and have many students who need coaching, you might schedule Self-Selected Reading at that time and have the helper coach students in their self-selected books. Many teachers like to schedule Guided Reading when they have help coming. The helper can coach students through the selection if it is close to their instructional level, or he can read that selection to them and coach them in material at their level.

Finding the time, people, and reading materials to do Coaching Groups is not easy. But, when you add regular coaching in instructional-level material to all of the good instruction struggling readers receive throughout the day, you will be amazed at the rapid progress struggling readers can make. In each grade level and in every class, students will need coaching to become better at decoding unknown words. You can use Coaching Groups with kindergartners who need help with print tracking and other early reading skills. Coaching Groups are also important for older students, particularly those who have not developed useful decoding skills for the many new words they will encounter in their texts. Change the composition of the Coaching Groups regularly and include some average readers for reading models. Teach students to be Word Coaches, and when a student is about to read a page aloud, let that student choose her own Word Coach. Even struggling readers can coach because they do not necessarily need to know the word, but they need to know how to give the right prompts.

Here is an example of a teacher with a Coaching Group. This small group might be "one ring" during a Three-Ring Circus, or it might be a small group that the teacher calls her After-Lunch Bunch. Some days, the teacher lets Self-Selected Reading last 10 minutes longer. Before conferencing with four or five students, she pulls her After-Lunch Bunch while the rest of the class enjoys a little extra Self-Selected Reading time and practices the skills taught in Guided Reading in their self-selected "just right" books.

The teacher is sitting at a small table with five students reading an easy version of *The Three Billy Goats Gruff*. After talking about the pictures on each page, the teacher says, "Now, read the page to find out what is happening to the three billy goats. Read it to yourself first, and I will choose someone to read it aloud."

Students read the page to themselves, pointing to each word and whispering it to themselves as first graders often do. Three students read more slowly than the others, getting stumped on and skipping a few words. The other two students read fluently. When students have finished reading to themselves, the teacher calls on Cooper to read the page aloud. She reminds everyone that one purpose of this group is for each student to learn how to be a word coach, and she says that she hopes Cooper will have at least one word with which he needs coaching.

Cooper reads the page and comes to a word with which he needs help. The teacher coaches Cooper to figure out the word. "Put your finger on the word and say all of the letters." Cooper puts his finger on the word and says, "f-i-e-l-d." "Now, use the letters and the picture clues." Cooper looks at the picture of the green grass on the other side of the bridge, says the sounds he hears in the letters, and figures out the word *field*. Students in this small group cheer! The teacher then leads the group in a quick retelling of what they read and has students read the page chorally before going to the next page. When they finish the whole book, they talk about the characters (the three goats and the troll), the setting, and what happens at the beginning, the middle, and the end.

One student in the group asks what the new book will be next time and if he can be in her After-Lunch Bunch again for the next book. She reminds him that everyone wants to join the group, so he will just have to wait and see who is called each time. She knows that some students need more coaching than others, and she will call those students to the group more often. But, she tells students, "Everyone will get a turn."

Coaching Groups

Coaching groups help students learn how to apply what you have been teaching when they need it. Try to choose material at the appropriate level for students who need coaching and include a few more-able readers in the groups. Once students know how to coach, let them be Word Coaches and occasionally let each reader choose her own word coach. These are the coaching steps:

1. Put your finger on the word and say all of the letters.
2. Use the letters and the picture clues.
3. Look for a rhyme you know.
4. Keep your finger on the word, finish the sentence, and pretend the word is the covered word.

Chapter 22

Partner Reading and Play-School Groups/Reading Teams

Collaborative Groups

So far, this part of the book has described teacher-led reading formats for the during-reading part of the Guided Reading. Shared Reading, Echo and Choral Reading, Everyone Read To . . ., and Sentence and Paragraph Detectives are ways to guide students through text while maximizing the amount of support and reading for every student. Most of the time, these formats are used with the entire class. Most teachers begin the year using these whole-class formats to teach students how to do Picture Walks, make and confirm predictions, make KWL charts and graphic organizers, do the Beach Ball, etc. Then, they teach students how to read with partners and in cooperative groups. By the time teachers put students with partners or in cooperative groups to read and come up with things to add to a web or prepare to answer the Beach Ball questions, webs and the Beach Ball are familiar activities. Now, students can focus on a new thing—how to teach and help each other while reading in groups.

Partner Reading, Play-School Groups/Reading Teams, Three-Ring Circus, Book Club Groups, and Literature Circles are wonderful formats when they work correctly, but that doesn't just happen. In the next chapter, you will discover some of the tricks of the trade and caveats for Partner Reading. Most of these tricks and caveats also apply to the other cooperative groups. There are times when groups work better than Partner Reading, and these times will be described in the appropriate chapters.

Partner Reading is when two students work together to read a selection and prepare for the after-reading activity. When four or five students read together in a cooperative group in first grade and in some second-grade classes, this format is called Play-School Groups. Young students often like to play "school" at home and be the teacher. More important, they have watched their teacher at school and know what to do and what to say! Play-School Groups are something students easily understand and can do without a lot of help. But, most students above first grade do not think that playing school is "cool." They do like being on a team, however, so the groups are called Reading Teams for older students.

Partner Reading

Partner Reading may follow the Shared or Echo Reading of a selection in the primary grades. Beyond first grade, it may follow Everyone Read To. Each time the class reads a selection, students need a new purpose. Partner Reading allows one student to provide support for another student who may find the text difficult to read and may need help with the after-reading activity. It also provides the opportunity for students to learn how to teach each other and work together, which are important life skills. Partnering requires some thoughtful planning. Here are some things to think about when planning Partner Reading for your class.

1. **Arrange the "partnerships" carefully.** Think about whom you will partner with whom— and whom you will not! If students are at the stage where boys can't stand girls, and girls think that boys are yucky, it may be best to do same-gender partnerships. Students who are feuding will probably not make good partners. The best reader in the class is probably not the best partner for the worst reader. Think about your struggling readers and who would be the best partners for them. Ask yourself: Who will be patient and not just tell them all of the words? Who will be able to coach them and get them to talk about their reading? In most classes, there are a few nurturing students who would love to help their struggling classmates. Try partnering these students with your readers who struggle the most.

2. **Think about how often to change partners.** Partner Reading seems to work better when the partners can work together long enough to establish a working relationship. There is not any real advantage to assigning new partners every time. When you begin Partner Reading, you may want to change the reading partners more frequently so that you can find the right matches. Once you have partnerships that work well, leave partners together for a while.

3. **Decide where the partners will read.** Some teachers have partners read at their desks, but this works only if partners already sit next to each other. Partners usually work best when they can sit in corners or sprawl out on rugs. They need some space, and they stay focused better if they cannot easily hear other pairs of students reading. Try designating Partner Reading spaces. Label each space with a number and the initials of the partners who will read in that spot on that day. A laminated poster works well for this display. Some spots are perceived as better than others, so rotate where partners will read. If you keep your partnerships together, students can rotate through the spots each time the class does Partner Reading, and they will eventually get to read in all of the spots.

Partner Reading Spots for Today	
Where?	**Who?**
1. Back corner	HR, JB
2. Reading table	JW, MM
3. By the sink	EH, MW
4. Teacher's desk	AB, CM
5. Beanbag chair	PC, RL
6. On the carpet	LP, PT
7. In the rocking chair	GH, MD
8. By the gerbil cage	WH, TM
9. Near the bookshelf	JR, BNF
10. You choose!	DL, BPF

4. **Decide how you will handle absent partners.** This may sound trivial, but many teachers spend a lot of time negotiating with students when a partner is absent. Some teachers have an "absent partners with absent partners" rule. If three partners are absent, a trio forms. Some teachers let students whose partners are absent join any other partnership. Some teachers let partnerless students decide if they want to read by themselves, with another partnerless student, or with another partnership. It does not matter which way you handle absent partners as long as you have a clear policy in effect, and time is not wasted negotiating.

5. **Always make sure that partners know how they will read the selection.** Depending on students' ages, teach students a variety of different Partner Reading formats, including the following:

   • **Take Turns:** One partner reads the first page, the other partner reads the second page, and so on. This is the most common, but not necessarily the most productive, way of Partner Reading.

- **Read and Point:** One partner points to the words on the page while the other partner reads. Then, they switch roles on the next page. Read and Point is particularly helpful when print tracking is a big issue with some students. You will be surprised at how quickly your students pick up print tracking when a nurturing, helpful partner is pointing to their words and making sure that they point to the words correctly when it is their turn. This format is not recommended once students become fluent, however, because it slows students down and can take their focus away from the meaning.

- **Ask Questions:** Both students read each page—silently if they can but chorally if they need help. Then, they ask each other questions about what they read.

- **Say Something:** Say Something is the simple notion that after partners read a page, they say something. If students do not have anything to say, they may have been concentrating too much on the words and not enough on the meaning. They may need to reread the page, thinking about what they might say about it. Some days, partners take turns—one partner reads a page, the other partner says something, and they reverse roles. On other days, partners read the page together, or silently, and each partner says something.

- **Echo Reading:** Once students know how to echo read, they will enjoy Echo Reading some sections. Give the student who is the echo in each partnership something to designate her status, or have partners read the selection twice, switching reading and Echo Reading roles. Make sure that struggling readers are the echo on the first reading.

- **Choral Whispering:** Choral Whispering is a variation of Choral Reading. Students whisper with their partners so that their reading will not distract partners seated nearby.

- **Everyone Read To . . .:** Students love doing ERT with each other. It is particularly effective as a rereading strategy when they know what the selection is about and they need a good purpose for rereading. Even students who are not fluent readers can usually find the answers to questions and pose good questions for their partners when they have already read the selection.

- **You Decide:** Once students have learned the different Partner Reading formats, you may occasionally want to declare a You Decide day when partners can decide to read together in any way they wish. Be stingy with your You Decide days, however, because you may want to decide the Partner Reading format according to the type and difficulty of the selection, whether this is the first, second, or third time students have read it, and which students are partnered.

6. **Always have partners read for a purpose.** The purpose for reading is not the same thing as the format. The format is how the partners will read a selection. Purpose is what students are getting out of the reading and what they should be ready to contribute to the after-reading activity. If students will do the Beach Ball after reading, partners should be reading and talking about their answers to the Beach Ball questions. If students will add to the KWL chart, they should be reading to find things to add to the L column. If students will do Figuring Out How and Why in discussions groups, they should be reading to answer the *how* and *why* questions. Remember that Guided Reading is when you teach students how to think about text—the comprehension strategies. Having a clear comprehension-oriented purpose for reading helps students become good thinkers who are good at comprehending.

7. **Set a time limit for reading.** Before students begin reading, tell them exactly how long they have to read the selection. Make it a reasonable amount of time, but do not give them longer than most of them will need. Most behavior problems during Partner Reading happen when students have extra time. Do not give students the same amount of time each day because some selections are longer and some rereading of selections can be done in less time. Do set a time and write it on the board and/or set a timer. Students pay more attention to unusual numbers, so tell them that they have 11 minutes, not 10, or 14 minutes, not 15. When the time is up, tell students that you are sorry if they did not finish, but you need them to join the group. Or, tell them that if they have not finished, they can finish before joining the group. It does not matter which way you do it as long as you are consistent and enforce your time limits. You will be amazed by how much more students can read and how much better they behave when the clock is ticking.

8. **Make sure that students have something to do if they finish reading before the time is up.** Always give a productive filler activity—what students should do if they finish reading before the time is up. Make this related to the reading purpose if possible. Here are some suggestions for students:

   - Take turns asking each other all of the questions on the Beach Ball and come up with some awesome answers.
   - Write things that you would like to add to a KWL chart.
   - Decide which character you would like to be when doing the book and practice what you will say and how you will act.
   - Write some *how* and *why* questions.
   - Practice reading your favorite page aloud until you can read it perfectly with terrific expression. If you still have time, practice reading your second-favorite page aloud.
   - Mark important or interesting information with sticky notes.

Having something students should do when they finish reading is essential for successful partner reading. If you do not have something to occupy them, some partners will rush through the reading and create problems because they're "all done!" Students are not usually in such a rush to finish reading first when they will have to think and prepare for the after-reading activity.

Do not make this preparation a requirement for everyone. Have students turn in the after-reading activity or give them time to finish it—that would put you right back in the they-don't-all-finish-at-the-same-time bind. The message you give to students as they read with partners should be perfectly clear:

> "Your job in these 13 minutes is to echo read the selection with your partner so that you are ready to prove which of our predictions are right and which are not. If you finish before the 13 minutes is up, write the number of each true prediction and the page number where you can read to prove it. If you still have time, rewrite the predictions that were wrong so that they are right."

9. **Before beginning Partner Reading, model and role-play the behaviors you want.**
   Call on a student to be your partner and model how to quickly find your reading spot. Then, model whatever kind of Partner Reading you have decided students should do. For the first month or two, before the beginning of every Partner Reading session, model how partners coach each other to figure out words and how partners explain things to each other to make sure that they understand what they read. This will take some time, but this time investment will pay off as the year goes on and your students begin to not only read the selection together but to also teach each other. Once Guided Reading is up and running, focus on a comprehension strategy before students read each day and follow it up after reading. Until students learn how to partner read, use the before-reading time to model and the after-reading time to discuss how the Partner Reading went and to comment on the good strategies you saw partners using.

10. **Circulate, "spy on," and coach the partners.** When you begin Partner Reading in your class, circulate as partners read and comment or make notes about the good strategies you see partners using. When the class reassembles, point out the examples of how partners coached each other with the words and helped each other understand what they were reading. Be specific about whom you saw doing what, and ask those partners to go back to that page and demonstrate for the group. Comment on how you knew that certain partners were focused on the purpose you gave them and how you noticed certain partners using their time wisely after they finished reading. Accentuate the positive by pointing out only good things.

Once students know how to partner read, shift your focus from how the partners are working to how individual students are reading. Stop for a minute to listen to each partner read and model how to coach partners to figure out words and how to explain what the words mean. Make anecdotal notes about students' reading fluency, their discussion, how they are figuring out words, and how they are helping each other. By stopping for just one minute and listening to each set of partners, you can monitor all students' reading in a 12–15 minute period.

An Example of Partner Reading

For this lesson, the teacher chooses the book *The Day Jimmy's Boa Ate the Wash* by Trinka Hakes Noble. Before the lesson starts, the teacher walks over to his "Today I will be reading with . . ." chart. He arranges the 24 wooden sticks into the 12 pockets. On each wooden stick, a name is written in black marker. Students learn who their partners are when they look at the chart. Some students are with the same partners they have worked with previously. For a few students, the teacher makes changes. He begins the lesson by telling students with whom they will work that day. When the names of two students are called, they sit together as partners on the floor and immediately begin previewing the pictures. The teacher begins by talking about the cover and taking a Picture Walk through the book. Then, he passes out a story map and reviews the sections with the class. He notices that Partner Reading has become routine and that everyone knows what to do without much direction. Still, he reminds them of their purpose: "Work together and alternate reading each page. When you finish the book, begin to fill in your story maps. Talk to each other about what you read and where things belong on the story map."

When students are reading, the teacher circulates from pair to pair. As he passes students, he listens and monitors their reading. He interrupts only when he is needed, and he coaches the partners on how to help each other. "Don't tell him the word. Use the coaching chart on the wall and help him figure out that word." When most partners are finished reading, the teacher notes a happy buzz in his second-grade classroom as students fill in information on the story map. Soon a timer dings and students return to the carpet in front of the teacher. They review the information on their story maps for their after-reading activity. The teacher calls on someone in each pair to share something on the story map or to answer a question.

Partner Reading

To make Partner Reading most effective, follow these guidelines:

1. Arrange the partnerships carefully.
2. Think about how often to change partners.
3. Decide where the partners will read.
4. Decide how to handle absent partners.
5. Always make sure that partners know how they will read the selection.
6. Always have partners read for a purpose.
7. Set a time limit for reading the selection and keep to it!
8. Make sure that students have something to do if they finish reading before time is up.
9. Before beginning Partner Reading, model and role-play the behaviors you want.
10. Circulate and coach the partners as they read.

Play-School Groups/Reading Teams

When two sets of partners join, they become a reading group. Sometimes, there may be five students in a group, but more than five can be too many. The guidelines for partners also apply to Play-School Groups/Reading Teams. Think about whom to assign to which groups, how long to leave the groups together, where they will meet, and other logistical variables. Students in Play-School Groups/Reading Teams usually work well together once they have used this format for a while. When groups get along and work well together, let them continue to work together and help each other. If there is a problem, it means that the groups need to be changed or the problem needs to be fixed in order for students to be successful. The groups should know what their purpose is, how long they have to read, and what they should do if they finish reading before the time is up.

In the beginning, circulate, comment, and take notes on how each group is functioning. Once students know how to work in Play-School Groups/Reading Teams, your focus shifts to noticing how individual students are reading—who needs help with the text and the activities and who is good at helping her classmates or team members.

Play-School Groups/Reading Teams is the format used for Doing the Book activities because the groups have more students. You can also do small-group discussions in these groups. After you have done a graphic organizer or KWL activity several times as a class, you can turn the activity over to the groups. Students contribute ideas and one student writes on the group's chart. Finally, all charts are compared and displayed.

Play-School Groups always have a "Teacher," and Reading Teams always have a "Coach." Give all students a chance to be the Teacher or Coach. You do not necessarily have to let everyone be the Teacher the same number of times, but the same bossy students cannot be the Teachers or Coaches every time! To get around this problem, consider which group formats do not require a super reader. Imagine that the class read a story and did an appropriate activity with it the preceding day. Today, they will reread the story to decide what the characters are saying and doing on each page in preparation for pantomiming the book. Divide your struggling readers and make them the Teachers or Coaches in the groups. The rest of each group will take turns reading the pages. Since you read it the day before and the struggling readers are not reading aloud, students should be able to fluently read their pages aloud. The Teacher or Coach tells everyone whose turn it is and asks, "Who is talking, and how would they act?"

If groups are doing Figuring Out How and Why, your struggling readers might be the Teachers because the Teacher is leading the discussion while the other students read the questions and talk about what they think the answers are. Struggling readers can also be the Teachers or Coaches for Choral Reading. For Echo Reading, on the other hand, you need one of your best readers to be the Teacher or Coach, and when groups do Everyone Read To …, they need a good reader to formulate the purposes for reading each page.

Play-School Groups/Reading Teams will be one of your students' favorite formats for reading and rereading selections if they are done correctly. With some clever thinking, you can allow all students to be Teachers or Coaches on various days. As students read, you can circulate and coach them when they need help with words or with the thinking required to fulfill their purpose for reading.

An Example of Play-School Groups/Reading Teams

For this lesson, the teacher chooses the book *Frogs* by Kevin J. Holmes. Before the lesson starts, the teacher tells students, "You will read an informational book about frogs, and we will use Reading Teams today." Like many informational books and content area textbooks, this book has a table of contents and an index that students need to know how to use. Some students will find the book difficult—especially since the book is all about frogs and they do not know much about frogs! The book enables the teacher to meet the Guided Reading goal of helping students learn to read informational text.

The teacher says, "Let's look in the table of contents. It is not numbered, but it is on page 3." She waits for students to locate that page. "A table of contents lets you know what is in a book. These chapters each have a picture on one page and text on the other page. You will read five chapters today: Photo Diagram, Frog Facts, Frogs, Appearance, and Homes."

Next, the teacher tells students which team they will work with that day. "Now, I will tell you who will be in each reading team. The first name I call is the Coach of the reading team." As the names of students are called and teams are formed, they sit together on the floor and immediately begin previewing the pictures and reading the captions at the bottoms of the pages.

When all teams are seated, the teacher reminds them of their purpose: "Work together to read each page. Talk about the picture and what you learn, and think about what you can add to our Frog Facts list." The Coach of each team leads the lesson for the team as if she were the teacher.

The teacher circulates from team to team as students read and talk. There is a happy buzz as these third graders find new and interesting facts about frogs.

When a timer dings, students return to the carpet in front of the teacher. They eagerly share their new information about frogs. The teacher calls on a student in each team to share something he learned. As students share what they learned, the teacher types the Frog Facts list on the classroom interactive whiteboard. Students watch the interactive whiteboard screen and read the sentences as the teacher types them. Each team is pleased as their information is added to the list. One student asks if they will all get copies of the information that the teacher is typing, and the teacher explains that she intends to print it for them to read to their families tonight as part of their homework.

Play-School Groups/Reading Teams

To make Play-School Groups/Reading Teams most effective, follow these guidelines and remind students of the rules for this format:

1. Arrange the Play-School Groups/Reading Teams carefully.
2. Think about how often to change the Play-School Groups/Reading Teams.
3. Decide where the Play-School Groups/Reading Teams will meet.
4. Make sure that each group knows who the Teacher or Coach is and the role of the Teacher or Coach.
5. Always make sure that Play-School Groups/Reading Teams know how they will read.
6. Always have Play-School Groups/Reading Teams read for a purpose.
7. Set a time limit for reading the selection and stick to it!
8. Make sure that students have something to do if they finish reading before time is up.
9. Before beginning partner or play-school Reading, model and role-play the behaviors you want.
10. Circulate and coach the groups as they read.

172

Chapter 23

Three-Ring Circus and You'se Choose

On some days during Guided Reading, some students read the selection on their own, others read it with partners, and the teacher meets with a small Coaching Group to guide their reading. Most of the time, the teacher decides who will read with whom. Because there are three formats being used simultaneously, this format is called Three-Ring Circus. Once students understand how Three-Ring Circus works, you can sometimes let them choose how they would like to read the selection. Those days are called You'se Choose days.

Three-Ring Circus

Once Partner Reading is working well, most teachers use the Three-Ring Circus format on some days. You may want to begin by explaining to students that there are advantages to all three types of reading. When students are reading by themselves, they can read at their own pace and focus on their own ideas. When they are Partner Reading, they have the advantage of getting help when they need it, and they have someone with whom to share ideas. Explain that you, the teacher, like to read with a small group of students so that you can see how each is progressing and so that you can coach them to apply the strategies they are learning. Make sure that students already know how to read with partners and have practiced the partner format you want them to use. Most teachers use an organizational chart so that students can quickly see how they will read the selection that day without wasting time waiting for the teacher to get everyone in the right place. Here is a Three-Ring Circus chart one teacher uses to let students know how they will be reading. On days when the teacher wants to have a Three-Ring Circus organization, the teacher places students' names in the appropriate rings.

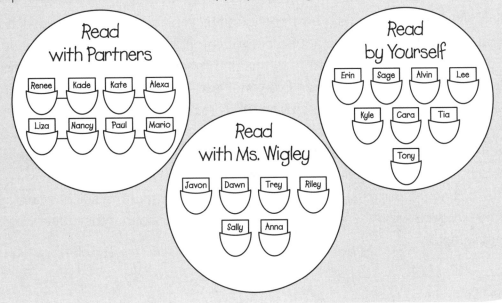

When deciding who should read in which format for a Three-Ring Circus, consider both the levels of your students and the selection. You may want to have your accelerated readers read the selection individually or with a partner of similar ability. Students who need support should be paired with supportive partners or assigned to the Coaching Group. Do not assign students who don't work well together to read in partnerships, and never assign a student to read individually unless you believe that he can successfully complete the reading on his own.

When deciding who should read with you in the Coaching Group, again look at the selection and think about the levels of your students. Including easier and average selections makes Guided Reading multilevel. While it might seem logical to include the struggling readers in your Coaching Group for the grade-level selections, this is usually not the case. These selections are probably above the instructional level of your struggling readers, who would profit more from being coached through the easier selections. Make sure that your struggling readers have nurturing partners, and in the Coaching Group, include grade-level readers who could profit most from being coached through the selection that is at their instructional levels. Try to include struggling readers in the Coaching Group when you are reading an easier selection.

Though it is important to include all students in Coaching Groups, you do not have to include them the same number of times. Accelerated readers do not need a lot of coaching and should be included occasionally, but not as often as struggling readers. This might seem unfair to your advanced readers, unless you remember that accelerated readers are generally happier reading selections on their own or with partners. Accelerated readers profit from Guided Reading as they learn a variety of comprehension strategies for all types of text. Their prior knowledge, understanding of concepts, and oral language skills increase as they participate in the before- and after-reading activities. But because accelerated readers are fast learners, they do not need a lot of coaching and reteaching.

While deciding which students could most benefit from coaching on a particular selection, keep in mind that your Coaching Groups are not fixed-ability groups. You may want to include different students for different reasons on different days. Imagine, for example, that you do the first reading of a selection with the whole class using an Everyone Read To . . . format. The next day, you plan to reread the selection for a different purpose using the Three-Ring Circus format. Two students who were absent the day before might be included in your Coaching Group so that you can support them in their first reading of the selection. There are also usually one or two students in every class who need help but do not work well with partners—particularly when the teacher is working with a Coaching Group and the partners are expected to function without the teacher circulating around the room. These students are often included in Coaching Groups so that the Three-Ring Circus format can run smoothly.

Guided Reading is hard to make multilevel. Any selection will be too hard for some, too easy for others, and just right for some. For that reason, many teachers who have help coming to their classrooms schedule Guided Reading during that time. In those classrooms, the Three-Ring Circus becomes a Four-Ring Circus in which two Coaching Groups go on simultaneously.

An Example of Three-Ring Circus

For this lesson, the teacher chooses the book *Baby Birds* by Helen Frost. Before the lesson starts, the teacher tells students, "Today, we will read an informational book about birds, and we will do a Three-Ring Circus." The teacher notices that several students are excited to be using this format again. She points to her Three-Ring Circus chart and tells students, "Five students will read with me and sit in front of the board, six pairs of partners will work together and sit around the room, and six of you will read by yourselves in your seats. We will all read the same book, *Baby Birds*." In a Three-Ring Circus, everyone reads the same book. Different students get different amounts of support, but everyone has the support she needs to be successful!

When the groups are in their places, the teacher says, "Look at the cover. What do you see? Do you see the author's name?" She then asks, "What do you already know about baby birds?" The teacher begins a KWL chart on a large sheet of chart paper and lists the things students tell her in the K column.

Baby birds hatch from eggs.

They live in nests.

They are fed by their mothers.

Then, the teacher asks students what they want to learn from reading this book and lists the things students tell her in the W column. Finally, she tells students, "If you are reading with a partner, take turns reading each page. If you are reading by yourselves, you will have to read all of the pages. When you finish reading, begin to list things you learned about baby birds from reading this book."

As the teacher leads her Coaching Group, she has students go on a Picture Walk with her. She asks them what they see in each picture, and she repeats their responses and prompts them for things they do not mention. In addition to identifying the items in each picture, the teacher has students say and stretch out one word, decide what letters they expect to see in the word, and find that word on the page before reading it. Students echo read each page. The teacher reads each sentence and cups her hand behind her ear as she listens for students to read it back just the way she read it. When they finish reading each page, the teacher and students talk about what they learned about baby birds on that page.

As the teacher works with her group, her eyes scan the room and she watches the partners read. These students know how to partner read. They take turns with each page, one student reading and the other pointing to the words. At the end of each page, the reader asks the pointer what he heard. As the partners take turns, it is clear that struggling readers are partnered with students who can help them. The partners do not tell each other the words but coach each other to figure them out.

After about 10 minutes, several sets of partners and almost all of the individual students finish reading, and the teacher signals all students to gather at the KWL chart. They have been writing some things that they think should be added to the L part of the chart. Students are eager to talk about what they learned from this informational book, and they share how much they liked the pictures of baby birds.

You'se Choose

If you were to enter a classroom and see some students reading with the teacher while other students were reading individually or with partners, you would probably assume that the format for reading that day was a Three-Ring Circus. Maybe, maybe not! Another format that looks the same and works the same is You'se Choose (in some Southern classrooms, it is referred to as Y'all's Call!), in which students decide with whom they want to read a selection.

Once you have the Three-Ring Circus format established, it is easy to tell students that on some days they will get to choose how they want to read the selection. Always establish the rule, however, that they must make good choices. As part of your before-reading activity, clearly establish the purpose for reading by making it clear to students what they will be doing in the after-reading activity. Then, tell them that they must be ready to contribute to the after-reading activity and ask them to preview the selection and decide how best to read it so that they can contribute. Tell students that they can read the selection with a friend, if both of them want to read it together, and they can prepare for the after-reading activity together. Explain that students can choose to read by themselves, with the same caveat—they must be able to handle it on their own. Finally, tell students that you would like some of them to choose to read with you and that together, you will read the selection and prepare to contribute to the after-reading activity.

Just as with Partner Reading and Play-School Groups/Reading Teams, make sure that students know what they are preparing to do and give them a filler task to do if they finish reading before the time is up. Relate that filler task to your after-reading activity (writing things to add to a time line, deciding which character they would like to be, practicing reading the parts a character would say in the way they think the character would say them, etc.). Give students the same amount of time to read that you want to spend working with students who choose to read with you. The rest of the class will work individually or with partners to begin the filler activity if they have time. Be sure not to make the filler activity something anyone has to complete or turn in. By doing so, you still would not have solved the problem of students taking different amounts of time to do things. When you have a good and clearly established filler activity, no one finishes before the allotted time is up! Having a filler activity solves some of the management problems that often occur when students are working in different configurations.

When you decide to do You'se Choose, it is important to let everyone make the choice for himself. But sometimes, this is easier said than done. The first time you do the activity, you may see some students who choose to read by themselves even though you know they cannot read the selection on their own and other students who have partners who will not be any help at all! You might casually ask the ones who have not chosen well, "Are you sure that you don't want to read with my group? I'd love to have you!" But, if they decline your kind invitation, let them do the reading the way they chose. When the class reassembles for the after-reading activity, call on these students for their contributions. Do not embarrass them, but make it clear that you expect them to be able to contribute. If they are unable to, take them aside privately and tell them that next time you will have to approve their choices. Be resolute with this and you will find your students making better choices. Don't be surprised if some of your more-able readers choose to read with you. You said that they could choose any way that would get them ready to contribute, and they have! Students have preferences about how they want to do things. Like adults, some students are more social than others. You'se Choose lets students express those preferences, and it is a favorite format in many classrooms.

You'se Choose is also a favorite format among older students who like to decide things for themselves and love to do things with their friends. Be sure that students have a purpose for reading and that they understand that they must make responsible choices. Students who choose to read on their own or with a partner, but who are unable to contribute to the after-reading activity, should be chosen by you for your group the next time. Then, give them the choice again the following time. Be resolute, and most students will learn to make good choices.

Three-Ring Circus and You'se Choose (Y'all's Call)

Both Three-Ring Circus and You'se Choose give you a lot of flexibility in how you support students during Guided Reading. When you do You'se Choose, you lose the advantage of being able to decide how much support students need, but you gain a lot of cooperation because students like to be in control! These formats should be used only after students know how to partner read and are familiar with the after-reading activity for which they are preparing. Most teachers begin with the Three-Ring Circus format and expand it to include You'se Choose when their students are used to the idea that some students read by themselves, others with partners, and others with the teacher.

1. If you are doing a Three-Ring Circus, decide who will read by themselves, with a partner, or with you. Think about how much support students will need to read based on the purpose you set. When you do You'se Choose, make sure that students understand that they must make responsible choices or they will lose the privilege of making choices the next time.

2. Set time limits just as you would for Partner Reading and Play-School Groups/Reading Teams.

3. If you have students who cannot handle the freedom to read on their own or with a partner while you work with a group, include them in the Coaching Group more often.

4. If you have help coming during Guided Reading, you might have two or more Coaching Groups, creating a Four- or Five-Ring Circus!

Chapter 24

Book Club Groups and Literature Circles

So far in this book, you have learned about formats for organizing students to read and reread text when they are all reading the same text. As your students become better and more independent readers, you can use Book Club Groups and Literature Circles to let them have some choices about what they read.

Book Club Groups

For Book Club Groups, you usually select four books that are tied together by author, genre, topic, or theme. When choosing the four books, try to include one that is easier and one that is harder than the others. (Do not tell students that some books are easier or harder!) Read aloud the first chapter or several pages of each book to students or preview the pictures with them. Then, have students indicate their first, second, and third choices for the books they would like to read. If students who are struggling readers choose the easier book as one of their choices, put them in the group who will read this book. If the more advanced readers choose the harder book for any of their choices, put them in that group. Each time you do Book Club Groups, the groups change, and while you consider the reading levels and choices of students when assigning them, the groups all have a range of readers and are not ability groups.

Once Book Club Groups are formed, they meet regularly to read and discuss the book. You rotate through the groups giving guidance, support, and encouragement. Each day, the groups report to the class what has happened or what they have learned in their book so far.

Book Club Groups with Dr. Seuss Books

Here is an example of Book Club Groups using four Dr. Seuss books. Many teachers find this a fun activity as March draws near and schools around the United States celebrate Dr. Seuss's birthday. Teachers often build up to this activity by reading Dr. Seuss books to students. Then, teachers encourage students to bring in their favorite Dr. Seuss books. When students bring the books to school, teachers often notice that there are many copies of several books. Teachers may be able to borrow these books from students, combine them with library and classroom copies, and use them for Book Club Groups.

The Dr. Seuss books chosen for this example are *Hop on Pop*; *The Foot Book*; *Ten Apples Up on Top*; and *One Fish, Two Fish, Red Fish, Blue Fish*. *Hop on Pop* is the easy selection because most of the pages have just two words with the same spelling pattern and a simple sentence using those two words. The pictures support the text and can be used by students to cross-check their reading. *The Foot Book* and *Ten Apples Up on Top* are a little more difficult than *Hop on Pop*, but they can easily be read by primary-grade students. The hardest of the four books is *One Fish, Two Fish, Red Fish, Blue Fish*. This book is harder than the others because there are more words in the book and more text on each page. Once again, the pictures support the text, and students can cross-check as they read. When you do Book Club Groups, make sure that you include a book that is a little more challenging than grade level for students who need the challenge.

Book Club Groups usually last several days. In the following example, the teacher decides that the Dr. Seuss Book Club Groups will last three days.

Book Club Groups with Dr. Seuss Books: Day One

The teacher begins Guided Reading the first day by telling students that she found four wonderful Dr. Seuss books for them to read in Book Club Groups. If this is the class's first time using this format, the teacher may talk about how grown-ups often read the same book and get together with friends to talk about it. She might tell about her own experience with a book club as an example. The teacher then explains that students are such good readers that they are now ready for Book Club Groups with their friends!

The teacher shows the covers of the books, one at a time, and lets students tell what they know about these books and some of their personal experiences with them. Using only the covers, she also gets students thinking about what they might read. She tells students that they have only three days to spend on these books and that they do not have enough time or enough copies of the books for each student to read all four books. She says that each Book Club Group will read one book and hear about the other three books from the other groups.

Next, the teacher gives each student an index card and asks students to write their names and the numbers 1, 2, and 3 on the cards. She then explains that they will have 20 minutes to preview the books—5 minutes for each book. At the end of the 20 minutes, students will return to their seats and write their first, second, and third choices. The teacher places all of the copies of each book in a corner of the room. Then, she divides the class into four groups and sends a group to each corner. She sets her timer for five minutes and tells students that when the timer buzzes, they must move to the next corner and the next group of books.

For the next 20 minutes, students busily try to read as much as they can and look at as many pages as they can. Each time the timer buzzes and they have to move, students groan. When the 20 minutes are up, students return to their seats to make their choices. It isn't easy! Most students protest that they want to read them all! They have trouble deciding which book is their first choice and which is their second choice. The teacher tells them not to worry too much about the order of choices because she cannot guarantee that they will get their first choice—or even their second choice. "I want the groups to be about the same size, and I need to put students together who work well together. I promise that I will give you one of your choices. I will try to give you your first choice, but I can't promise that you will get it!"

After school, the teacher looks at all of the cards. First, she looks at the cards of the struggling readers. Four of her five struggling readers chose *Hop on Pop* as one of their choices, so she puts them in the *Hop on Pop* group with two more-able readers who also chose *Hop on Pop*. One struggling reader chose *Ten Apples Up on Top* as his first choice, and the teacher puts him in the *Ten Apples Up on Top* group. Next, she looks at the choices of her most able readers. Four of these students have chosen *One Fish, Two Fish, Red Fish, Blue Fish*, so she puts them in a group with two fairly able readers. She puts the other 11 students in the remaining two groups, five in the *Ten Apples Up on Top* group and six in *The Foot Book* group.

Book Club Groups with Dr. Seuss Books: Day Two

The second day, students read the whole book with their Book Club Groups. Before passing out the books, the teacher tells students how they will read the books and what their purpose for reading is. The teacher explains that during reading today, they will echo read the book and read and point. Students know this means that the leader of each group will read each page first while the other students point to the words. Then, the group will echo read, reading exactly the way that the leader did. (Read and Point is used in the early reading stages to help students stay focused and track print.)

The students' purpose is to read the book with good expression, emphasizing the funny words and the rhyming words, and to think about what they like best about the book. Which pictures do they like best? Which words? What is really funny? What is really silly? The teacher explains that they will think more about this tomorrow, but if students finish before the time is up, they should go back through the book and begin to talk about what they like best.

The teacher passes out the books. As she hands each group their books, she says, "The person who gets the book with the index card in it is the leader today." She makes sure that a fluent reader who is a responsible student is given that book.

As students read, the teacher circulates, listens, coaches if needed, and moves on. She monitors most closely the *Hop on Pop* group, visiting them at the beginning and making sure that they know what to do and how to do it. After she monitors the other Book Club Groups, the teacher returns to the *Hop on Pop* group and coaches them some more if needed.

As the groups finish reading, they begin to discuss what they like about the book. Students like the funny pictures, the rhyming words, and the silly things that Dr. Seuss writes about in his books. The leader will share these things with the class in the after-reading phase of this lesson.

Book Club Groups with Dr. Seuss Books: Day Three

On the third day, students reread the books with their Book Club Groups. This time, they read the books chorally. Each student's purpose is to find his favorite page to read to the group. Each student is given a bookmark, and as students chorally read the pages, he can insert his bookmark to mark his favorite page. As they continue reading and he comes to a "more favorite" page, he can move the bookmark. Once the whole book is read chorally, each student will practice reading his favorite page. The leader in each group makes sure that each student can read the page fluently and can explain why he chose it. If several students in a group have chosen the same page, they practice reading that page chorally.

The Guided Reading lesson ends with all students reading aloud and explaining their choices. They talk about the pictures, what the author is saying on the page, and how the text is illustrated. The teacher hears members of other Book Club Groups say, "I liked those funny fur feet too!" and "The house on the mouse was the best illustration in that book, but a mouse can't really carry a real house!" It is apparent from their faces and their comments that students want to read and reread these books.

The teacher ends the lesson by telling the class that although the Book Club Groups are finished, she wants to borrow these books a little longer. If the owners let her, she will put one book from each group in each book basket so that everyone has a chance to read or reread his favorite Dr. Seuss book during Self-Selected Reading.

Book Club Groups with Biographies

You learned in Chapter 3 that it is important for students to learn to read different kinds of text, including biographies. Biographies are interesting to most students. Students who like to read informational text enjoy biographies because they depict events that really happened. Students who like to read stories like biographies because they are true stories of people's lives.

For this Book Club Group example, the teacher has chosen four biographies by David A. Adler. Each book has 25 pages and ends with a page of important dates and events. The easiest biography chosen is *A Picture Book of Abraham Lincoln*. It follows the life of the popular U.S. president from his childhood on the frontier to his assassination after the American Civil War. Most pages have two to four lines of text and illustrations. Some pages have only illustrations. Most students who have been in school in the United States for at least one year know something about Abraham Lincoln.

Students' prior knowledge about Lincoln, combined with shorter text and more illustrations, makes this biography easier than the others.

Two biographies that are a little harder than the one about Abraham Lincoln are *A Picture Book of Martin Luther King, Jr.* and *A Picture Book of Jackie Robinson*. Each of these books has more text on the pages than the biography of Abraham Lincoln. Also, some students may not be as familiar with these two historic figures as they are with Lincoln. The hardest biography is *A Picture Book of Rosa Parks*. The vocabulary is the most difficult of the four biographies by far, including words such as *boycott*, *protest*, *humiliated*, *segregated*, and *discrimination*. There is also more text on each page, and there are several pages that have text without illustrations.

The biography Book Club Groups will last four days. Students will preview and make their choices on the first day, read the book over the next two days, and do a summary writing activity on the fourth day.

Book Club Groups with a Biography: Day One

The first day of a Book Club Group's cycle is always the previewing and choosing day. The teacher gathers students and tells them that they will focus on biographies this week, and he says that he has four great biographies from which they can choose. He shows students the covers of the four biographies and lets them tell what they know about each person. He then reads aloud the first six or seven pages of each biography. After the teacher previews the books, students indicate their first, second, and third choices on index cards. The teacher reminds students that he may not be able to give them their first or even their second choice, but he will give them one of their choices.

After school, the teacher looks at students' choices. He looks first at the choices of his struggling readers. Three of them chose *A Picture Book of Abraham Lincoln*, and the other three chose *A Picture Book of Jackie Robinson*. The teacher gives all of these students their first choices. Next, he looks at the choices his advanced readers made. Four of the advanced readers chose the Rosa Parks book, and the rest of the advanced readers chose the Jackie Robinson and Martin Luther King Jr. books. The teacher gives the remainder of the class their first, second, and sometimes third choices so that each group has five or six members.

When students come to school the next day, they immediately check the posted list of Book Club Groups. Some are disappointed that they did not get their first choices. The teacher sympathizes but points out that he was able to give them one of their choices. He also tells students that he will keep the books in the room for the next week, and they can read them during Self-Selected Reading.

Book Club Groups with a Biography: Day Two

On the second day of Book Club Groups, students gather in the front of the room and huddle around the teacher. There are four sheets of chart paper taped to the board behind him. He shows students that each sheet has the name of one book and the names of the students in that group. He explains that he wrote the name of the person they will read about in the oval in the center of the chart paper. There are four lines that come from the center and have circles at the ends. There are spokes, or lines, coming from each small circle. In the small circles, the teacher has written *family*, *birth/early years*, *work*, and *later years/death*.

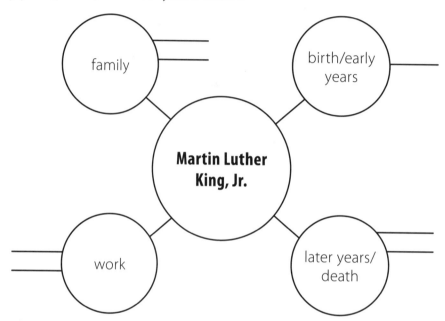

Students have helped complete webs before, so they understand that their purpose for reading is to find important facts related to each subtopic and write them on the appropriate spokes. The teacher points out that he drew a star beside the name of the student in each group who will write on the web and be the "Teacher." In each group, the teacher has appointed one of the more-able readers and writers for this task. He gives markers to the member of each group whom he has chosen to do the writing and tells students that the writer will also be the Teacher and lead the group, just as he does when the class completes webs together.

In preparation for this activity, the teacher has placed the books in the four corners of the room. He used large paper clips to clip together the pages in the second half of each book so that students would not read beyond that point on the first day. The groups go to their corners and have 20 minutes to read the first half of the book and add information to the spokes on their webs.

As the groups work, the teacher walks around and listens to them read. He stops and coaches individuals who need help and monitors the reading of many others. At the end of 15 minutes, one group has not begun writing any information on their web, so the teacher signals to them that with only five minutes left, they should be discussing and writing things on their web. He adds that some groups will have to move a little faster. The last 10 minutes of Guided Reading ends with each group sharing their web and telling what they have learned so far.

Book Club Groups with a Biography: Day Three

On the next day, the teacher meets with the class and makes sure that they know what they will do. He says, "Review what you have learned so far and read the remaining pages of your biographies." Each group must have its web completed by the end of 20 minutes and be ready to share details from the life of the person about whom the book is written. The teacher uses the same procedure as he used the previous day to support their reading, giving a little extra time to those who need it. (He remembers his friend's motto: "Being fair isn't giving everyone the same thing; being fair is giving each student what she needs!") At the end of the allotted time, the teacher reassembles the class, and they share the new information from their finished webs.

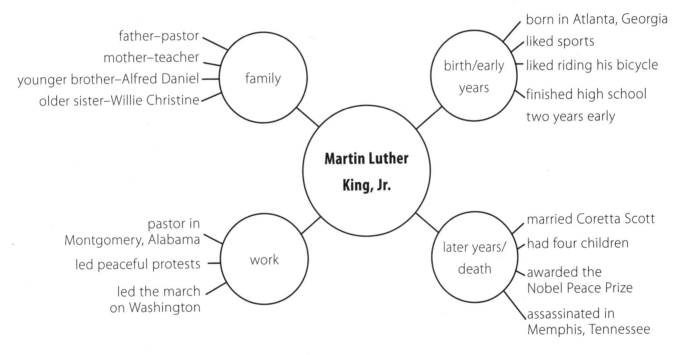

Book Club Groups with a Biography: Day Four

On the final day, the teacher tells students that each group will write a paragraph summarizing some of the important things that they learned about the historic person. He shows students the paragraph frame that he wrote on the board, and they read and discuss each sentence.

I learned a lot about _____ . I learned that (s)he was born _____ . I learned _____ . (S)he is remembered for _____ . The most important thing I learned was _____ .

The teacher gives each student four sticky notes and shows students how they can use the sticky notes to mark the places in the text to which they will want to refer when they complete their paragraphs. They can reread the books by themselves or with partners, and they can write their own summaries or write them with partners if they can agree on what they want to say.

As students read, the teacher visits each student or pair of students and asks them to read a page aloud. He makes notes about their fluency and word identification and is pleased to see that all students are able to read their biographies with good fluency and adequate word identification. As students begin writing, they use both the books and the webs to help them. Have the webs and books available for support and have the frame to help structure their writing. Because students know so much about their topics, each student writes a good paragraph to share with the class.

> I learned a lot about Rosa Parks. I learned that she was born in Tuskegee, Alabama, in 1913. I learned that she lived and worked on her grandparents' farm as she was growing up. She is remembered for being the mother of the Civil Rights Movement. The most important thing I learned was that it is against the law to discriminate against people because of their race or skin color.

> I learned a lot about Martin Luther King, Jr. I learned that he was born in Atlanta, Georgia, in 1929. I learned that he won the Nobel Peace Prize. He is remembered for leading the famous March on Washington. The most important thing I learned was that he helped end the unfair treatment of African Americans.

Biographies make history come alive and thus are natural social studies links. The biographies listed in the example are appropriate for students from late second grade and beyond. There are many biographies written for older students. Some biographies of athletes include *Shaquille O'Neil: Big Man, Big Dreams* by Mark Stewart; *Emmitt Smith: Finding Daylight* by Ted Cox; and *Derek Jeter: Shortshop Sensation* by Brendan January. Some other books about athletes include Therese Shea's *Hockey Stars, Basketball Stars, and Soccer Stars* and Virginia Buckman's *Baseball Stars and Football Stars*.

Book Club Groups with Plays

Most students love to be in plays. Many publishers make it easy to do plays with students reading on their own levels. For this Book Club Group's example, the teacher has chosen four books from Rigby's collection. Each book has 20 pages for the story and an 11- or 12-page play. *The Three Billy Goats Gruff* is easier. *Robin Hood and the Silver Trophy* is more challenging than *Goldilocks and the Three Bears* and *Town Mouse, Country Mouse*. This round of Book Club Groups will last five days.

Students will preview and make their choices on the first day, read the stories and plays over the next three days, and perform the plays on the final day.

Book Club Groups with a Play: Day One

The teacher begins Book Club Groups by sharing the covers of the books and explaining that each book contains both a story and a play. Most students smile because they know what comes next—Doing the Book! The teacher explains that on this first day, they will look at all of the books. He asks students to think about which characters they would like to play as they look at the books and to read a few lines to see if they sound like a good match for any characters. After previewing the four books, the students will write which books they want to read. The teacher has placed eight copies of each title in a corner of the room. Students have six minutes to preview each book and six minutes to decide and write their choices.

As students are previewing the books, the teacher circulates and spends a few minutes in each corner. He gives some attention to the struggling readers, who are mixed in with the other readers in all four corners. He reads a page or two with them and helps them think about which books they like best and which characters they would want to play.

When students have previewed all of the books, they write their three choices. Most students like all of the books and want to do all of the plays. A few students have particular books they want to read and characters they really want to be, and they write pleading notes to the teacher on their choice sheets. The teacher looks at students' choices and divides the class into groups. Given that students will do the plays, he also decides who will be which character, but he does not tell students their parts until they have read the books. He puts six students in the Goldilocks group, which needs five actors and a narrator, and five students in the Billy Goats group, which has four characters and a narrator. He assigns students to the Mouse group and puts all of the other students in the Robin Hood group, which has a lot of characters, including several with very few lines. He assigns two students several small parts to round out this cast.

Book Club Groups with a Play: Day Two

The teacher has written the names of the students in each group on an index card and hands the card to the leader/director/narrator of the play. The leader calls out the names on her list and leads students to the appointed area. Each group will read a two-page spread and discuss what happens on the pages. Students begin to read these familiar tales two pages at a time. They follow the procedure set up by the teacher—read and discuss, read and discuss, and so on. When the class gets together at the end of the lesson, one student in each group reports what has happened in his group's book so far.

Book Club Groups with a Play: Day Three

The whole class gathers before the lesson, and one student in each group retells what has happened in each story so far. The teacher congratulates each student for her accurate retelling and praises her for telling the events in the correct sequence. Each group follows the same procedure as the day before to finish reading and discussing the book. One student in each group finishes retelling the tale when the class reassembles at the end of the reading lesson.

Book Club Groups with a Play: Day Four

On the fourth day, the Book Club Groups read the plays in the backs of the books. The teacher gives the leader in each group a list of who will read which parts. The groups begin reading the play with each student reading his appropriate part. (Depending on your class, you may let each group decide who will play each part if this can be done amicably and quickly.) The teacher circulates as students read and coaches them to read with appropriate expression. Students enjoy the reading and compete to see who can be the "hammiest." The teacher lets students take the books home to practice reading their parts so that they can read them fluently the next day. Many students discuss their plans to read the whole play at home, giving everyone at home a part to read!

Book Club Groups with a Play: Day Five

The fifth and final day begins with the teacher clearing some space in the front of the room and declaring it their stage. The leader/narrator/director in each group draws a straw on which the number 1, 2, 3, or 4 has been written. The numbered straw tells whether the groups will be first, second, third, or fourth to perform their play. The first group comes forward, and the rest of the class becomes an eager audience. Students begin reading and acting out their parts. After the applause, one student in each of the other three groups tells something she liked about the performance: "I like the way each of the goat's voices sounded different." "The troll walked just how a big troll would!"

Each group takes a turn reading and performing their plays. When all of the plays have been done, students take out their reading response logs and write about which play—other than their own—they liked best and why. Students demand to keep the books in the room for a while, and several students ask to check out books so that they can read all of the plays at home with their family and friends!

Book Club Groups

Here are the important things to remember for Book Club Groups:

1. Select four books that are tied together by author, topic, genre, or theme. Try to include one book that is easier and one that is more challenging than the others.
2. Let students preview books and indicate their choices.
3. Form groups considering the choices students made, the reading abilities of students, and the difficulty of the books.
4. For Book Club Groups, have students read for the purpose you determine and the amount of time you allow each day.
5. Have each group share what they have read with the other groups.
6. Make the books available for Self-Selected Reading so that students who want to read the other books can.

Literature Circles

Literature Circles are similar to Book Club Groups in that students choose books and meet in small groups to discuss them. Unlike in Book Club Groups, students in Literature Circles read on their own rather than with a group. For this reason, you should do Literature Circles only when you are sure that students can read their books without help, or you may modify the Literature Circles format to allow students who have picked a book with which they may need help to partner read.

Another major difference between Literature Circles and Book Club Groups is that the whole group has the same purpose for reading in Book Club Groups, while students in Literature Circles have different roles and can choose the role they want. These roles determine their purpose for reading. There are a variety of roles, but the most commonly used ones are Character Sketcher, Author Authority, Plot Person, Conflict Connector, and Solution Suggester. A student who likes drawing can become the Character Sketcher and sketch the characters in the story that his group is reading. Another student who knows a lot about the author can become the Author Authority. The Plot Person makes sure that everyone in the group understands what has happened in the story so far. To carry out this task, the Plot Person must keep track of who the characters are, what they want, what happens, and how the problem is solved. The Conflict Connector helps the group understand the conflicts that exist (character versus character, character versus nature, character versus society, etc.) and how the characters work through the conflicts. These roles help students discuss the books they are reading and share what is happening in the stories with the whole class.

To help students choose roles, you can give them a role sheet. Here is a role sheet one teacher used:

Discussion Director: Your job is to develop a list of questions that your group might want to discuss about today's reading. Determine what is important about the text. Focus your questions on big ideas.

Passage Master: Your job is to locate a few special sections of the reading that the group should revisit. You should help your group notice the most interesting, funny, puzzling, and important parts.

Vocabulary Enricher: Your job is to be on the lookout for a few especially important words that your group should remember or understand. You should look for new, interesting, strange, important, and puzzling words.

Connector: Your job is to find connections between the material you are reading and yourself or other students. You should look for connections to the world and to other books we have read.

Illustrator: Your job is to draw a picture related to the reading. It can be a sketch, diagram, flow chart, or stick figure scene.

You will find more roles and their descriptions in the books *Literature Circles* by Harvey Daniels and *25 Reproducible Literature Circle Role Sheets for Fiction and Nonfiction Books* by Christine Boardman Moen.

An Example of Literature Circles in Fifth Grade

The teacher chooses four biographies for Literature Circles. All of these biographies of early Americans are written by David A. Adler. The teacher's goal is to give students more information about American history, one of their social studies topics this year. Students will also learn more about biographies and write a biography as a writing assignment. There will be six students in each Literature Circle.

"Today, we will begin Literature Circles with the same groups as last time, but instead of reading a fiction book, you will be reading a biography. The biographies are about people you have read about or will read about in social studies. Here are the roles I will assign for each group and from which you will choose."

The teacher gives students the following role sheet.

Discussion Director: Your job is to develop a list of questions that your group might want to discuss about the biography. Determine what is important about the text. Focus your questions on the important things that happened in the person's life.

Passage Master: Your job is to locate a few special sections of the reading that the group should revisit. You should help your group notice the most interesting, historic, and important parts.

Vocabulary Enricher: Your job is to be on the lookout for a few especially important words that your group must understand to learn more about this person's life. You should look for new, interesting, strange, important, and puzzling words.

Connector: Your job is to find connections between the material you are reading and other books or materials we have read in social studies.

Illustrator: Your job is to draw a picture related to the reading. It can be a sketch of the person, a drawing of something that happened in her life, or a diorama or time line of the events in her life.

"You will spend five days reading the chapters at home and in school and working on your role. On the sixth day, you will prepare to give a presentation to the class. Every group will have five presentations to give about their biography." (This lesson can also be done in one day when reading a picture book at any grade level.)

Older students love Book Club Groups and Literature Circles because they get to choose their own books. If you offer a group of books that includes an easier and a harder book, this Guided Reading format is multilevel. Book Club Groups and Literature Circles are a favorite way to organize Guided Reading once students read well enough that you can find multiple books tied together in some way. Most teachers find that students participate eagerly in these groups and that the books students did not get to read are the most popular selections during Self-Selected Reading the following week. It is not unusual for students to read all three books that their group did not read. Students' knowledge of each book is greatly increased by each group sharing information with the class. Students are often able to read books at a higher level because of their increased knowledge of the topic and writing style.

Literature Circles

Here are the important things to remember for Literature Circles:

1. Select four books that are tied together by author, topic, genre, or theme. Try to include one book that is easier and one that is more challenging than the others.
2. Let students preview the books and indicate their choices, or assign books to different groups.
3. Form groups considering the choices made by students as well as the difficulty of the books.
4. Let students choose their roles, but ensure that each role is covered.
5. Let groups decide how much to read each day and use role sheets that fit the age and sophistication of your students.
6. Have each group share what they learned with the other groups.
7. Make the books available for Self-Selected Reading so that students who want to read the other books can.

Chapter 25

Pick a Page

Pick a Page is a fluency-building activity in which each student is given one or two pages of a story to read and practice. Students practice reading their pages in groups of "same pagers." Next, new reading groups are formed that contain one reader for each page. Pick a Page can be done as a rereading activity, but it is more fun to do it as a first reading. Part of the intrigue as each student is practicing his page is not knowing what happens or how the story ends.

You can do Pick a Page with any story. It is more dramatic to cut apart selections from old reading textbooks or inexpensive paperback books, because everyone really has to wait until the reading group gathers to find out the rest of the story (no one can look back or peek ahead). If students are reading their pages and the rest of the story is available, make a firm "no peeking" rule and deal quickly with anyone who peeks! Take a "No peeking or else!" stance and have an appropriate "or else" in mind.

An Example of Pick a Page

For this lesson, the teacher chooses the book *A Chair for My Mother* by Vera B. Williams. The copy comes from an old reading textbook, so the teacher cut it apart. The selection has 15 pages, and the teacher decides to distribute the pages so that each student is reading two pages, printed front and back on one sheet. The last page has words on only one side, so she groups it with the preceding two pages, which do not have much text on them. There are 23 students in the class, so the teacher decides to create two reading pairs who will chorally read their pages.

Before beginning, the teacher explains to students how Pick a Page works. She tells students that they will read a story but that each reader will know only a small part of the story. First, each student will practice reading his page with other students who have the same page until they can read it well. Then, students will form three groups to read the whole story and find out how their part fits into the whole.

The teacher distributes the pages to students. The pages have page numbers on them, and the teacher has written *A*, *B*, or *C* on each page. Once students have their pages, she asks them to raise their hands if they have pages 17–18. Three students raise their hands, and she explains that they are the practice group for those pages. She then asks students who have pages 19–20, 21–22, 23–24, 25–26, 27–28, 29–30, and 30–32 to raise their hands.

"Now, I will give you seven minutes to practice reading your pages and to think of a good question to ask everyone once the whole story is read. First, I want all of the A's to raise your hands, now all of the B's, and finally all of the C's. When the time is up, the A's will gather at the back table, the B's will gather on the rug, and the C's will gather in the computer area to read the story. I want you to practice your pages using good partner-reading strategies so that you can read them well and with expression. You can read the pages chorally or you can echo read them, taking turns until you can all read them well. When you can all read the pages, remember to think of a good question."

Students get into their practice groups. The teacher goes quickly to each group that has an extra student and explains that the numbers did not work out exactly. She tells them that the two students with the same letter will join that group and read their pages chorally. The teacher then circulates and makes sure that students are practicing the page several times and that they are coaching and helping each other.

Next, the A, B, and C groups assemble. The teacher tells them to get in the proper order, according to page numbers, and to listen as each student reads his pages aloud. "When you finish, ask each other the good questions you thought of. You may not have time to ask them all, but ask as many as you can." As students read, the teacher circulates and notices that all of the students are paying unusually good attention. She realizes that no one knows how the story really goes, so they are all genuinely interested in listening to each other read!

Pick a Page is a nice change of pace for Guided Reading. It can be combined with many different before- and after-reading activities. Like all stories, students can do the Beach Ball or complete a story map. *A Chair for My Mother* has many characters, and students would enjoy pantomiming the book and ad-libbing some of the lines as described in Doing the Book. Students often have strong feelings about the mother, the grandmother, and the fire in this story. You may want to have students write a response in their response journals, comparing the lives of the people in the story to their own lives.

Pick a Page

Pick a Page is a fluency-building activity. It is most successful when it is the first reading of a story—particularly a story with some interesting twists. Remember the following:

1. Choose a selection that your students will enjoy and that has enough pages.
2. Divide the selection into pages. If you can cut apart the story, students can read the front and back of the page. If not, it works best if they can read the two-page spread.
3. Let students know which pages they will read. If you are using a cut-apart story, write *A*, *B*, *C*, *D*, etc., on the each page so that the student will know to which group she will read her pages. If you are using an intact book, give each student a strip of paper with the page numbers and letter designation on it.
4. Have students gather by page numbers and practice reading their pages. Enforce the "no peeking" rule!
5. Have students gather by the letters of their groups and let each student read his pages aloud.

Part Four

Chapter 26

Research on Reading Comprehension

Reading Comprehension Is Not Being Taught (Much)

Since a classic study (Durkin 1978–1979), it has been clear that regardless of how important everyone agrees reading comprehension is, little time is actually spent teaching students how to comprehend better. A good deal of comprehension *assessment* occurs—some of it high stakes—but comprehension instruction is rare in most schools and classrooms.

After their extensive observations of reading and writing instruction in fourth- and fifth-grade classrooms, Pressley, Wharton-McDonald, Mistretta-Hampston, and Echevarria (1998) concluded that not much had changed since Durkin's study. They found that intermediate students were frequently asked to comprehend, but received few comprehension lessons. In addition, their study was completed before the increased emphasis on phonological awareness, phonics, and oral-reading fluency mandated by Reading First. The situation is almost certainly worse today.

In 2002, the RAND Reading Study Group concluded—based on the research they reviewed—that the quantity and quality of reading comprehension instruction in most schools are inadequate.

The Need for More and Better Comprehension Instruction

Buly and Valencia (2002) gave a battery of tests to fourth graders who had failed their state reading assessment. Results indicated that fewer than half had done poorly because of inadequate phonics knowledge or lack of oral-reading fluency. In a landmark report, Biancarosa and Snow (2006) summarized the current situation in America's schools:

"Approximately eight million young people between fourth and twelfth grade struggle to read at grade level. Some 70 percent of older readers require some form of remediation. Very few of these older struggling readers need help to read the words on a page; their most common problem is that they are not able to comprehend what they read." (p. 11)

Allington and McGill-Franzen (2008) reviewed a number of studies from different lines of research and concluded that many struggling readers need good reading comprehension instruction and would benefit from it were they to receive it. Of course, students who do pass their state reading assessments also need effective comprehension instruction so that they can excel in the challenging reading they must do in middle and high school.

Why This Matters

This book includes a wide variety of reading comprehension lesson frameworks. Each framework helps your students learn one aspect of how to comprehend. This book exists for one purpose: to enable you to provide more and better reading comprehension instruction to all of your students.

The Need for Earlier Comprehension Instruction

Most teachers are not surprised to learn that students who are behind in reading in first or second grade are likely to remain behind as they move through the grades (Juel 1988; Phillips et al. 2002). What often does surprise teachers, however, is that a number of the students who were at grade level in reading in first or second grade have fallen significantly behind by fourth or fifth grade (Chall and Curtis 2003).

Paris (2005) has distinguished between constrained reading skills, which are eventually mastered by almost everyone, and unconstrained skills, which are never mastered by anyone and determine who will be the better and worse readers in the long run. Word identification and prior knowledge are more important than strategies in determining whether a reader will comprehend a particular text in second through fourth grade, but strategy use is more determinative of comprehension than either word identification or prior knowledge in fifth and sixth grade (Willson and Rupley 1997).

It is important to maintain the progress of students who get off to a good start in reading in first and second grade. Moreover, it is important not to get discouraged about students who struggle at first, because many of them can become successful readers and students later (Jimerson, Egeland, and Teo 1999).

Why This Matters

Unlike many books about how to teach comprehension, this book includes lesson frameworks and examples that spread across the range of first through sixth grade. Why? By the time it becomes apparent that students are behind in reading comprehension, it is often too late to help them catch up. Focusing on the constrained skills of phonics and sight words is essential in first and second grade, but there must also be a strong secondary emphasis on comprehension and meaning vocabulary. Otherwise, in the long run, many students who started off well will end up as struggling readers. This book can help you provide more and better reading comprehension instruction earlier.

Young students love Doing the Book, and because they are demonstrating characters and plot, it helps them focus on what the play or story means rather than on just saying the words correctly. The Beach Ball is also an enjoyable comprehension lesson framework for young students. It helps them develop the sense of story that good story comprehension requires. Think-Alouds help young students understand what it means to comprehend while they read—that they are not just saying the words but also *thinking* about what the words are saying! Other comprehension lesson frameworks described in this book can also be used in first and second grade.

This book also offers ways to organize young students to provide extra support for their comprehension of text that you are asking them to read. For example, Everyone Read To . . . (ERT) can be used with young students to guide their reading comprehension and help them learn to make inferences. Students like ERT, and it enables them to have success because of the amount of guidance provided. Other effective ways to organize young students for reading comprehension instruction are also explained in this book.

What Is Reading Comprehension?

One of the first questions you should ask of the research literature on reading comprehension is not how to teach it, but what is it? Unless you have a clear sense of what good comprehension consists of, your instructional efforts may not have the best goals or priorities. For example, in recent years, many teachers have been told that when they are teaching fluency (oral-reading accuracy at a satisfactory rate), they are teaching comprehension! Such a massive misunderstanding of what comprehension is cannot possibly lead to effective comprehension instruction.

There is a field in cognitive science called text comprehension. This field began in the 1970s and continues to grow. The research on text comprehension in cognitive science over the past several decades paints a general picture of the comprehension process that can serve as a guide to what the major emphases in comprehension instruction should be.

The following account of what it means to comprehend well represents a consensus of research in cognitive science on text comprehension over the years. However, because terminology sometimes differs between researchers, we present this account in terms used by Walter Kintsch (1998), one of the founders and arguably the most important researcher of text comprehension in the history of the field.

Comprehension Is Building Memory Models of the Text

According to research on text comprehension in cognitive science, good readers build representations in memory, or "memory models," of the text while reading it. Just as a model car is made to represent or resemble a real car in certain ways, readers' memory models are constructed to represent specific aspects of the text we are reading.

While we remember some of the exact words of the text, at least for a few seconds, by far most of our efforts at comprehending are spent on constructing what the text means and the situations it is about. During reading, good readers are simultaneously and constantly constructing three important representations:

- A memory model of the meaning of the last few sentences (the micro-textbase model)
- A memory model of the meaning of the entire text so far (the macro-textbase model)
- A memory model of the situation the entire text is about so far (the situation model)

Constructing the micro-textbase model (memory of the meaning of the most recent few sentences) is when the ongoing work of sentence comprehension takes place. Sentence comprehension is when word meanings are accessed and integrated using syntactic and cohesion cues provided by the text. Building the micro-textbase memory model is not about getting main ideas; it is about understanding what the text probably means word by word, phrase by phrase, and sentence by sentence.

Readers gradually build their macro-textbase memory model (the meaning of the entire text so far) from their micro-textbase model as both models change moment by moment. For example, when reading an informational selection about hydroelectric power, readers who are good at comprehending are sensitive that some of the ideas being added to their micro-textbase memory are repeats. The exact wording may or may not recur, but some of the same concepts are in sentences that were read earlier. There are probably several references throughout the hydroelectric power text to dams, rivers, reservoirs, power grids, etc. To put it most simply, concepts referred to in only one sentence probably do not get moved from a good reader's micro-textbase into the macro-textbase, but concepts referred to in a number of sentences throughout the selection do become part of a good reader's memory model for the entire text so far. Primarily, the repetition of references to the same concepts (including objects, characters, places, events, and abstract ideas) throughout a reading selection determines whether those concepts end up in the macro-textbase memory model or are forgotten.

While building the two related textbase memory models (micro and macro), good readers also use prior knowledge and experiences to infer aspects of the situation in the text. Integrating our prior knowledge, our experiences, and these inferences with the macro-textbase constructs the situation memory model for a text. This is the hardest comprehension memory model to understand because we are used to thinking of comprehension as answers to questions.

The situation model is why most of us read! For example, imagine that someone who has never been to Alaska is considering taking a cruise there. To help her decide, she buys and reads a book about Alaska. While doing so, she constantly maintains a micro-textbase model for the meaning of the most recent sentences and moves the most repeated concepts into her growing macro-textbase model for the book so far. Yet, the most important (and enjoyable) thing she is doing while reading is imagining what Alaska is like—not mere terminology or facts about it (they're in her textbase), but what it looks like, sounds like, feels like, and even smells like. Her developing situation model for the Alaska portrayed in the book consists of her macro-textbase enriched by all of the relevant knowledge and experience she has retrieved and integrated with it. Her situation model for the book is a construction in her memory of the situation in the book (in this case, Alaska). If her situation model is sufficiently appealing to her, she will book the cruise. Of course, if she actually goes to Alaska, she may find that some of the situation model she built while reading that book was accurate but that some of it was not. As a result, she will modify her knowledge of Alaska so that correct information based on experience replaces incorrect information or inferences based on reading.

For another example, imagine that a novel you recently read and loved has been made into a movie. Imagine also that the movie—unlike some—closely follows the plot and includes all of the characters from the novel. You may love the movie too, or you may hate it. Why? When you see a movie made from a novel, you are usually seeing the director's situation model for that novel (or the screenplay based upon it). If the director's situation model is consistent with yours in important ways, you will probably be pleased with the movie. If not, you may say, "The personality of the main character just didn't feel right to me." Or, you may say, "The town where the movie took place seemed too small and isolated compared to the one in the book." Or, you may say, "I really liked the main character's mother in the novel, but I couldn't stand her in the movie."

The evidence in cognitive psychology and psycholinguistics supports that comprehension is the building of mental representations in memory while reading. The evidence for the textbase and situation memory models is so strong that few researchers question it (Fletcher 1994). When you are comprehending well, you are building representations of text meaning (micro and macro) as well as a representation of the real or imagined situation in the text. The memory models you build simultaneously as you read are the reason why you can pick up a book right where you left off last night or several days ago without skipping a beat. You do not have to start reading from page one again every time your reading is interrupted by sleep or life!

Why This Matters

The consensus view in cognitive science about what comprehension is has two major implications for how to teach it. First, students should ordinarily be expected to remember what they have comprehended. Why? Comprehension is building representations of text meaning in memory. Unfortunately, this means that students who spend a lot of time doing tasks that resemble a standardized reading test are not learning much about how to comprehend. While a few comprehension lesson frameworks do have students complete the comprehension task with the book open, the most effective comprehension lesson frameworks have students perform the task after reading with the book closed. Students who know that they must complete the after-reading task with their books closed are more likely to build better memory models while reading than those who know that they will be allowed to do the task with their books open.

In Chapter 10, you read about a family of comprehension lesson frameworks each built around a graphic organizer (web, data chart, Venn diagram, time line, and causal chain). In each case, students are given the skeleton of the particular graphic organizer before reading so that they will know what to focus on during reading. After reading, they work together at first and later individually to complete the graphic organizer with specific information from the text they read. They always do this task with the text closed. Only when they have finished the task do they open their books to correct mistakes and fill in gaps. Over time, this process increases students' efforts to understand and remember what they have read. That is what it means to comprehend better. The second major implication for teaching comprehension is that the research in cognitive science on comprehension acknowledges not what good readers remember, but what they *forget* when they read. Good readers tend to forget the details in what they are reading except for those that are repeated enough to indicate that they are important to the text's overall meaning. Consequently, detail questions asked after students read "to find out whether they read it carefully" are counterproductive to the development of

(continued from page 201)

real comprehension ability. Unfortunately, if students know that they will be held accountable for isolated details, they will focus on those during reading and not devote much effort to building the macro-textbase or situation memory model. Higher-order questions and tasks focusing on the macro-textbase and situation models get students to emphasize the building of those memory models while they read. None of the comprehension lesson frameworks in this book hold students responsible for unimportant information when the text is closed. All of the lesson frameworks in which the after-reading task is completed with books closed give students a preview before they read that targets specific information in the text. In these lesson frameworks, the before-reading activity—the preview—makes some of the information in the text important enough to remember. The other information can safely be forgotten by students.

When a lesson framework in this book does focus on low-level information, students always complete the task with their books open. For example, the family of mini comprehension lesson frameworks called Sentence and Paragraph Detectives (Chapter 20) helps students learn how to use capitalization, punctuation, pronouns, and other syntactic and cohesion cues to process sentence and paragraph structures. Because these are things that most good readers would soon forget, each of these lesson frameworks has students complete the task with open texts.

Comprehension Requires Prior Knowledge and Meaning Vocabulary

Educational research in general supports the value of students' prior knowledge in helping them perform any academic task, including reading comprehension or learning from text (Dochy, Segers, and Buehl 1999). Research on reading comprehension has long found a strong association between students' meaning vocabulary and their reading comprehension (Cutting and Scarborough 2006).

Research supports that readers' prior knowledge and meaning vocabulary are especially helpful to their comprehension when the text they are reading is difficult or poorly written (Goldman and Rakestraw 2000).

Why This Matters

If the story or informational text you will use for a comprehension lesson has several pictures, taking students on a Picture Walk before the lesson begins can help them connect appropriate prior knowledge and meaning vocabulary to that text. It can also provide you with the opportunity to teach or review a few important word meanings that will help students be more successful during your comprehension lesson.

Comprehension lesson frameworks that have students predict what may happen or what they may learn also help them connect (access appropriate prior knowledge) before they read. During and after reading, as they consider whether their predictions were confirmed by the text, students must attempt to integrate their prior knowledge with the textual information. Using the lesson frameworks Prove It!, Rivet, Guess Yes or No, Preview-Predict-Confirm, and KWL helps students get in the cognitive habit of connecting (accessing what they know already about what they are reading).

Because Rivet is a lesson framework that asks students to predict what will happen in a story, it helps students both access appropriate prior knowledge before reading and attempts to integrate prior knowledge with textual information during and after reading. Rivet also helps students access or learn word meanings when reading a story.

Because examining and thinking about pictures is a way students acquire knowledge, Preview-Predict-Confirm does not only help your students access appropriate prior knowledge and word meanings for a text but also teaches them new knowledge and vocabulary.

Ten Important Words may be the most powerful comprehension lesson framework for building meaning vocabulary while reading. By attempting to determine the 10 most important words in an informational text, students are integrating main idea comprehension with a focus on the most informative words. That way, students are more likely to learn both the words and the richer meanings for them.

Good Readers Have Learned to Understand Texts in Terms of Their Structures

The most promising interventions to prepare readers for texts have attempted to teach students to process text structures at one level or another (sentence/paragraph/passage) for one type of text or another (story/exposition). Most of these interventions have consistently increased subjects' reading comprehension ability, at least on measures related to the structures students were taught how to process (Cunningham 1994).

Research supports that readers' familiarity with the structures of a text is especially helpful to them when they lack relevant prior knowledge and when the comprehension task is challenging (Fox 2009).

Good Readers Have Learned to Process Texts in Terms of Their Genre and Organization

Texts take many forms. There are poetry, drama, and prose. Usually, you need to only glance at the way the print is arranged on the page to determine which of those three forms a text is. Prose texts can be divided into story and informational text. A story has chronological organization and elements of fiction or fantasy. Within stories, there are many genres: mystery, historical fiction, fantasy, science fiction, etc. Within informational text, the content is organized in different ways— overall and in each of its major sections. Some of these informational organizations are main idea/ details, compare/contrast, sequential or chronological, and cause/effect (Chapter 2).

Good readers have learned to read a story as a story, not as an essay. They have learned to read a text comparing and contrasting as such, rather than as a story or as a text organized mainly by main idea/details. For comprehension, it does not matter whether students can talk about these different genres and organizational patterns, but it does matter whether they are sensitive to these overall structures as they read (Cunningham 1994).

Why This Matters

Story Map and the Beach Ball teach students to think their way through stories as a genre. As a result, students' abilities to comprehend and discuss stories gradually improves.

Because Prove It! and Rivet have students predict what will happen in a story and read to determine which predictions are confirmed, they help students think about the structure of stories. Students must learn what kinds of characters, settings, and events take place in stories to gradually become better predictors of what will happen in particular stories. This knowledge of story structure is both accessed and built during Prove It! and Rivet lessons.

The overall text structure helps good readers determine whether to focus on similarities and differences between subjects, the sequence of events or steps, the cause-and-effect relationships, or something else in an informational piece. The family of comprehension lesson frameworks built around a graphic organizer (web, data chart, Venn diagram, time line, and causal chain) does more than anything else you can do to help all students become sensitive to the ways informational texts are organized.

Good Readers Have Learned to Process Syntactic and Cohesion Structures

Not only do texts have an overall structure (story, compare/contrast, sequential), but sentences have syntactic structure, and paragraphs have cohesion that connect them to previous sentences and paragraphs. Readers who lack successful experience comprehending written language often fail to be aware of or process the syntax of the sentences they read (Chiappe, Siegel, and Wade-Woolley 2002; Goldman and Rakestraw 2000). Readers can also have comprehension problems if they are not sensitive to the words or phrases that refer back to information in previous sentences and do not distinguish them from the words or phrases that refer to new information (Clark and Clark 1977). In contrast, successful readers are good at determining which concepts pronouns and other anaphora refer back to (Van der Schoot, et al. 2008).

Why This Matters

The family of mini comprehension lesson frameworks called Sentence and Paragraph Detectives is a powerful tool for helping students learn how to comprehend sentences and paragraphs by processing their syntactic and cohesion structures. Repeated opportunities to participate in the various types of these lessons teach students how to use capitalization, punctuation, pronouns, and other syntactic and cohesion cues to process sentence and paragraph structures.

The Most Successful Comprehension Instruction Emphasizes Higher-Order Thinking

The most consistently effective teachers of elementary students in high-poverty classrooms are those who emphasize higher-order thinking (Taylor et al. 2003). Unfortunately, the opposite also holds true: "The more that routine, practice-oriented approaches to teaching important comprehension processes were observed, the lower the growth in reading comprehension" (Taylor et al. 2003, 23).

Why This Matters

Even young or struggling readers can learn how to make inferences while reading from participating in Everyone Read To . . . (ERT) lessons.

Figuring Out How and Why is a powerful comprehension lesson framework for helping students learn to make inferences while reading.

The comprehension lesson framework What Do You Think? helps students develop critical reading and discussion abilities. Relative to comprehension, it helps them become more aware and thoughtful of their use of the evaluating thinking strategy.

Doing the Book, whether acting out a play, preparing and doing a Readers' Theater or pantomiming (with just a little speaking), is a powerful and underused tool to help students build the situation model for a story. Think of the visualizing and inferring you have to do to turn any play or story into a performance. The play or story gives the words the characters say, but the actors (and director—you!) still have to decide how to say them. The play or story rarely gives much indication about how the characters should move around the stage. When Doing the Book, you and your students have to imagine—visualize and infer—facial expressions, gestures, tones of voice, movements, where and how to stand or sit, etc. Cognitive scientists call that part of comprehension "building the situation model." It is the kind of higher-order thinking good readers always do when reading a piece of literature. They do the book in their minds while reading!

Giving Readers a Purpose for Reading

Giving students a specific purpose for reading can increase both their interest in and recall of a text (Schraw and Dennison 1994).

Why This Matters

Every comprehension lesson framework in this book has a before-reading activity that gives students a purpose for reading or rereading the text.

Two of the formats for organizing students for comprehension lessons—ERT and Sentence and Paragraph Detectives—also provide specific purposes to guide students' reading of segments (paragraphs or pages) of a longer text.

Reading Comprehension Engagement and Motivation

In elementary and middle school classrooms, increased engagement of students with comprehension tasks can be accomplished by a combination of efforts on the part of the teacher. Providing large amounts of positive motivation and making sure that instruction does not undermine student motivation to read are both important (Bogner, Raphael, and Pressley 2002; Pressley 2002). To refine these efforts, research supports two major emphases: building students' intrinsic motivation to comprehend and building their self-efficacy in comprehension.

Intrinsic Motivation in Reading Comprehension

"Intrinsic motivation concerns the performance of activities for their own sake, in which pleasure is inherent in the activity itself. . . ." (Gottfried, Fleming and Gottfried 2001, 3). Extrinsic motivation is engaging in an activity in order to receive a reward. Anything you choose to do out of interest, enjoyment, curiosity, or desire for self-improvement is intrinsically motivated. Students in third grade and higher who are intrinsically motivated tend to get better grades and score higher on standardized tests (Gottfried, Fleming and Gottfried 2001; Lepper, Corpus, and Iyengar 2005). However, the earlier in school that teachers begin building students' intrinsic motivation, the more likely the approach is to work (Gottfried, Fleming and Gottfried 2001). Reducing the use of extrinsic rewards has been shown to help build students' intrinsic motivation (Cameron and Pierce 1994).

Why This Matters

To help students begin to acquire intrinsic motivation in reading comprehension, nothing is more important than the attitude you regularly express toward your reading and theirs. Your enthusiasm about what you are having students read can be contagious and shows students that reading does not have to be a chore but should be seen as an opportunity to learn something interesting, important, or fun.

Some comprehension lesson frameworks are fun for most students, such as Doing the Book or the Beach Ball. Whenever a comprehension lesson can be fun, either because of the lesson framework used or because of the text itself, it builds students' intrinsic motivation for reading.

Comprehension lessons that elicit student predictions are another way of building or tapping into intrinsic motivation. When readers make predictions, they want to find out whether their predictions were right. Prove It! and Rivet are comprehension lesson frameworks that ask students to predict what may happen in the story they will read. Guess Yes or No, Preview-Predict-Confirm, and KWL ask students to predict what they may learn from the informational text they will read. In each case, you will find students more willing to read the text simply because they want to find out which predictions were right. That is intrinsic motivation because they are not doing it for grades, praise, or tangible rewards, but to satisfy their curiosity.

One of the opposites of intrinsic motivation is boredom! In this book, we have included a large number of lesson frameworks in part to prevent students (and you!) from becoming bored with any one of them. For example, if you find that students really like Prove It!, you will keep it fresh longer if you alternate it with Rivet and other appropriate lesson frameworks for guiding the reading comprehension of stories. Likewise, if students keep asking for the Beach Ball, alternate it with Story Map and other lesson frameworks to prevent students from becoming tired of it.

Self-Efficacy in Reading

People used to think that motivation was all about feelings. Research in recent decades has shown that beliefs are also an essential component of motivation. In particular, self-efficacy has been shown to contribute to student engagement and success with academic tasks. "*Self-efficacy* refers to beliefs a person has about his or her capabilities to learn or perform behaviors. . . ." (Schunk and Zimmerman 1997, 34). Self-efficacy in reading comprehension is very important. If a student believes that he can be successful with the comprehension task he will be given after reading, he is more likely to be willing to read, to try hard when he reads, to persist if the going gets tough, and to avoid feeling stressed when reading under pressure. If he believes that he may fail on the comprehension task, he is more likely to try to avoid reading, or if he can't avoid it, to finish it quickly with as little effort as possible. The lack of self-efficacy in comprehension is especially a problem for struggling readers. Research has also shown that students who have had difficulties with reading in the past have lower perceptions of their own abilities to read, and to learn to read better, than other students have (Wilson, Chapman, and Tunmer 1995).

Research has found at least four mutually supportive ways that you can build students' self-efficacy in reading. The first way is to increase their reading successes and reduce their reading failures (Schunk and Zimmerman 1997). Students who have usually been successful in their reading expect to be successful next time, and students who have usually failed expect to fail next time (Walker 2003). It will not always be possible for you to ensure success or prevent failure, but successful teachers consider what they do and say to their students in light of how it may affect their self-efficacy. It is also helpful when teachers give feedback to students about their reading comprehension in terms of the improvements they are making rather than their shortcomings (Bandura 1997).

Why This Matters

To help students increase their comprehension successes and reduce their comprehension failures, always express enthusiasm for some aspect of the students' performance on a comprehension task. Teach comprehension strategies, but have tolerance for imperfection! Teach students to respond positively to each other's comprehension and consider any derogatory remark by one student about another's comprehension to be a discipline problem. Help students compare their reading comprehension now with their performance in the past so that they can see their improvement.

One of the most underused ways of increasing success and reducing failure during a comprehension lesson is to give students a good preview before they read of what the comprehension task will be after they read. For example, students who have seen and understood the Venn diagram before they start reading will be better able to fill it in correctly after they read than students who did not know that there would be a Venn diagram until they were given it to fill in! This is one reason almost every comprehension lesson framework in this book begins with a clear preview of the after-reading task.

The second proven way to build students' self-efficacy in comprehension is to teach them strategies they can use to perform better while reading (Schunk and Zimmerman 1997). Learning specific comprehension strategies contributes to a student's belief that she can learn how to read better and helps her have more success when she reads, which contributes additionally to her self-efficacy in reading. In fact, raising students' skill levels in a way that gives them more genuine success experiences with a particular aspect or type of reading comprehension is probably the best way to build their self-efficacy.

Why This Matters

This book is filled with reading strategy instruction, not only because research says that it is effective in improving reading comprehension but also because research says that it builds self-efficacy in reading. For both reasons, it is vital to teach students the essential strategies of reading and not assume that they can learn how to read well by just reading.

The third way to boost your students' self-efficacy in reading is to use modeling. Research has found that modeling how to cope when having trouble is more effective than modeling mastery (Schunk and Zimmerman 1997). That is, teachers who model having difficulty and overcoming it with effort, persistence, or a specific strategy build students' self-efficacy better than teachers who model the task without error.

Why This Matters

To have self-efficacy, students must know how to overcome problems without thinking that having problems is an indication of failure. There is no better way to teach them that than to model it. For example, teachers who introduce a comprehension lesson framework like Prove It! by modeling it with a short text, will help their students more if they make at least one prediction that students realize cannot possibly be right and at least one sensible prediction that turns out to be wrong. Such modeling helps prevent your students from getting discouraged simply because they have difficulties in comprehension.

The fourth way to increase self-efficacy is to teach students to monitor their own performance. Providing students with specific criteria that they can use to evaluate their reading helps build their self-efficacy (Schunk 2003). When students see specific opportunities to improve their performance on comprehension tasks by applying strategies you have taught them, their self-efficacy improves. "Negative self-evaluations will not diminish self-efficacy and motivation if students believe they are capable of succeeding but that their present approach is ineffective. . . ." (Schunk and Zimmerman 1997, 40). Rather, finding errors or missing elements in their own reading comprehension provides opportunities for students to set their own specific short-term goals that can be met and that contribute to self-efficacy when they are met (Schunk and Zimmerman 1997).

Why This Matters

Nothing is more helpful to students' self-efficacy in reading than to be held responsible for opening their books after they have completed a comprehension task and correcting their own task performance. By finding and fixing their own mistakes and filling in gaps in what they remembered, students learn how to monitor their comprehension better, which is one of the essential thinking processes and a major contributor to better self-efficacy.

Students often believe themselves to be efficacious in one kind of reading comprehension, but not another, and on comprehending one type of text, but not another. Your students will benefit significantly over time if you apply these four ways to build their self-efficacy to each area of comprehension and as you teach them to read each major type of text.

etptn

ᵉᵉᵉenᵉes

Research Bibliography

Allington, R. L., and A. McGill-Franzen. 2008. Comprehension difficulties among struggling readers. Ed. S. E. Israel and G. G. Duffy, *Handbook of Research on Reading Comprehension* (pp. 551–568). New York: Routledge.

Bandura, A. 1997. *Self-efficacy: The exercise of control*. New York: W. H. Freeman.

Biancarosa, C., and C. E. Snow. 2006. *Reading Next—A Vision for Action and Research in Middle and High School Literacy: A Report to Carnegie Corporation of New York* (2nd ed.). Washington, DC: Alliance for Excellent Education.

Bogner, K., L. Raphael, and M. Pressley. 2002. How grade 1 teachers motivate literate activity by their students. *Scientific Studies of Reading*, 6, 135–165.

Buly, M. R., and S. W. Valencia. 2002. Below the bar: Profiles of students who fail state reading assessments. *Educational Evaluation and Policy Analysis*, 24, 219–239.

Cameron, J., and W. D. Pierce. 1994. Reinforcement, reward, and intrinsic motivation: A meta-analysis. *Review of Educational Research*, 64, 363–423.

Carr, E., and D. Ogle. 1987. K-W-L plus: A strategy for comprehension and summary. *Journal of Reading*, 30, 626–631.

Chall, J. S., and M. E. Curtis. 2003. Children with reading difficulties. Eds. J. Flood, D. Lapp, J. R. Squire, and J. M. Jensen, *Handbook of Research on Teaching the English Language Arts* (2nd ed.; pp. 413–420). Mahwah, NJ: Erlbaum.

Chiappe, P., L. S. Siegel, and L. Wade-Woolley. 2002. Linguistic diversity and the development of reading skills: A longitudinal study. *Scientific Studies of Reading*, 6, 369–400.

Clark, H. H., and E. V. Clark. 1977. *Psychology and Language*. New York: Harcourt Publishers.

Cunningham, J. W. 1994. Reading comprehension research studies. Ed. A. C. Purves, *Encyclopedia of English Studies and Language Arts* (A Project of the National Council of Teachers of English) (pp. 993–998). New York: Scholastic, Inc.

Cutting, L., and H. Scarborough. 2006. Prediction of reading comprehension: Relative contributions of word recognition, language proficiency, and other cognitive skills can depend on how comprehension is measured. *Scientific Studies of Reading*, 10, 277–299.

Dochy, F., M. Segers, and M. M. Buehl. 1999. The relation between assessment practices and outcomes of studies: The case of research on prior knowledge. *Review of Educational Research*, 69, 145–186.

Durkin, D. 1978–1979. What classroom observations reveal about reading comprehension instruction. *Reading Research Quarterly*, 14, 481–533.

Fletcher, C. R. 1994. Levels of representation in memory for discourse. In M. A. Gernsbacher (Ed.), *Handbook of Psycholinguistics* (pp. 589–607). San Diego: Academic Press.

Fox, E. 2009. The role of reader characteristics in processing and learning from informational text. *Review of Educational Research*, 79, 197–261.

Goldman, S. R., and J. A. Rakestraw (2000). Structural aspects of constructing meaning from text. Eds. M. Kamil, P. B. Mosenthal, P. D. Pearson, and R. Barr, *Handbook of Reading Research* (Vol. 3, pp. 311–335). Mahwah, NJ: Erlbaum.

Gottfried, A. E., J. S. Fleming, and A. W. Gottfried. 2001. Continuity of academic intrinsic motivation from childhood through late adolescence: A longitudinal study. *Journal of Educational Psychology*, 93, 3–13.

Jimerson, S., B. Egeland, and A. Teo. 1999. A longitudinal study of achievement trajectories: Factors associated with change. *Journal of Educational Psychology*, 91, 116–126.

Juel, C. 1988. Learning to read and write: A longitudinal study of 54 children from first through fourth grade. *Journal of Educational Psychology*, 80, 437–447.

Kintsch, W. 1998. *Comprehension: A Paradigm for Cognition*. New York: Cambridge University Press.

Lepper, M. R., J. H. Corpus, and S. S. Iyengar. 2005. Intrinsic and extrinsic motivational orientations in the classroom: Age differences and academic correlates. *Journal of Educational Psychology*, 97, 184–196.

Paris, S. G. 2005. Reinterpreting the development of reading skills. *Reading Research Quarterly*, 40, 184–202.

Phillips, L. M., S. P. Norris, W. C. Osmond, and A. M. Maynard. 2002. Relative reading achievement: A longitudinal study of 187 children from first through sixth grades. *Journal of Educational Psychology*, 94, 3–13.

Pressley, M. 2002. What I have learned up until now about research methods in reading education. Eds. D. L. Schallert, C. M. Fairbanks, J. Worthy, B. Maloch, and J. V. Hoffman, *51st Yearbook of the National Reading Conference* (pp. 33–44). Oak Creek, WI: National Reading Conference.

Pressley, M., R. Wharton-McDonald, J. Mistretta-Hampston, and M. Echevarria. 1998. Literacy instruction in 10 fourth- and fifth-grade classrooms in upstate New York. *Scientific Studies of Reading*, 2, 159–194.

RAND Reading Study Group. 2002. *Reading for understanding: Toward an R&D program in reading comprehension.* Santa Monica, CA: RAND.

Schraw, G., and R. S. Dennison. 1994. The effect of reader purpose on interest and recall. *Journal of Reading Behavior,* 26, 1–18.

Schunk, D. H. 2003. Self-efficacy for reading and writing: Influence of modeling, goal setting, and self-evaluation. *Reading and Writing Quarterly,* 19, 159–172.

Schunk, D. H., and B. J. Zimmerman. 1997. Developing self-efficacious readers and writers: The role of social and self-regulatory processes. Eds. J. T. Guthrie and A. Wigfield, *Reading Engagement: Motivating Readers through Integrated Instruction* (pp. 34–50). Newark, DE: International Reading Association.

Taylor, B. M., P. D. Pearson, D. S. Peterson, and M. C. Rodriguez. 2003. Reading growth in high-poverty classrooms: The influence of teacher practices that encourage cognitive engagement in literacy learning. *The Elementary School Journal,* 104, 3–28.

Van der Schoot, M., A. L. Vasbinder, T. M. Horsley, and E. C. D. M. van Lieshout. 2008. The role of two reading strategies in text comprehension: An eye fixation study in primary school children. *Journal of Research in Reading,* 31, 203–223.

Walker, B. J. 2003. The cultivation of student self-efficacy in reading and writing. *Reading and Writing Quarterly,* 19, 173–187.

Willson, V. L., and W. H. Rupley. 1997. A structural equation model for reading comprehension based on background, phonemic, and strategy knowledge. *Scientific Studies of Reading,* 1, 45–63.

Wilson, M. G., J. W. Chapman, and W. E. Tunmer, W. E. 1995. Early reading difficulties and reading self-concept. *Journal of Cognitive Education,* 4, 33–45.

Yopp, R. H., and H. K. Yopp. 2004. Preview-Predict-Confirm: Thinking about the language and content of informational text. *The Reading Teacher,* 58, 79–83.

Yopp, R. H., and H. K. Yopp. 2007. Ten important words plus: A strategy for building word knowledge. *The Reading Teacher,* 61, 157–160.

Teacher Resources Bibliography

Allington, Richard L. *What Really Matters in Response to Intervention: Research-Based Designs.* (Allyn & Bacon, 2008)

Daniels, Harvey. *Literature Circles.* (Stenhouse Publishers, 2002)

Emberley, Ed. *Ed Emberley's Drawing Book of Animals.* (LB Kids, 2006)

Fountas, Irene and Gay Su Pinnell. *Matching Books to Readers: Using Leveled Books in Guided Reading.* (Heinemann, 1999)

Fredericks, Anthony D. *African Legends, Myths, and Folktales for Readers Theatre.* (Libraries Unlimited, 2008)

Fredericks, Anthony D. *Fairy Tales Readers Theatre.* (Libraries Unlimited, 2009)

Fredericks, Anthony D. *Mother Goose: Readers Theatre for Beginning Readers.* (Libraries Unlimited, 2007)

Fredericks, Anthony D. *Nonfiction Readers Theatre.* (Libraries Unlimited, 2008)

Fredericks, Anthony D. *Silly Salamanders and Other Slightly Stupid Stuff for Readers Theatre.* (Libraries Unlimited, 2008)

Keene, Ellin Oliver and Susan Zimmerman. *Mosaic of Thought: The Power of Comprehension Strategy Instruction.* (Heinemann, 2007)

Long, Don. *Speak Out! Readers' Theater* series. (Pacific Learning, 2006)

Moen, Christine Boardman. *25 Reproducible Literature Circle Role Sheets for Fiction and Nonfiction Books.* (Lorenz Corporation, 2004)

Pugliano-Martin, Carol. *15 Plays for Beginning Readers: Famous Americans.* (Scholastic, 2009)

Pugliano-Martin, Carol. *25 Just-Right Plays for Emergent Readers.* (Scholastic, 1999)

Pugliano-Martin, Carol. *25 Spanish Plays for Emergent Readers.* (Scholastic, 1999)

Pugliano-Martin, Carol. *Folk and Fairy Tale Plays for Building Fluency: 8 Engaging, Read-Aloud Plays Based on Favorite Tales to Help Boost Students' Word Recognition, Comprehension, and Fluency.* (Scholastic, 2010)

Pugliano-Martin, Carol. *Greek Myth Plays: 10 Readers Theater Scripts Based on Favorite Greek Myths That Students Can Read and Reread to Develop Their Fluency.* (Scholastic, 2008)

Pugliano-Martin, Carol. *Just Right Plays: 25 Emergent Reader Plays for Around the Year.* (Scholastic, 1999)

Pugliano-Martin, Carol. *Read-Aloud Plays: Tall Tales.* (Scholastic, 2000)

Wheeler, Kathryn. *Act It Out with Readers' Theater: Build Fluency with Multilevel Plays!* (Carson-Dellosa Publishing, 2009)

Recommended Children's Books Bibliography

Adler, David A. *Cam Jansen: The Chocolate Fudge Mystery.* (Puffin, 2004)

Adler, David A. *A Picture Book of Abraham Lincoln.* (Holiday House, 1990)

Adler, David A. *A Picture Book of Jackie Robinson.* (Holiday House, 1997)

Adler, David A. *A Picture Book of Martin Luther King, Jr.* (Holiday House, 1990)

Adler, David A. *A Picture Book of Rosa Parks.* (Holiday House, 1995)

Barton, Byron. *Little Red Hen.* (HarperFestival, 1994)

Bernard, Robin. *Creepy Crawlies.* (Teaching Resources, 2003)

Bernard, Robin. *Insects.* (National Geographic Children's Books, 2001)

Bernard, Robin. *Penguins.* (Teaching Resources, 2003)

Branley, Franklyn M. *Tornado Alert.* (HarperCollins, 1990)

Brenner, Barbara. *Wagon Wheels.* (HarperCollins, 1984)

Brown, Marc. *Arthur's Pet Business.* (Little Brown, 1993)

Browne, Anthony. *Things I Like.* (Dragonfly, 1990)

Buckman, Virginia. *Baseball Stars.* (Children's Press, 2007)

Buckman, Virginia. *Football Stars.* (Children's Press, 2007)

Buffington, Kate. *Whales.* (Teaching Resources, 2003)

Byars, Betsy. *The Summer of the Swans.* (Puffin, 1981)

Cocca-Leffler, Maryann. *Missing: One Stuffed Rabbit.* (Albert Whitman and Company, 2000)

Cole, Joanna. *The Magic School Bus at the Waterworks.* (Scholastic, 1988)

Cole, Joanna. *The Magic School Bus in the Time of Dinosaurs.* (Scholastic, 1995)

Cole, Joanna. *The Magic School Bus Lost in the Solar System*. (Scholastic, 1992)

Cowley, Joy. *Mrs. Wishy-Washy*. (McGraw Hill, 1998)

Cox, Ted. *Emmitt Smith: Finding Daylight*. (Children's Press, 1994)

Cronin, Doreen. *Click, Clack, Moo: Cows That Type*. (Atheneum, 2000)

DiCamillo, Kate. *Because of Winn-Dixie*. (Candlewick Press, 2009)

Drew, David. *Caterpillar Diary*. (Rigby, 2007)

Dussling, Jennifer. *Bugs! Bugs! Bugs!* (DK Children, 1999)

Eastman, P. D. *Are You My Mother?* (Random House, 1988)

Esbaum, Jill. *Apples for Everyone*. (National Geographic Children's Books, 2009)

Esbaum, Jill. *Everything Spring*. (National Geographic Children's Books, 2010)

Esbaum, Jill. *Seed, Sprout, Pumpkin, Pie*. (National Geographic Children's Books, 2009)

Eugene, Toni. *Exploring Space*. (National Geographic Children's Books, 2001)

Fox, Mem. *Hattie and the Fox*. (Aladdin, 1992)

Fox, Mem. *Zoo-Looking*. (Mondo, 1996)

Frost, Helen. *Baby Birds*. (Capstone Press, 1999)

Frost, Helen. *Cats*. (Capstone Press, 2001)

Galdone, Paul. *The Little Red Hen*. (Sandpiper, 2006)

Geisel, Theodor Seuss (Dr. Seuss). *The Foot Book*. (Random House, 2003)

Geisel, Theodor Seuss (Dr. Seuss). *Hop on Pop*. (HarperCollins, 2003)

Geisel, Theodor Seuss (Dr. Seuss). *One Fish, Two Fish, Red Fish, Blue Fish*. (HarperCollins, 2003)

Geisel, Theodor Seuss (Dr. Seuss). *Ten Apples Up on Top*. (HarperCollins, 2003)

Gibbons, Gail. *Bats*. (Holiday House, 2000)

Gibbons, Gail. *Cats*. (Holiday House, 1996)

Gibbons, Gail. *Dogs*. (Holiday House, 1996)

Gibbons, Gail. *Owls*. (Holiday House, 2006)

Gibbons, Gail. *Penguins*. (Holiday House, 1999)

Gibbons, Gail. *Sea Turtles.* (Live Oak Media, 1999)

Giles. *Goldilocks and the Three Bears.* (Rigby, 1992)

Giles. *Robin Hood and the Silver Trophy.* (Rigby, 1999)

Glasscock, Sarah. *Laura Ingalls Wilder: An Author's Story.* (Steck-Vaughn, 1998)

Glasscock, Sarah. *My Prairie Summer.* (Steck-Vaughn, 1998)

Gomi, Taro. *My Friend.* (Chronicle Books, 1995)

Goodman, Susan E. *Pilgrims of Plymouth.* (National Geographic Children's Books, 2001)

Grimm, Jacob and Wilhelm. *The Bremen Town Musicians* (any version)

Grossman, Bill. *My Little Sister Ate One Hare.* (Dragonfly, 1998)

Guarino, Deborah. *Is Your Mama a Llama?* (Scholastic, 2006)

Halpern, Jerald. *A Look at Spiders.* (Steck-Vaughn, 1998)

Henkes, Kevin. *Lilly's Purple Plastic Purse.* (Greenwillow Books, 1996)

Hoff, Syd. *Arturo's Baton.* (Sandpiper, 2002)

Holmes, Kevin J. *Frogs.* (Capstone Press, 2000)

Howard, Elizabeth Fitzgerald. *Aunt Flossie's Hats (and Crab Cakes Later).* (Clarion, 2001)

Hutchins, Pat. *The Doorbell Rang.* (Houghton Mifflin, 1996)

January, Brendan. *Derek Jeter: Shortstop Sensation.* (Children's Press, 2000)

Johnson, Angela. *One of Three.* (Scholastic, 1995)

Lester, Helen. *Tacky the Penguin.* (Houghton Mifflin, 2006)

Ling, Mary. *Amazing Fish.* (Knopf, 1991)

Lobel, Arnold. *Days with Frog and Toad.* (HarperCollins, 1984)

Lobel, Arnold. *Frog and Toad Are Friends.* (HarperFestival, 1990)

Lobel, Arnold. *Frog and Toad Together.* (HarperFestival, 1999)

Martin Jr., Bill. *Brown Bear, Brown Bear, What Do You See?* (Henry Holt & Co., 2008)

Mayer, Mercer. *There's an Alligator Under My Bed.* (Dial Books, 1987)

McNaughton, Colin. *Suddenly.* (Sandpiper, 1998)

Mead, Katherine. *How Spiders Got Eight Legs.* (Steck-Vaughn, 1998)

Munsch, Robert. *Purple, Green and Yellow.* (Annikins, 2007)

Noble, Trinka Hakes. *The Day Jimmy's Boa Ate the Wash.* (Puffin, 1992)

Polacco, Patricia. *Applemando's Dreams.* (Putnam Juvenile, 1997)

Polacco, Patricia. *The Butterfly.* (Puffin, 2009)

Polacco, Patricia. *Chicken Sunday.* (The Putnam & Grosse Group, 1992)

Polacco, Patricia. *Just Plain Fancy.* (Dragonfly Books, 1994)

Polacco, Patricia. *The Keeping Quilt.* (Aladdin, 2001)

Polacco, Patricia. *Pink and Say.* (Philomel, 1994)

Rudy, Lisa Jo. *Ocean Life.* (Teaching Resources, 2003)

Saunders-Smith, Gail. *Clouds.* (Capstone Press, 2000)

Saunders-Smith, Gail. *Lightning.* (Capstone Press, 1998)

Saunders-Smith, Gail. *Rain.* (Capstone Press, 1998)

Saunders-Smith, Gail. *Sunshine.* (Capstone Press, 1998)

Shea, Therese. *Basketball Stars.* (Children's Press, 2007)

Shea, Therese. *Hockey Stars.* (Children's Press, 2007)

Shea, Therese. *Soccer Stars.* (Children's Press, 2007)

Smith. *The Three Billy Goats Gruff.* (Rigby, 1997)

Spinelli, Jerry. *The Library Card.* (Scholastic, 1998)

Spinelli, Jerry. *Loser.* (HarperCollins, 2003)

Spinelli, Jerry. *Maniac Magee.* (Little Brown, 1999)

Spinelli, Jerry. *Stargirl.* (Laurel Leaf, 2004)

Stewart, Mark. *Shaquille O'Neal: Big Man, Big Dreams.* (Children's Press, 1999)

Stewart, Mark. *Tiger Woods: Driving Force.* (Children's Press, 1999)

Stone, Jon. *The Monster at the End of This Book.* (Golden Books, 2004)

Van Allsburg, Chris. *The Sweetest Fig.* (Houghton Mifflin, 1993)

Waters, Kate. *Sarah Morton's Day: A Day in the Life of a Pilgrim Girl.* (Scholastic, 1993)

Waxman, Laura Hamilton. *Dr. Seuss.* (Learner Publications, 2010)

White, E. B. *Charlotte's Web.* (HarperCollins, 2001)

Williams, Sue. *I Went Walking.* (Live Oak Media, 2000)

Williams, Vera B. *A Chair for My Mother.* (Greenwillow Books, 1984)

Yolen, Jane. *Commander Toad in Space.* (Putnam, 1996)

Yolen, Jane. *Owl Moon.* (Philomel, 1987)